TEXTURED ART

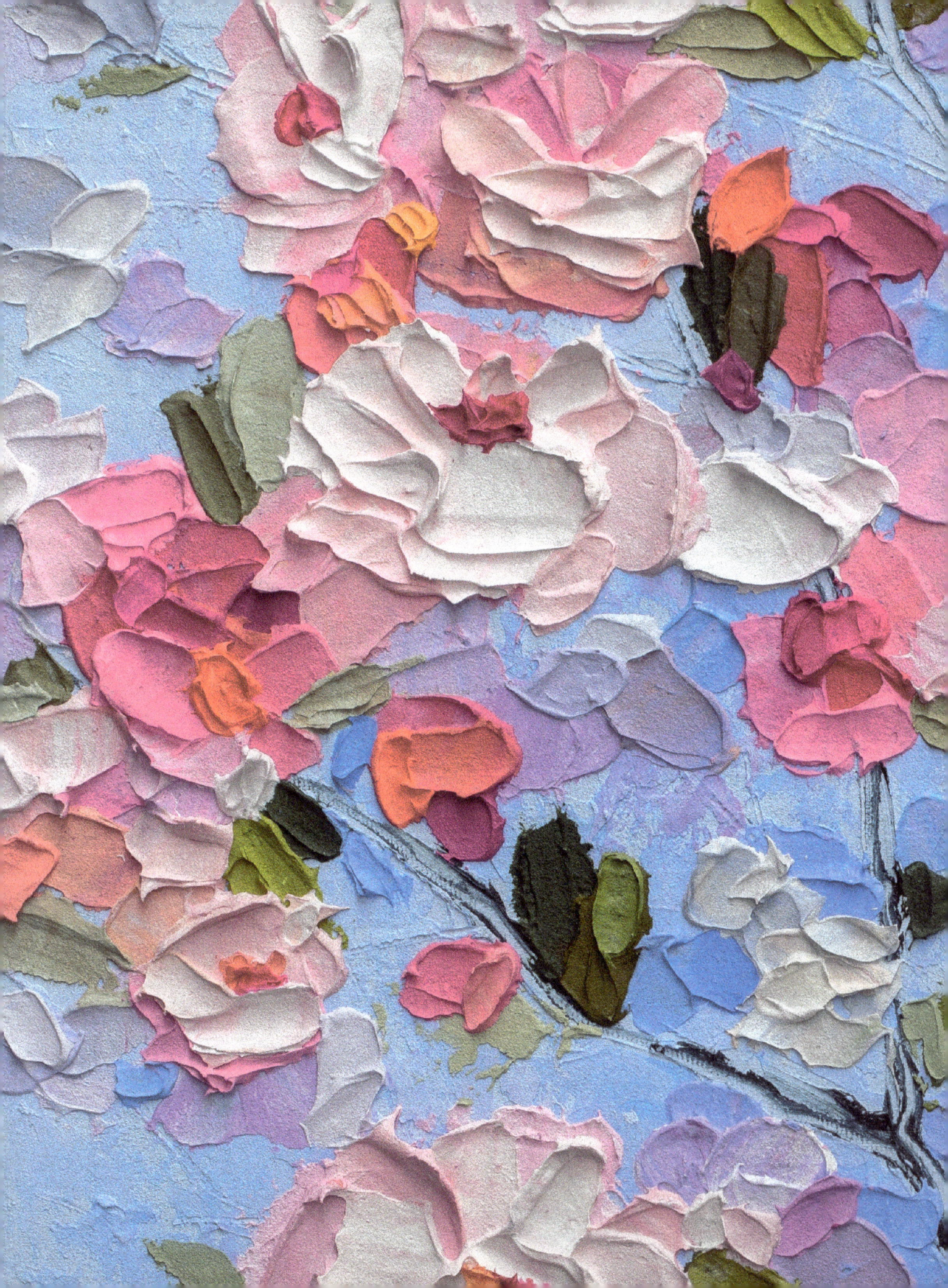

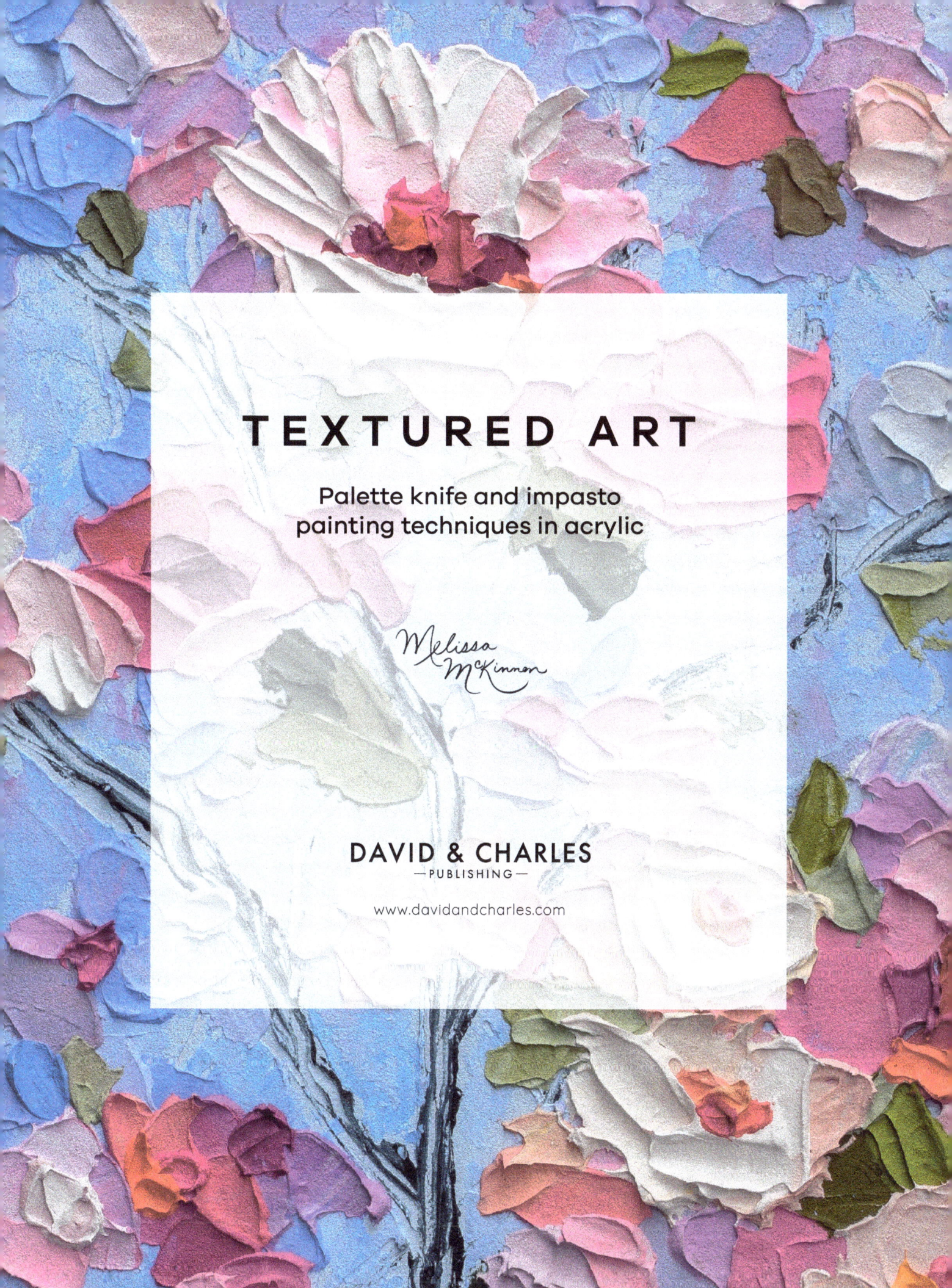

TEXTURED ART

Palette knife and impasto
painting techniques in acrylic

Melissa McKinnon

DAVID & CHARLES
— PUBLISHING —

www.davidandcharles.com

Contents

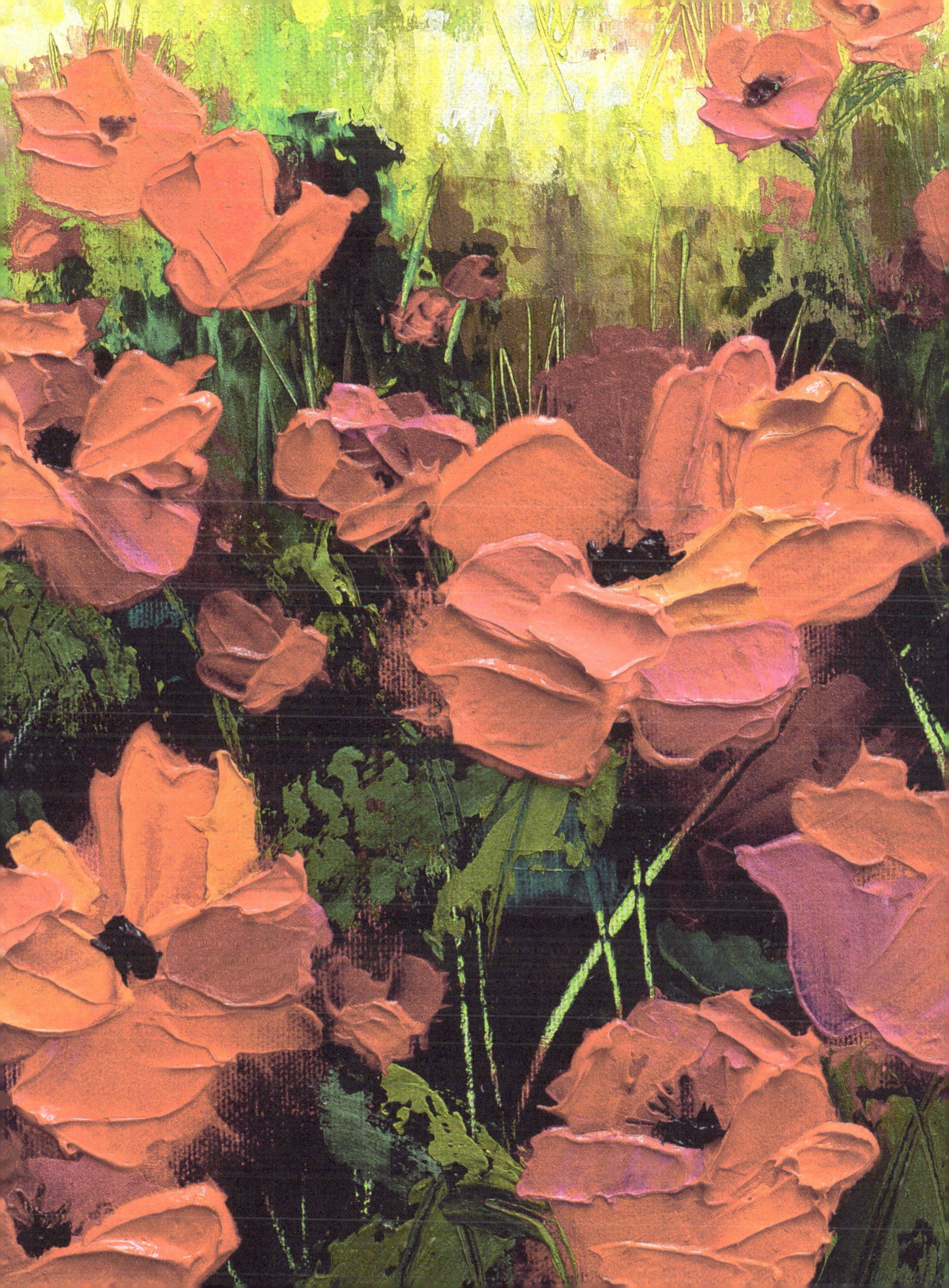

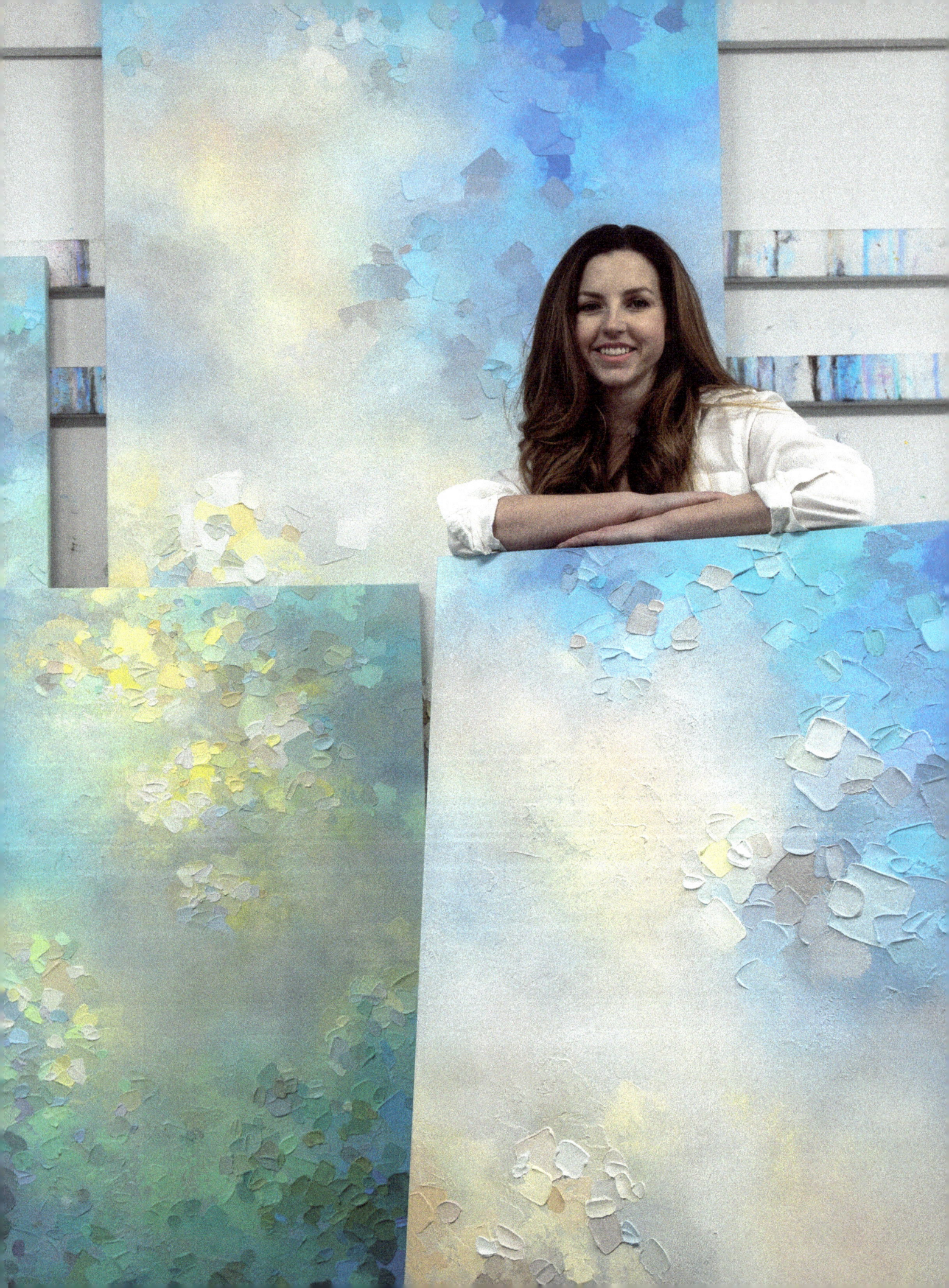

Introduction

For as long as I can remember, 'painter' has been part of my identity.

As a child, art was a way for me to make sense of the world. It allowed me to create beauty in the dark, find quiet in the chaos, and develop a sense of optimism that has carried me to where I am today. My earliest experiences with art gifted me the ability to express myself, and I loved the feeling of freedom that expression gave me so much that I made it my profession. Even now, in a messy world constantly in crisis, I stand before my canvas with the same unrelenting optimism that pulled me out of the deepest, darkest parts of my life with an artist's sense of duty to show others that all of life becomes art when you choose to see the beauty in it.

I love to travel. Everywhere I go, I gather inspiration and find something to fall in love with. Whether it's a sunset, a breathtaking vista, or a dense forest, those who see my paintings often see themselves in the same scene, instantly transported to a time in their life or a memory that brings them happiness. When you look at my artwork, you'll see the visual evolution of the many journeys I've taken, the places I've been, and the joy in my soul – all expressed through paint.

Stand back and take in all the trees, mountains, and oceans, or step forward and put your nose to the canvas to immerse yourself in the dozens of individual strokes that support each other in telling a larger story.

My painting style is unique, using abstraction, expressive color, and texture to draw viewers into nature's stunning moments and their own intimate memories. The gentle rustling of a wooded breeze, the sun-drenched sway of leaves and petals, the sensual light in a sunset fading fast... my paintings feel at once like real destinations and imagined dreamscapes.

I like to think that my paintings give people the same sacred permission to dream in color that art gave me so many years ago in pieces that serve as reminders, on walls and in homes, in workspaces and in schools, that beauty is ours for the taking if we're brave enough to train our eye to it.

As you explore the techniques and paintings in this book, practice your own observation. What catches your breath as much as it catches your eye? What causes you to pause, lean in closer, or zoom in a little further? Let yourself be drawn to the beauty you take in – and when you're ready to – make it yours.

Thank you for learning with me, for supporting my dream, and for dreaming in color with me.

Yours in creativity,

Melissa McKinnon

Find Melissa at
www.melissamckinnonart.com
Instagram: @melissamckinnonart
Facebook: MelissaMcKinnonArt
Pinterest: mmckinnonartist

How to use this book

I've designed this book to take both the beginner and experienced artist on a journey into impasto painting. I'll start by describing everything you need to know about the paint and mediums, as well as the tools and materials we'll be using. We'll take a look at color and how to mix it, which is an important part of the process.

There are simple practice exercises to get you comfortable using a palette knife and LOTS of paint. Using lots of paint is essential to creating eye-catching, thickly textured paintings. The more layers of paint you use, the more depth and interest your painting will have. This is the essence of impasto painting.

Practice is vital to achieving success with a palette knife. Sculpting and molding large amounts of paint can be intimidating and unwieldy at first. But once you get the hang of it, there is so much you can do to control the paint and create stunning textural effects. I'm going to show you several mark making techniques that you can use alone or in combination to create your own expressive, textured paintings.

Once you feel confident with the tools and paint, I'll show you how I create my textured landscapes, florals, and abstracts with step-by-step instructions. I've designed a series of paintings that will help you put all of the techniques and color theory you've learned into action.

There's no right or wrong when it comes to painting. Every person is different and has their own way of seeing and expressing the world around them. There are no rules – even though we see the grass as green and the sky as blue, it doesn't mean that it must look that way in your painting. I encourage you to learn and master the techniques but when it comes to creating your own paintings, allow yourself the freedom to indulge in the process, choose colors you love, and be expressive with your strokes. Be brave and be bold!

I hope this book gives you a solid foundation to identify what works best for you and the courage and freedom to develop your own unique style. I hope you will feel challenged and inspired.

Happy painting!

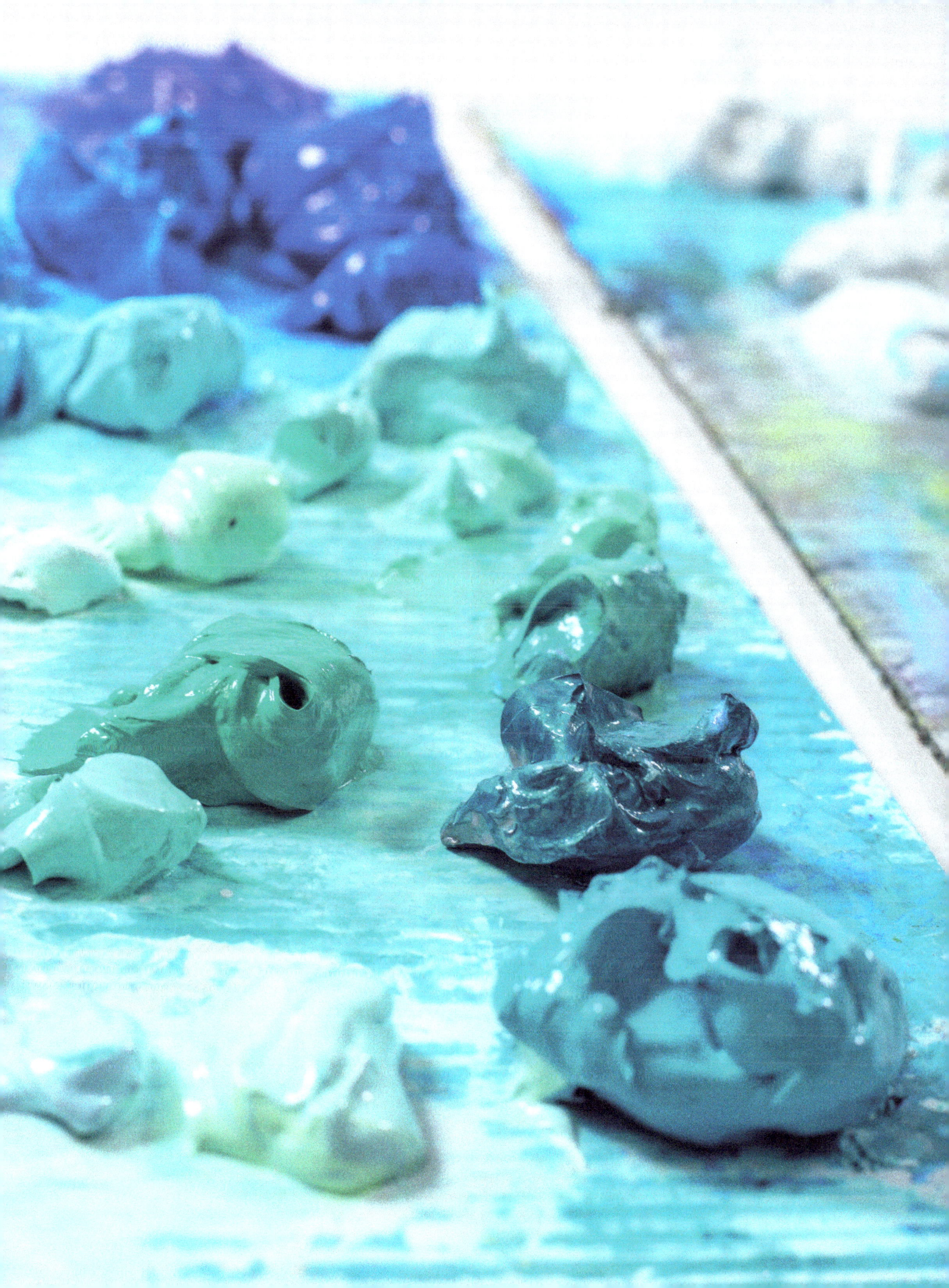

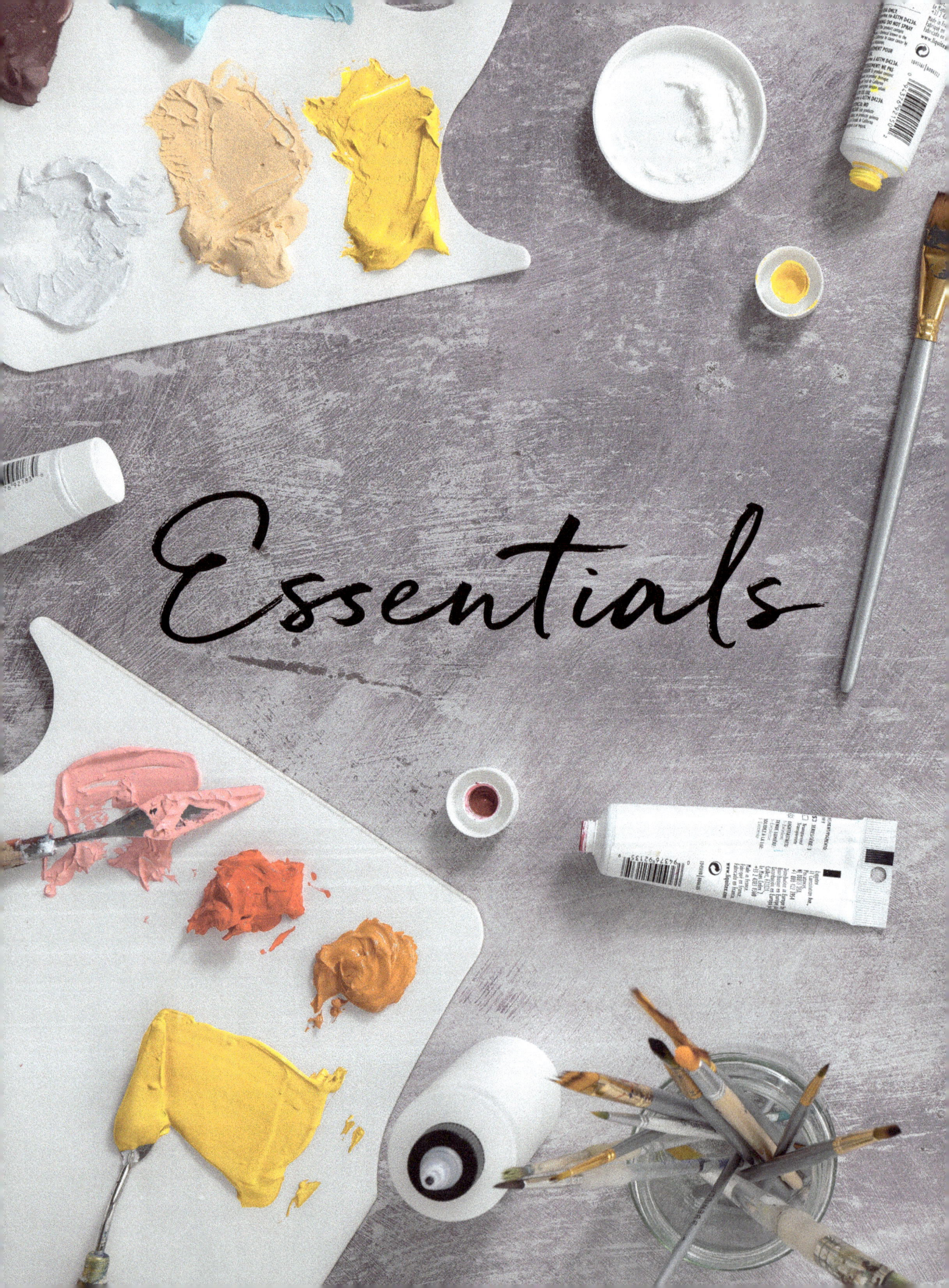

Essentials

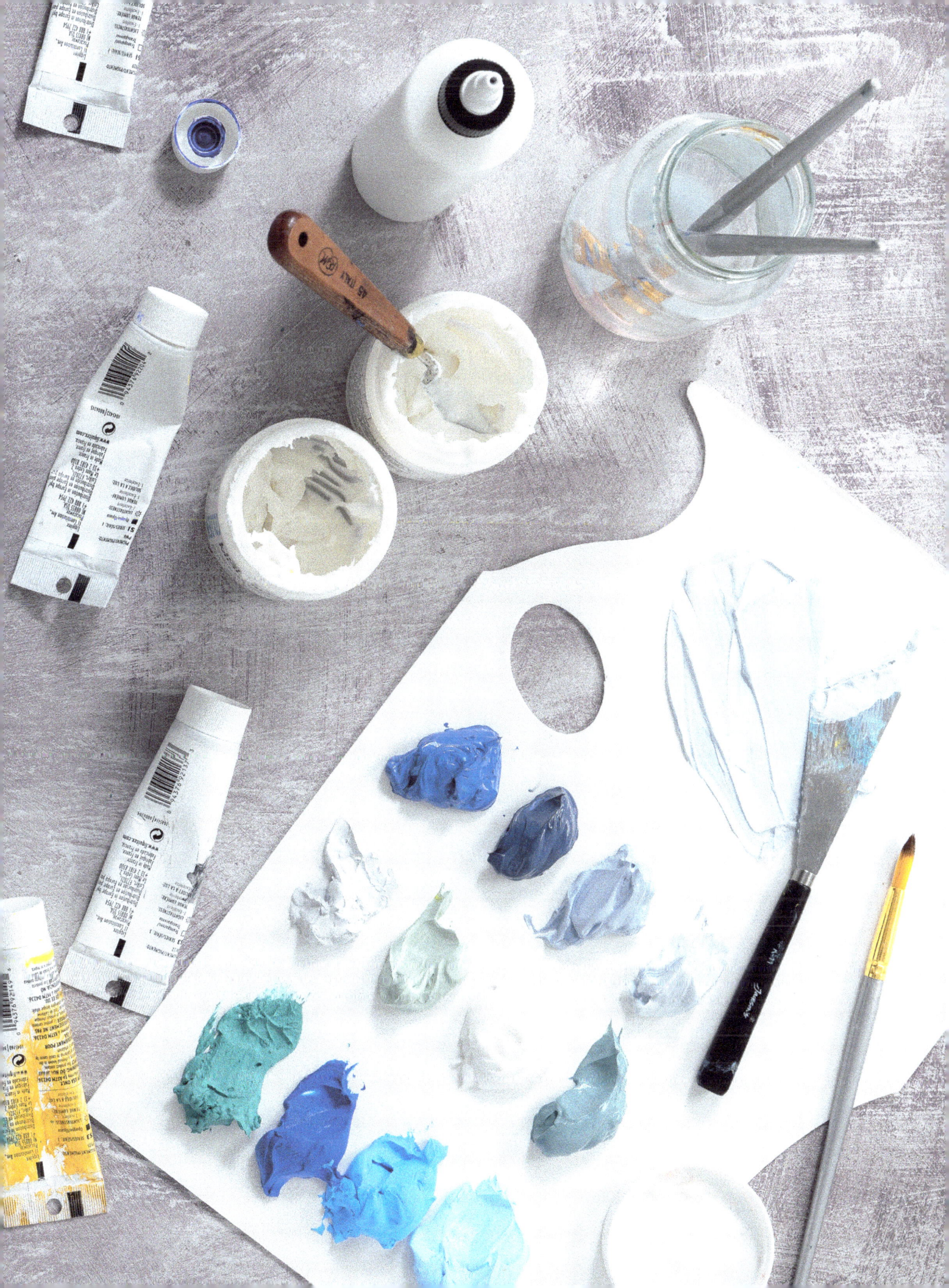

Overview

Here are the essential supplies you'll find useful on your painting journey. As you work through the exercises and projects in this book, you can refer to these lists to help guide your choices. I've listed everything I've used in detail but feel free to substitute anything with supplies you have on hand.

Acrylic paint and mediums

This list covers the types and brands of paint and medium that I use, and I'll talk more about these crucial elements later on in this section.

- Acrylic paint
- Fluid acrylic paint or acrylic ink
- Gel medium
- Molding paste
- Crackle paste
- Glaze medium
- Clear acrylic polymer to seal wood panels

OTHER USEFUL SUPPLIES

- Cloth or paper towels for wiping off knives
- Jar of water for cleaning brushes or tools
- Table, easel, or any sturdy surface to work on
- Masking tape for horizon lines
- Pencil or chalk for sketches
- Rubbing alcohol to remove paint
- Spray bottle of water

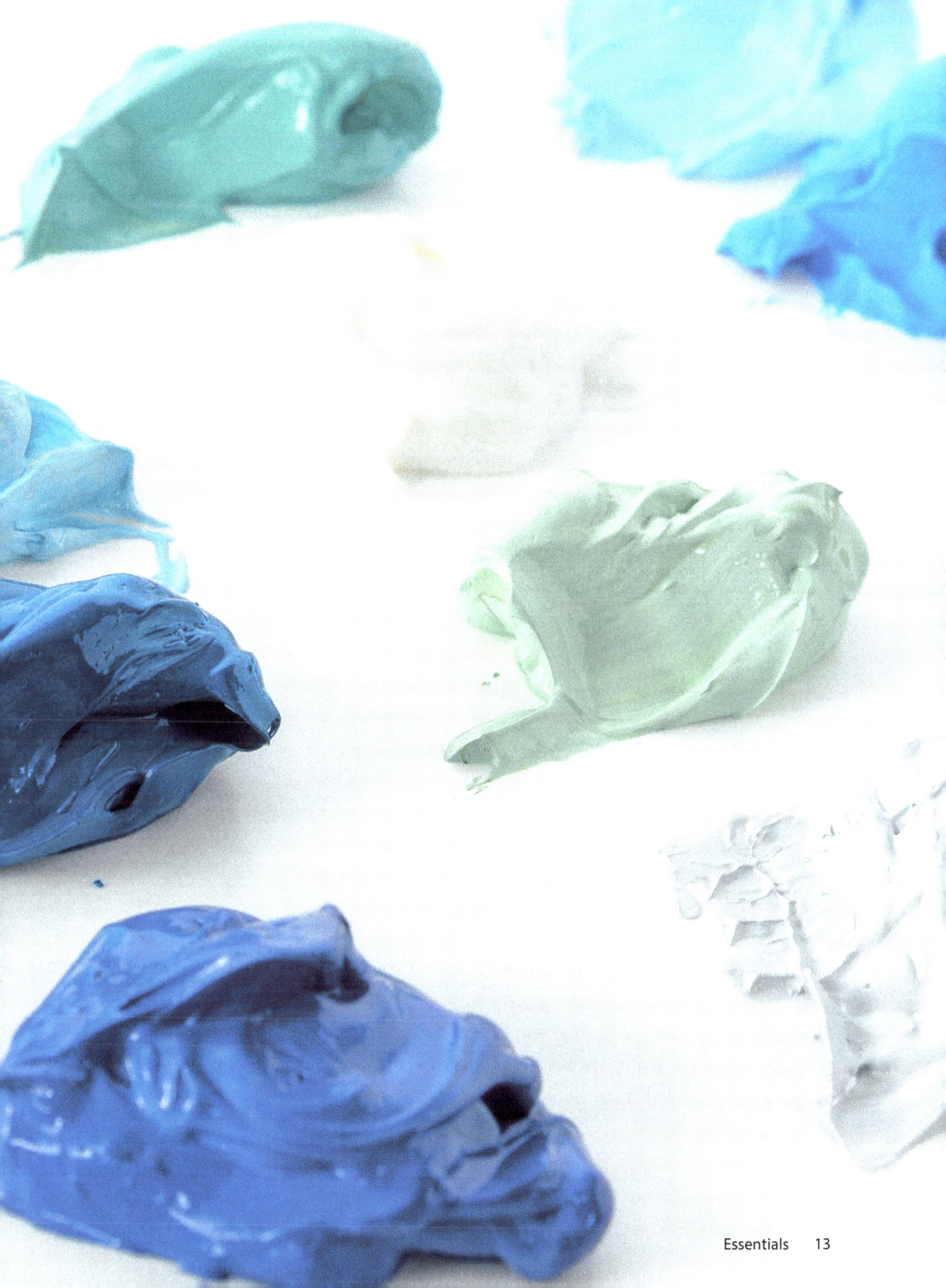

Palettes

You will need a non-porous surface to mix and store your paints. Acrylics dry quickly so you'll want to keep your paint moist. You can purchase a stay-wet palette or easily make your own. Here's how.

Use a plastic tray lined with several paper towels. Soak the paper towels with water and place a sheet of wax paper or parchment paper over the top, and add your paint. The moisture from the paper towels will keep your acrylic paint moist without diluting the paint and making it runny.

To prevent your paint from drying out and forming a skin, lightly mist with water to keep it moist.

I use this tray palette for my fluid paint mixing. The raised edge keeps the paint contained and prevents it from flowing off the sides. For my thicker paints, I use sheets of corrugated plastic cut to size to fit under an overturned plastic tub. Since impasto painting requires a lot of paint, I usually have several palettes on the go at a time. A light mist of water sprayed inside the tub will keep your paint moist for days if not weeks. You can also pre-mix your colors with medium and store them in sealed jars or plastic containers.

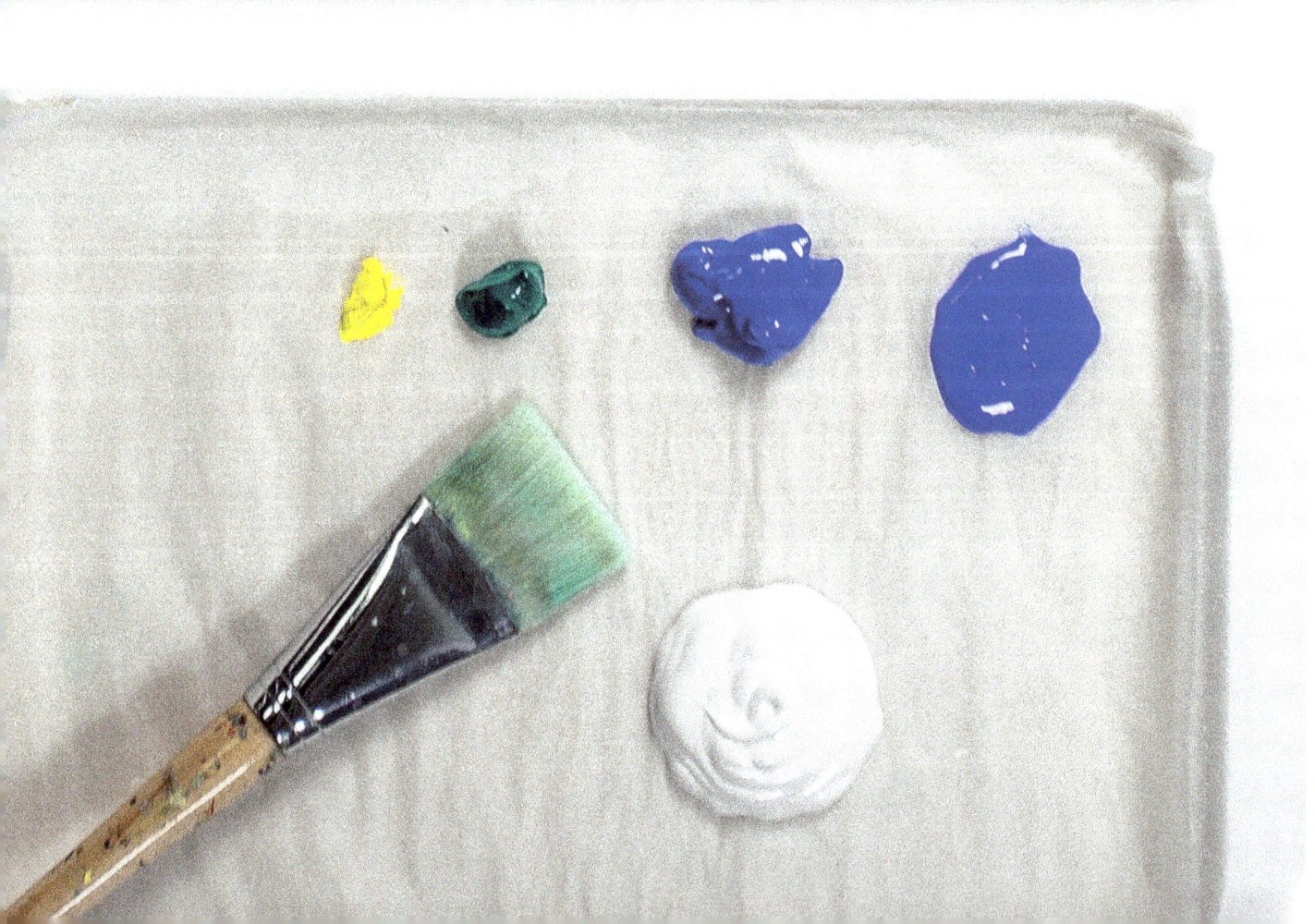

Brushes and palette knives

Brushes and palette knives come in many shapes and sizes. Although you can create an entire painting using just one palette knife or brush, adding additional shapes and sizes to your tool kit will offer you more variety and save time wiping off your knife each time you change colors.

PALETTE KNIVES

1 Large rounded metal knife
(2in or 50mm)

2 Large spade-shaped metal knife
(1½in x 4in or 40mm x 100mm)

3 Medium spade-shaped metal knife
(1¼in x 3¼in or 32mm x 82mm)

4 Small diamond-shaped metal knife
(2in x ¾in or 50mm x 20mm)

5 Small oval-shaped metal knife
(¾in x 1½in or 20mm x 40mm)

6 Angled straight-edged metal or plastic knife
(1½in or 38mm)

BRUSHES

7 Large flat synthetic brush (4in or 100mm)

8 Medium flat synthetic brush (2in or 50mm)

9 Large round natural bristle brush (size 50)

10 Small flat synthetic brush (1in or 25mm)

11 Small round natural bristle brush (size 8)

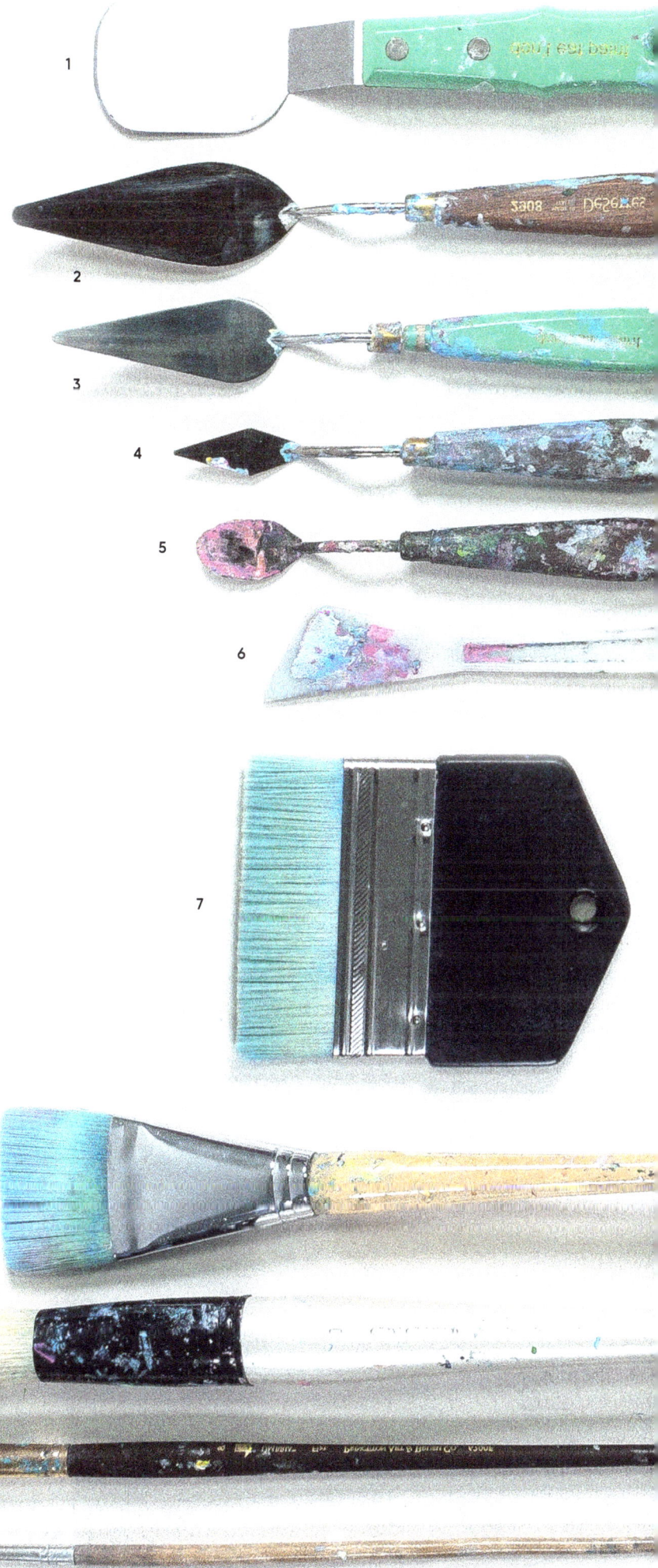

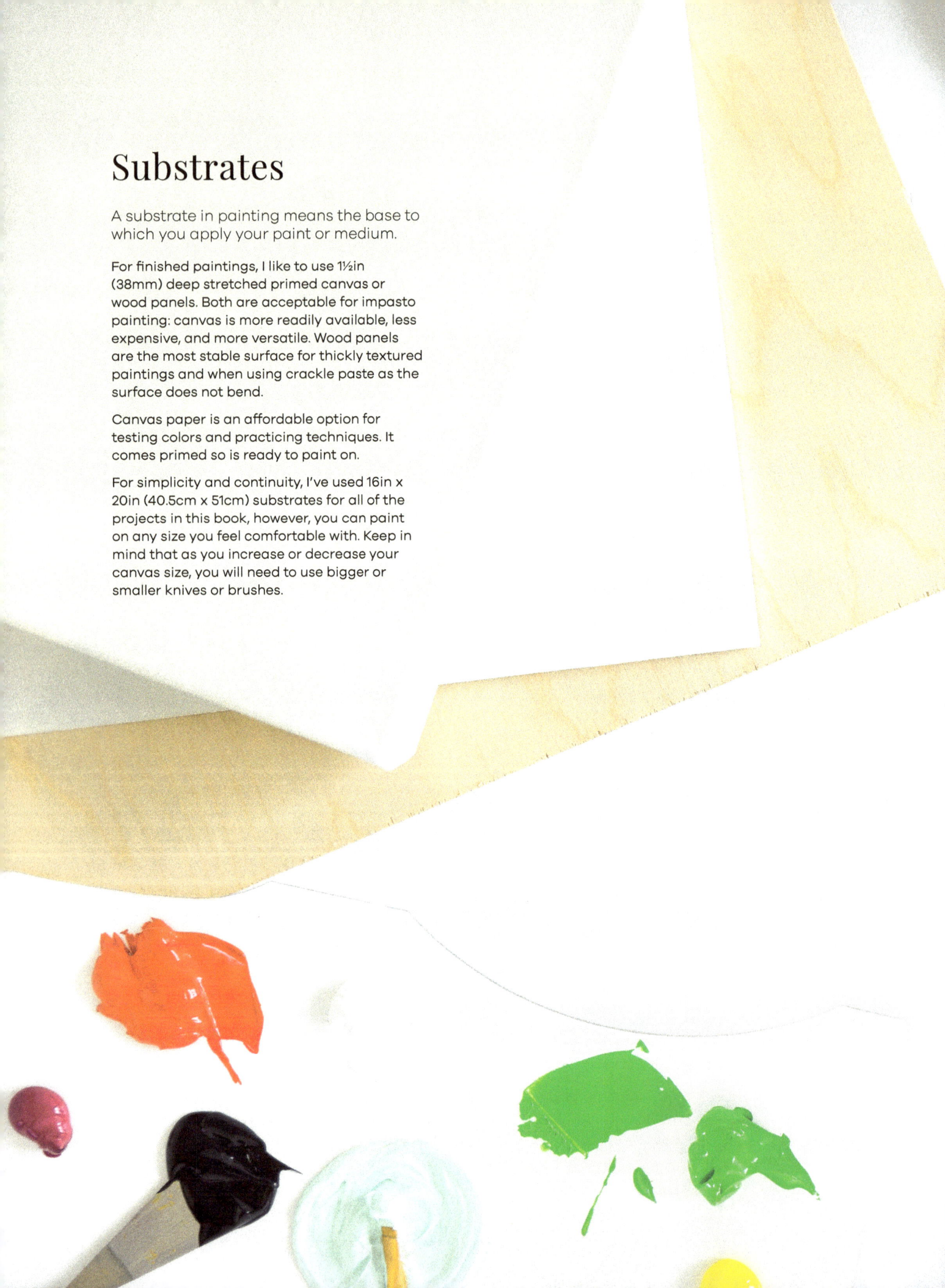

Substrates

A substrate in painting means the base to which you apply your paint or medium.

For finished paintings, I like to use 1½in (38mm) deep stretched primed canvas or wood panels. Both are acceptable for impasto painting: canvas is more readily available, less expensive, and more versatile. Wood panels are the most stable surface for thickly textured paintings and when using crackle paste as the surface does not bend.

Canvas paper is an affordable option for testing colors and practicing techniques. It comes primed so is ready to paint on.

For simplicity and continuity, I've used 16in x 20in (40.5cm x 51cm) substrates for all of the projects in this book, however, you can paint on any size you feel comfortable with. Keep in mind that as you increase or decrease your canvas size, you will need to use bigger or smaller knives or brushes.

Paint

Investing in good quality paint is essential to an enjoyable process and achieving the best results. I recommend using the best quality art supplies you can afford, but if you're just starting out and don't want to make a big investment, student grade paints are fine for practice.

Professional grade or artist quality heavy body paints are much thicker and more highly pigmented than student grade paint. If you're starting with a student grade paint, choose a brand that offers the thickest consistency. We will be adding mediums to thicken the paint but they can dilute the color pigment, so try to choose a good quality brand that offers the thickest consistency. Nova Color Acrylic Paints are a highly pigmented artist quality paint that come at an affordable price. I'll be using colors from this brand for most of the paintings in this book.

If the brands I use aren't available where you live, you could try: Golden, Liquitex, Amsterdam, Utrecht, Matisse, or Studio3. For fluid acrylic paint or acrylic ink, try Daler-Rowney as well as the brands above.

Acrylic paints come in a variety of consistencies. From ink (like water), fluid (like heavy cream), regular acrylic, and heavy body (like soft butter). I prefer heavy body consistency for impasto painting. For one

of the projects, Under the Desert Sky, we'll be using inks and high flow acrylic to paint on a textured background. However, these are optional, as you could always use acrylic paint thinned with water or glazing medium instead. See Mediums for more on this.

Keep in mind that acrylic paints tend to dry a shade darker and shrink in size when dry. It can be disappointing to mix a color exactly the way you want only for it to dry a much darker shade. It's helpful to test your colors first. Lay down a color on a scrap piece of paper or canvas and let it dry to see if it's still the color you want. Practice color mixing (see Color Mixing) and always mix more than you think you'll need.

Acrylic paint cleans with soap and water. Keep tools wet to assist cleaning and never let paint dry on your brush. If paints dry on the palette, wet the surface and wait a few minutes, then peel or scrape the paint off with a straight-edged palette knife.

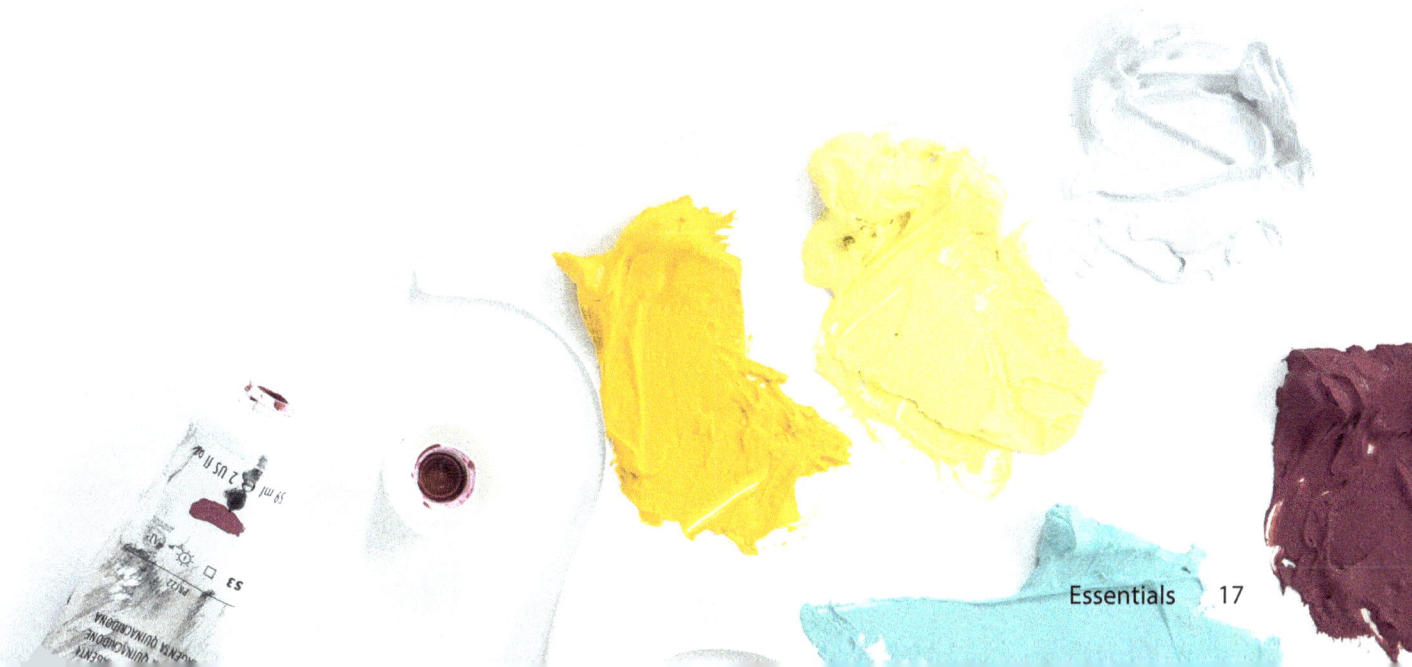

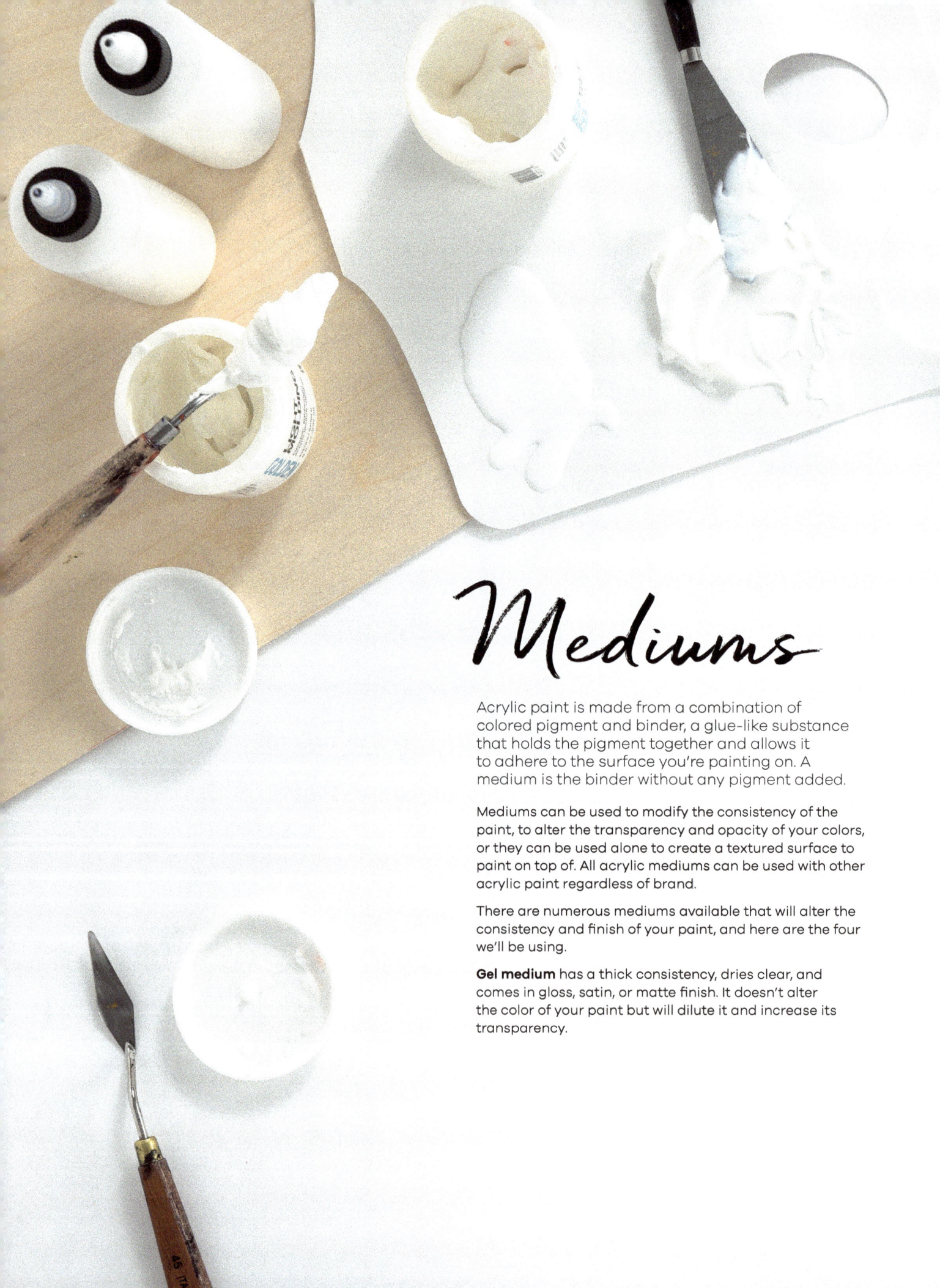

Mediums

Acrylic paint is made from a combination of colored pigment and binder, a glue-like substance that holds the pigment together and allows it to adhere to the surface you're painting on. A medium is the binder without any pigment added.

Mediums can be used to modify the consistency of the paint, to alter the transparency and opacity of your colors, or they can be used alone to create a textured surface to paint on top of. All acrylic mediums can be used with other acrylic paint regardless of brand.

There are numerous mediums available that will alter the consistency and finish of your paint, and here are the four we'll be using.

Gel medium has a thick consistency, dries clear, and comes in gloss, satin, or matte finish. It doesn't alter the color of your paint but will dilute it and increase its transparency.

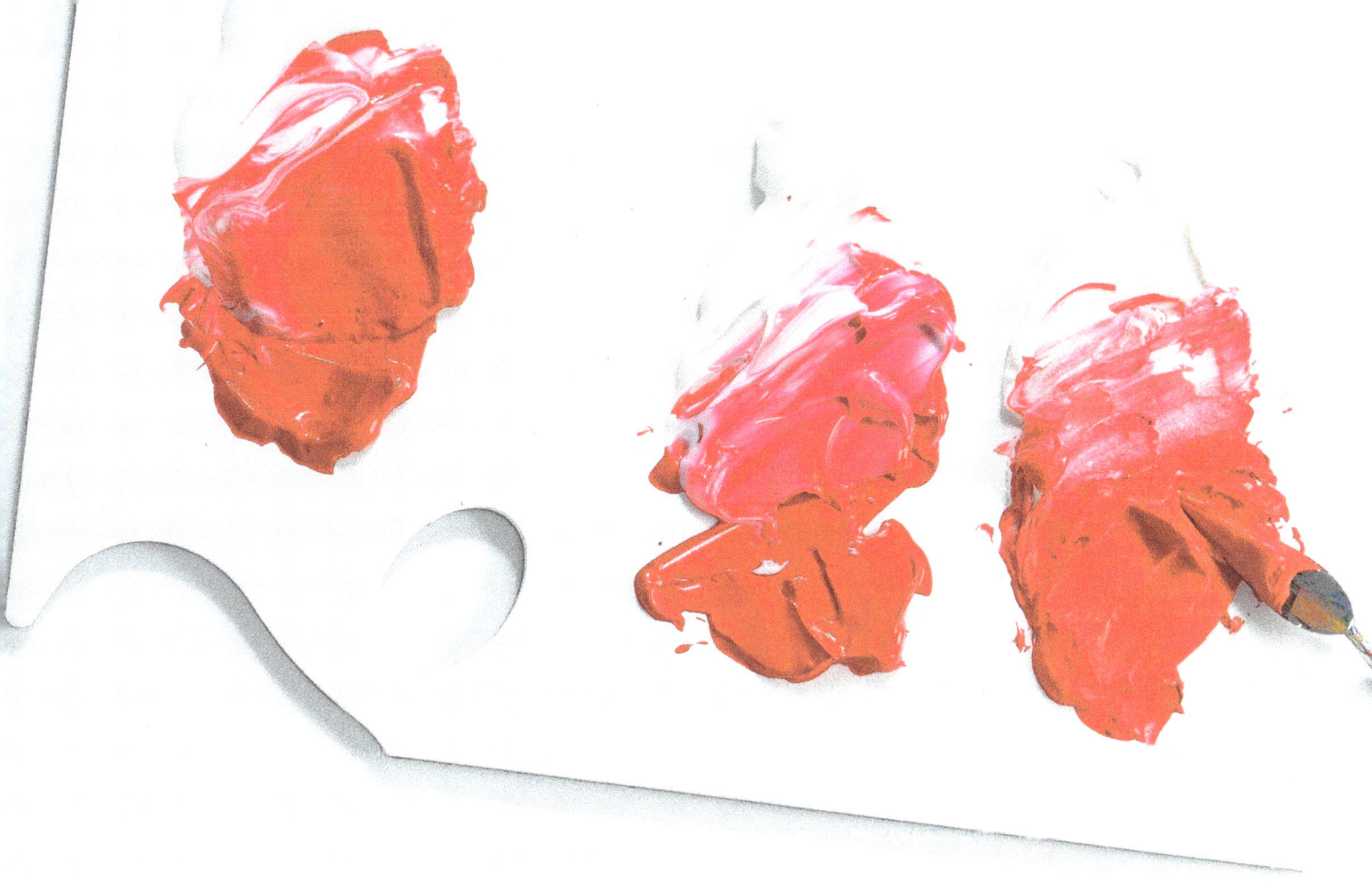

Consistency

Molding paste dries to an opaque, matte finish with an absorbent surface. It lightens your paint color making it more pastel. Gel medium and molding paste are largely interchangeable, depending on personal preference. Try both and see which one you prefer.

Crackle paste is a thick, opaque material that forms cracks as it dries. The size of the cracking pattern depends on the brand, thickness of application, and environmental conditions during drying. It dries to an opaque, matte finish, with an absorbent surface suitable for acrylic paints and mediums.

Glaze medium increases the fluidity and transparency of your paint. It slows drying time, making it easier to glaze layers of color and blend acrylics together wet-on-wet. It can be thinned with up to 20 percent water, and although it looks milky when wet, it dries clear.

Consistency is key to creating thick, animated layers of paint. Heavy body paint is much thicker than regular acrylic and is highly recommended for impasto painting. However, you can still use regular acrylic paint with the addition of a thickening medium such as molding paste or gel medium.

Mix a small amount of paste or gel to each of your paint colors before you start painting and keep them ready to go on the palette. Since each brand of acrylic paint can vary widely in consistency, there isn't an exact recipe. Usually adding 15 to 25 percent medium will be enough to thicken it without diluting the color too much. Ideally you want your paint to feel like buttercream frosting. It should be thick enough to scoop with a knife and hold its shape once applied to the canvas.

Remember to do this for all of the projects in the book if you are using regular acrylic paint, unless heavy body paint is specified.

Color

It might be tempting to purchase a tube of every color you see at the art store but I promise you that if you learn to mix your own colors, you will develop an intuitive knowledge of how to use color effectively and be able to create harmony in your paintings.

I believe it's better to buy fewer tubes of high-quality paint than a large inexpensive set.

Be aware that the hue and strength of a color can differ between manufacturers. For example, mixing a yellow and a blue from two different manufacturers can give you two slightly different greens. Experiment and get to know your colors before you begin painting: the colour wheel is an excellent place to start.

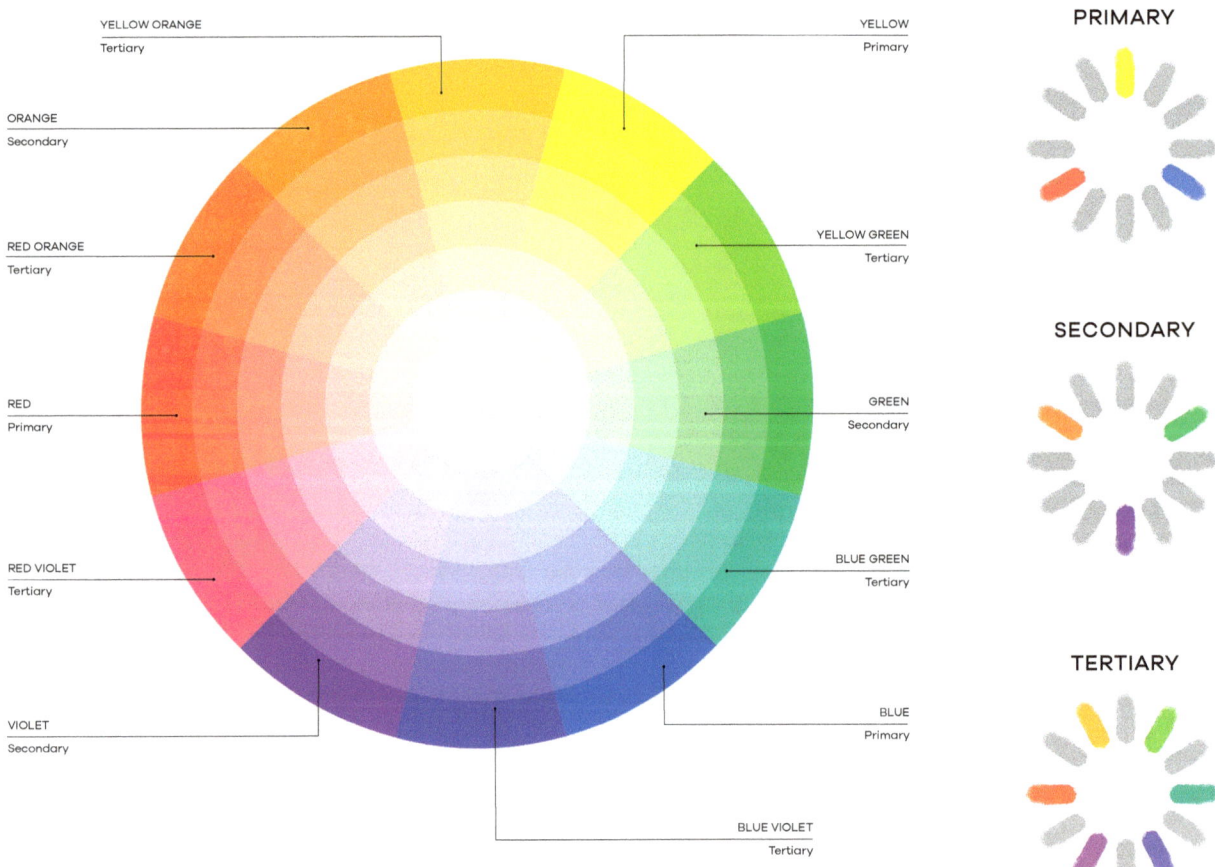

YELLOW ORANGE
Tertiary

ORANGE
Secondary

RED ORANGE
Tertiary

RED
Primary

RED VIOLET
Tertiary

VIOLET
Secondary

YELLOW
Primary

YELLOW GREEN
Tertiary

GREEN
Secondary

BLUE GREEN
Tertiary

BLUE
Primary

BLUE VIOLET
Tertiary

PRIMARY

SECONDARY

TERTIARY

Choosing a color palette

There are many approaches to selecting a color palette and every artist has their favorite way to mix color. If you're new to acrylic painting, I recommend starting with a warm and cool version of each of the primary colors and titanium white.

ESSENTIAL COLOR PALETTE

These are the colors I use most, either straight from the tube or mixed with a small amount of titanium white.

 Titanium white

 Cadmium yellow light (cool yellow)

 Cadmium yellow medium (warm yellow)

 Cadmium red medium (warm red)

 Ultramarine blue (warm blue)

 Phthalocyanine blue - green shade (cool blue)

 Quinacridone magenta (cool red)

EXTENDED COLOR PALETTE

These are additional colors you might want to consider buying for experimenting with your palette.

 Yellow ochre

 Cadmium orange

 Quinacridone red

 Permanent green light

 Phthalocyanine green

 Olive green, Hooker's green or deep green

 Raw sienna

 Burnt sienna

 Payne's gray

 Ivory black

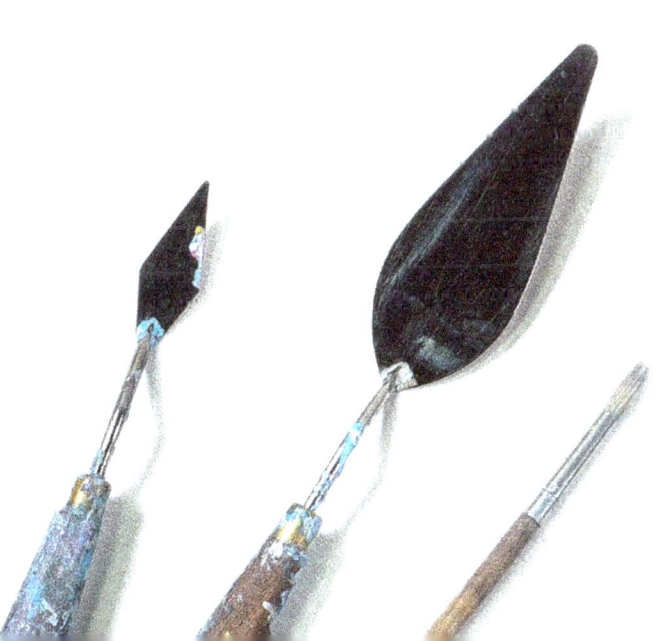

Color terminology

There are countless books on color theory and design principles, and you can spend a lifetime learning, so I won't get too deep here, but there are a few ideas you should familiarize yourself with. Let's start with some basic terminology.

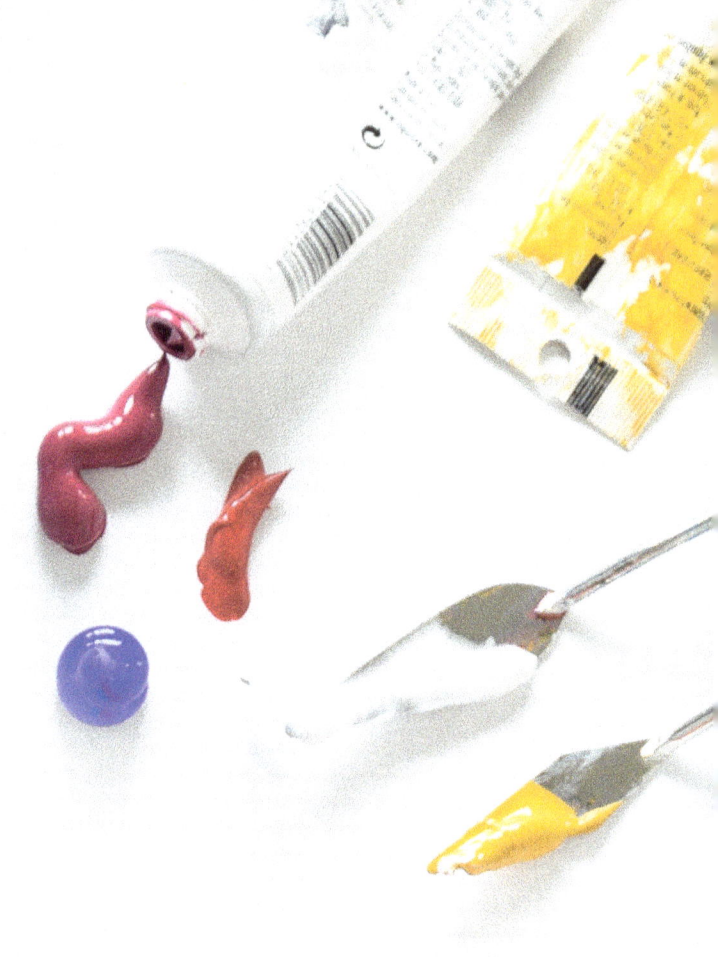

Hue

The name given to a color to distinguish it from another such as red, yellow, blue, etc.

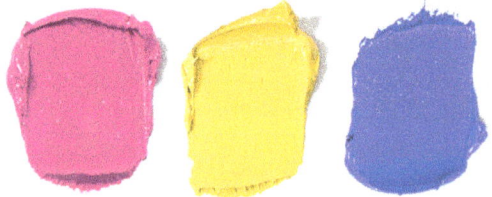

Chroma or saturation

The purity or intensity of a color. Mixing a pure hue with any other color reduces its purity and lowers the strength of the original hue (known as desaturated color). For example, adding a small amount of red to desaturate pure green colors will create more natural greens.

Value

The lightness or darkness of a color, defined by how close it is to white or black. Changes in value can be achieved by adding either black or white to any color. Strive to use a full range of values in your paintings.

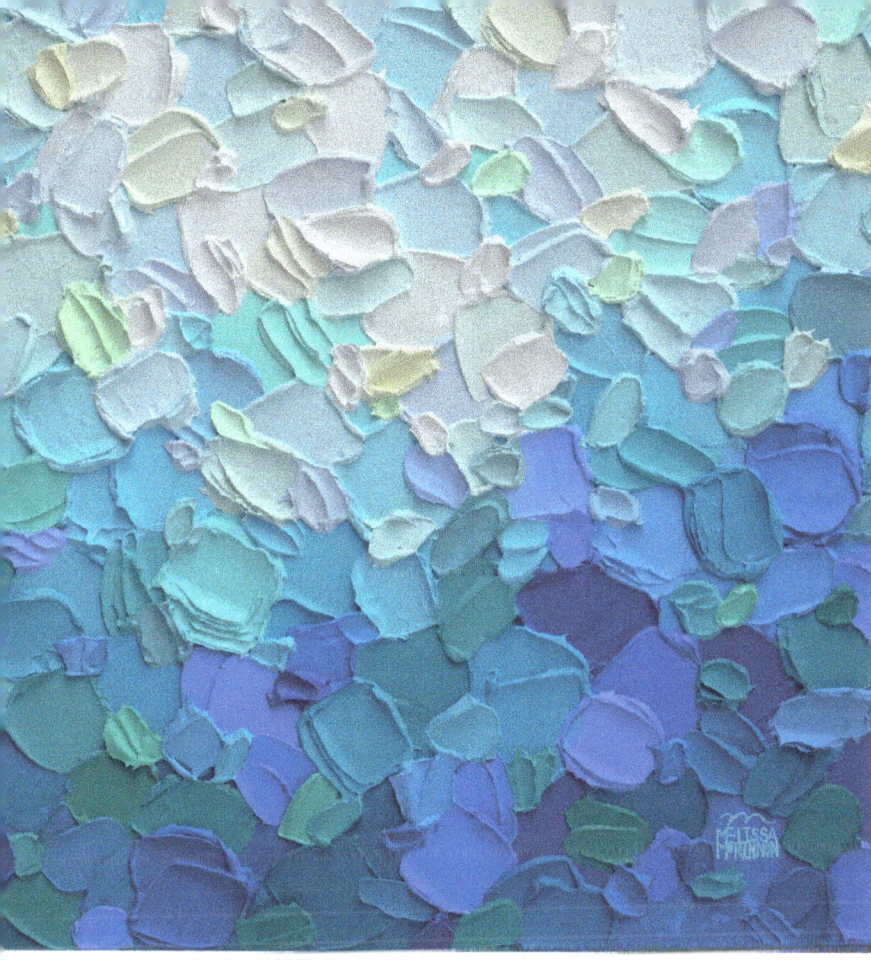

Harmony

Mixing a small amount of one color in with all of your other colors creates harmony, as now each color shares a similarity and relates to all the others.

Variety

Subtle differences within one color hue adds variety. Rather than filling the canvas with only two shades of blue (ultra and phthalo) you can mix small amounts of other colors (red, magenta, yellow) to shift the blue to become slightly warmer or cooler. Now you have several blues to work with (see Color Mixing). Additionally, once you start adding increasing amounts of white, you multiply the number of colors on your palette exponentially.

Contrast

The juxtaposition of difference, used to intensify the properties within the work, or when opposing elements are placed together. Examples of contrast include:

- Color: red v green
- Value: light v dark
- Saturation: saturated v desaturated
- Texture: smooth v rough
- Size: large v small

Color mixing

Here is a simplified version of my approach to color mixing to ensure you have a variety of color and value in your paintings. It's worth practicing this skill so that you feel confident with your color choices.

For each primary color chosen for your palette, start by mixing three piles of paint in three different values: dark, mid-tone, and light.

For example, let's mix three values of cool red:

- Dark cool blue = phthalo blue + a very small amount of titanium white.

- Mid-tone cool blue = phthalo blue + titanium white until it becomes a mid-value.

- Light cool blue = phthalo blue + lots of titanium white (when mixing light values it's easier to add a small amount of color to white rather than the other way around).

Essentially, add white until the color reaches the desired value. If you are new to painting, this simplified method allows you to work easily from dark to light without having to decipher between all ten values on the value scale.

Once you have mixed three values of each color on your palette, you can take small amounts from these piles and mix them with other colors on the palette, creating even more variations of color and value.

This is an easy way to achieve variety of color and interest in a painting without mixing dozens of colors on your palette at the beginning of a project. Starting with only a few essential colors in three different values ensures that all of the colors produced from mixing are harmonious and look good next to each other.

Often beginners default to mixing a variety of mid-tone colors and use them for the entire painting. This results in a flat, monotone painting with little contrast or interest. To increase the chance of creating a successful painting, remember to add those light and dark values.

It's also worth noting that some colors straight from the tube can be very dark and will need to be mixed with a small amount of titanium white to bring out the true color of the paint.

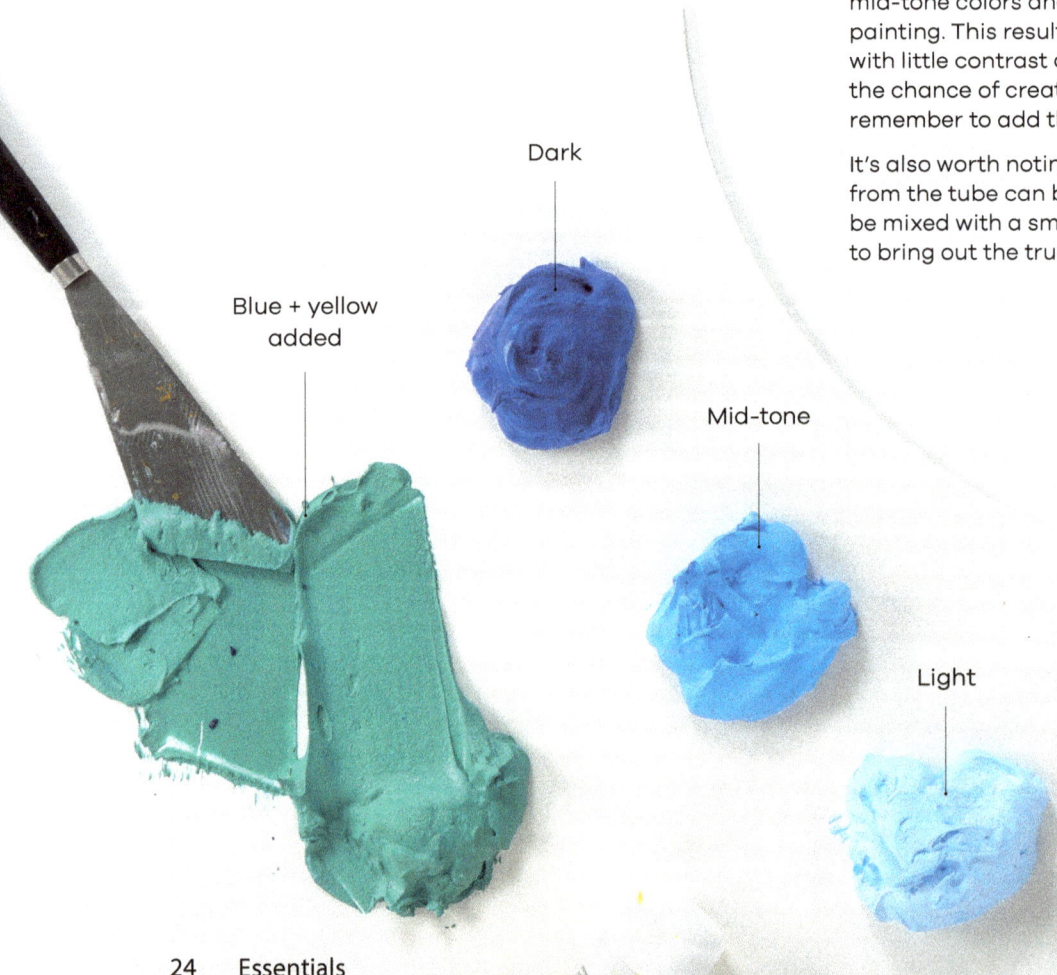

Dark

Blue + yellow added

Mid-tone

Light

MIXING CHROMATIC BLACK AND GRAY

I rarely use black straight from the tube in my paintings and prefer to mix my own chromatic black and gray. Mixing complementary colors (those that are opposite each other on the color wheel) will create a rich black. Adding titanium white will lighten the value and create a beautiful range of grays. You can use these colors on their own or add them to others to reduce their saturation.

We will be using chromatic black and gray in several projects throughout the book. You can mix a large quantity and store it in an airtight container or mix small amounts as you go. If you prefer not to mix your own colors, ivory black and Payne's gray are acceptable substitutions.

To create a rich chromatic black:

Mix a blue, red, and yellow from your chosen palette of colors (ultramarine blue, quin magenta, and cad yellow medium in our example). Adjust the quantity of each primary color to skew the temperature making it more cool or warm. Add titanium white to create a range of grays.

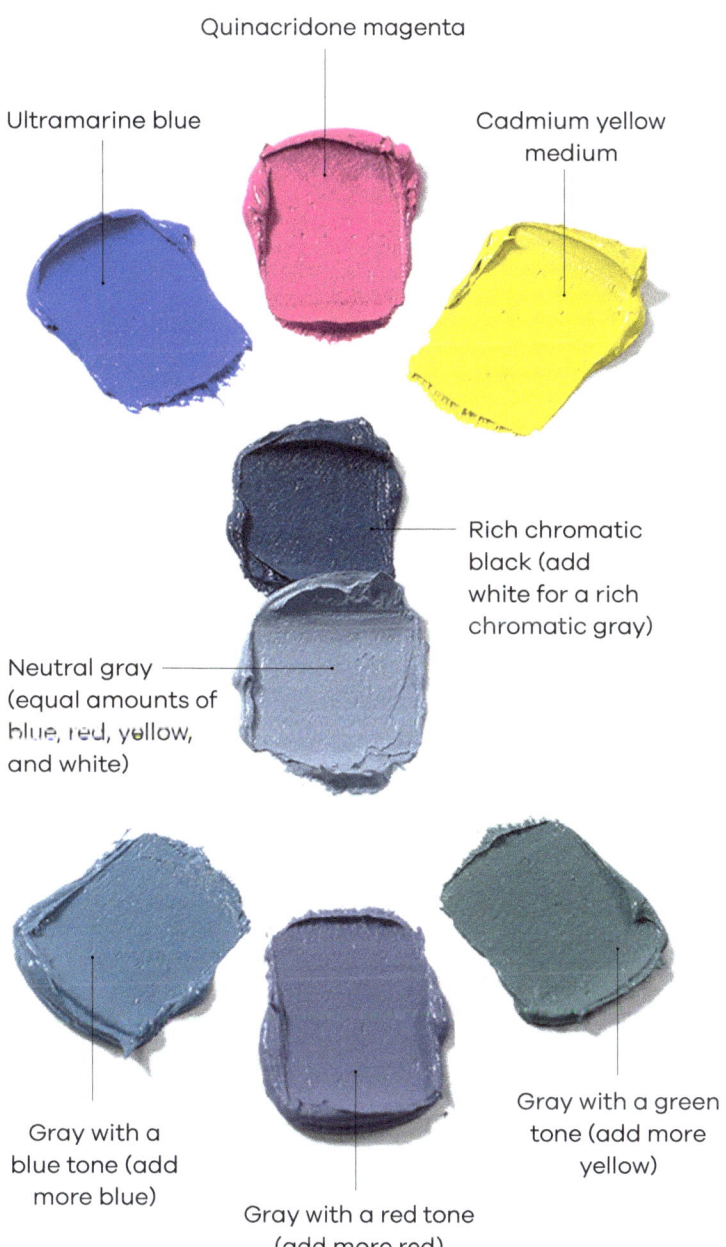

Quinacridone magenta

Ultramarine blue

Cadmium yellow medium

Rich chromatic black (add white for a rich chromatic gray)

Neutral gray (equal amounts of blue, red, yellow, and white)

Gray with a blue tone (add more blue)

Gray with a red tone (add more red)

Gray with a green tone (add more yellow)

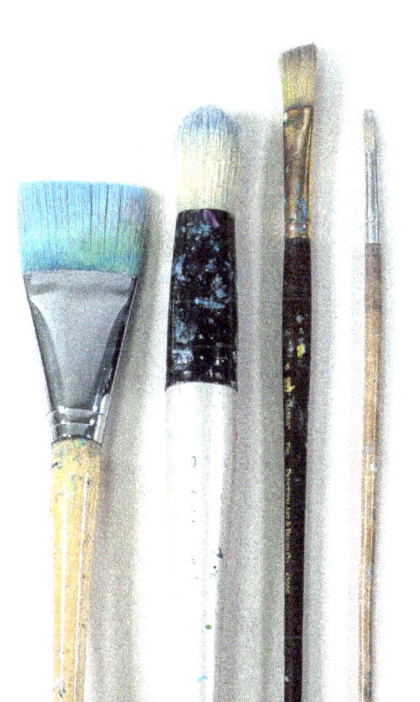

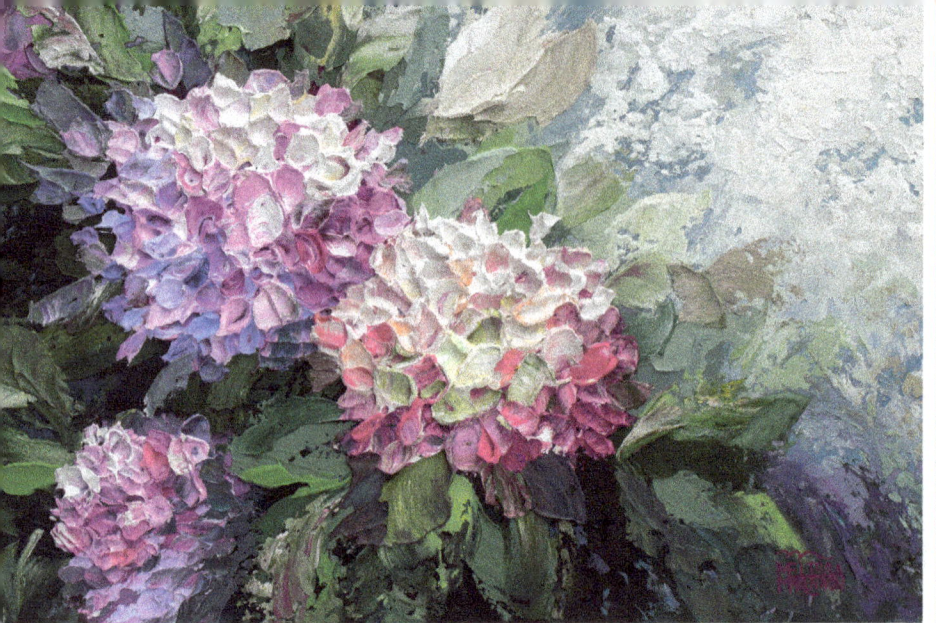

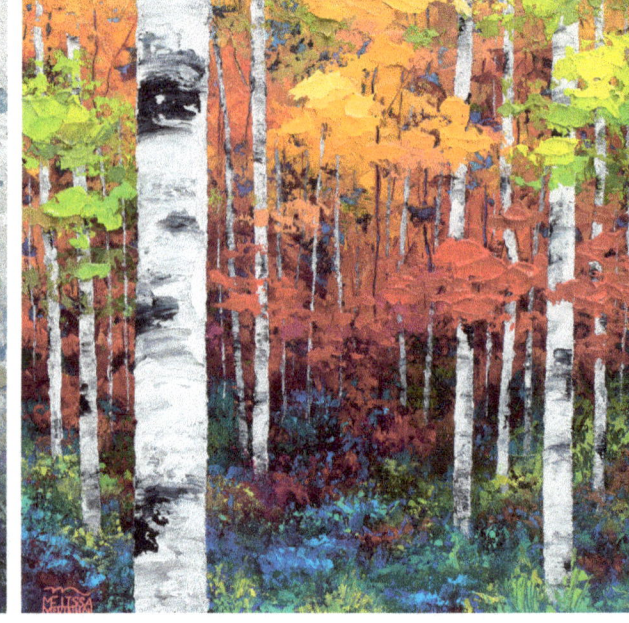

Composition

SKETCHES

Sketching is a useful tool to establish composition before you begin painting. Sometimes I'll create four or five small thumbnail sketches (roughly 1in to 2in or 25mm to 50mm in size) and other times, I'll use pencil or chalk to sketch directly on the canvas. I prefer chalk because it's easy to erase with a finger or damp cloth. You can make your sketches as detailed as you like. I prefer to keep mine quite simple and loose to avoid getting stuck in the details.

THE RULE OF THIRDS

The rule of thirds is a simple and effective way of creating an interesting and balanced composition. Divide your canvas into three horizontal rows and three vertical columns and at the points where the vertical and horizontal lines intersect is where your focal points should be.

Dividing landscape elements into thirds – for example, two-thirds sky and one third land or vice versa – creates drama, and provides interest and balance in your composition.

There are many principles of composition to choose from, so feel free to explore them further if this topic interests you.

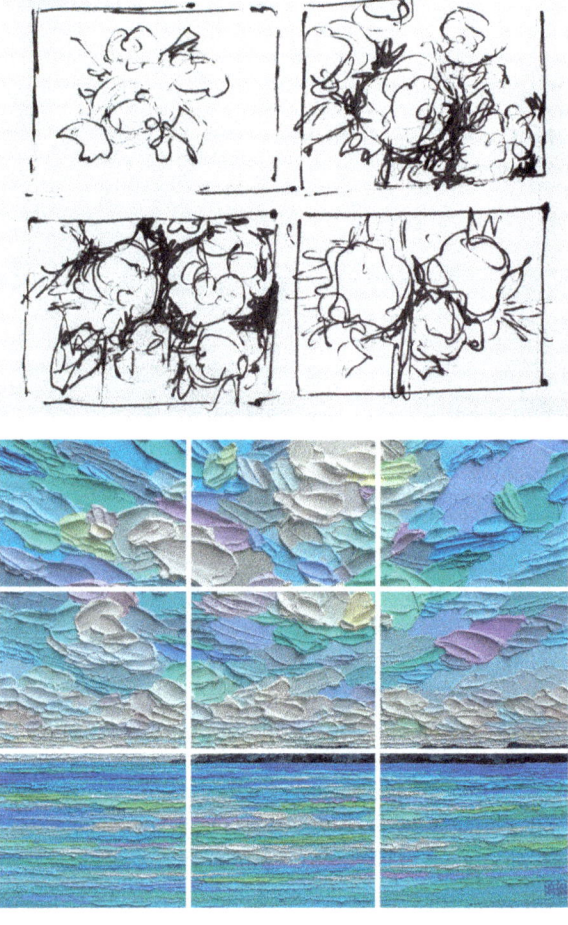

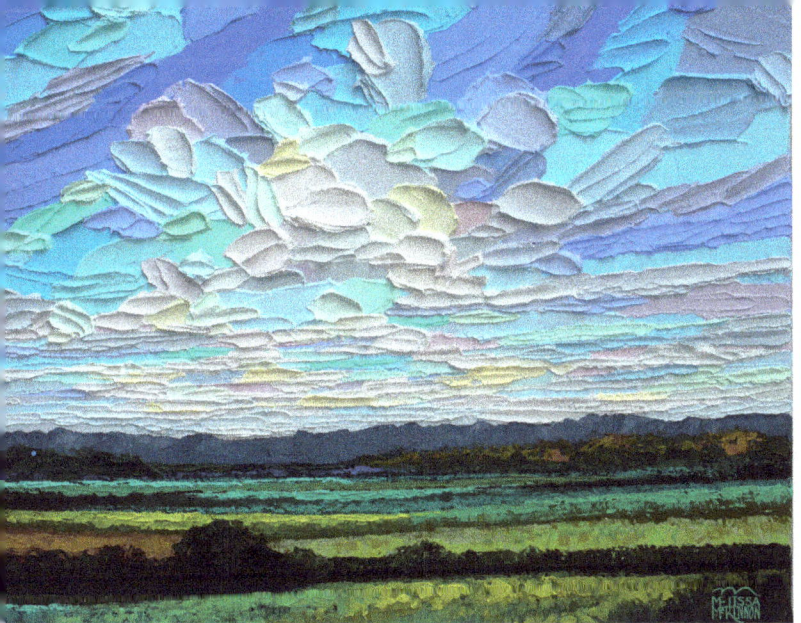

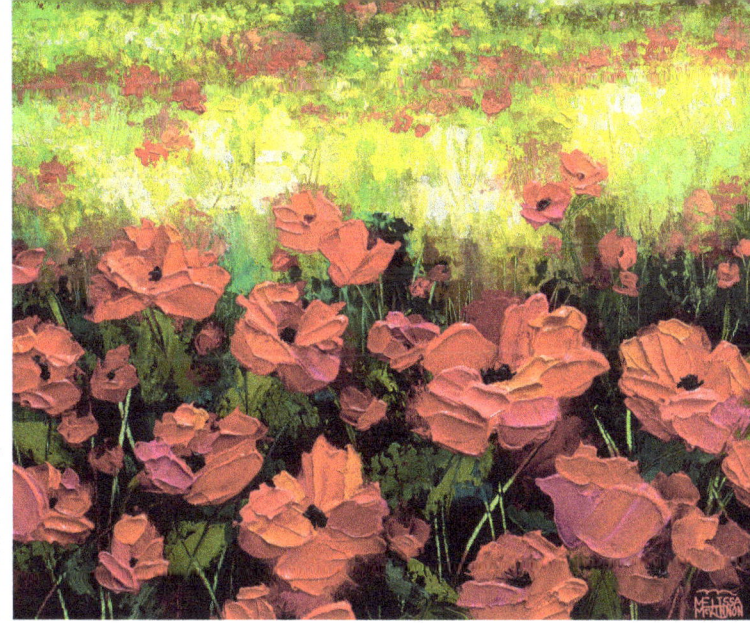

ELEMENTS

Think about the scale of the elements within your painting. Objects such as fields, trees, and flowers in the distance should appear smaller as well as cooler and more desaturated in color, while elements that are in the foreground should appear larger, warmer, and more saturated.

Keep the following in mind when choosing where to place colors and shapes in the sky. When you observe the sky, you'll notice that it appears to have a lighter and warmer shade of blue near the horizon and progressively gets darker and cooler the higher up you look. In terms of perspective, the cloud shapes generally appear to get smaller near the horizon as the clouds move further away.

When painting flowers, think about how you group them. Odd numbers are pleasing to the eye so groups of one, three, or five are a great starting point. Spread your largest blooms around the canvas to encourage the viewer's eye to move around the composition, and think about overlapping big and small flowers. Beginners often paint individual flowers all the same size and spaced evenly apart, which looks unnatural. Overlapping flowers of different sizes, shapes, and directions, and placing them in small groups, is an easy way to overcome that tendency and make the painting more believable and interesting.

WHILE YOU WORK

Assess your painting as it develops. You want to look for flow – does your eye travel around the canvas, or does it get stuck in one main area? Ideally, areas of interest and high contrast are balanced with areas of calm to allow the eye to rest. Perhaps there is an area of your painting that you want to draw attention to – you could add some interest there such as contrasting shapes, color, value, or texture.

I often start with one color and place it in several areas around the canvas, then pick up another color and add that in several more places, and repeat this with additional colors, lightening their value as I go. Placing the same color in multiple places throughout your painting will help draw the viewer's eye around the composition.

I get asked all the time, "how do you know when a painting is finished?" For me, it's when I look at the painting and the composition is balanced and has a good flow, as well as having a good range of color and value. It's when I don't see anything distracting that leaps out. If it does, I may need to tone it down or add something to balance it somewhere else in the painting. It's also finished when I don't feel the need to add anything else. It's better to leave the painting 95 percent complete rather than over working it and adding too much.

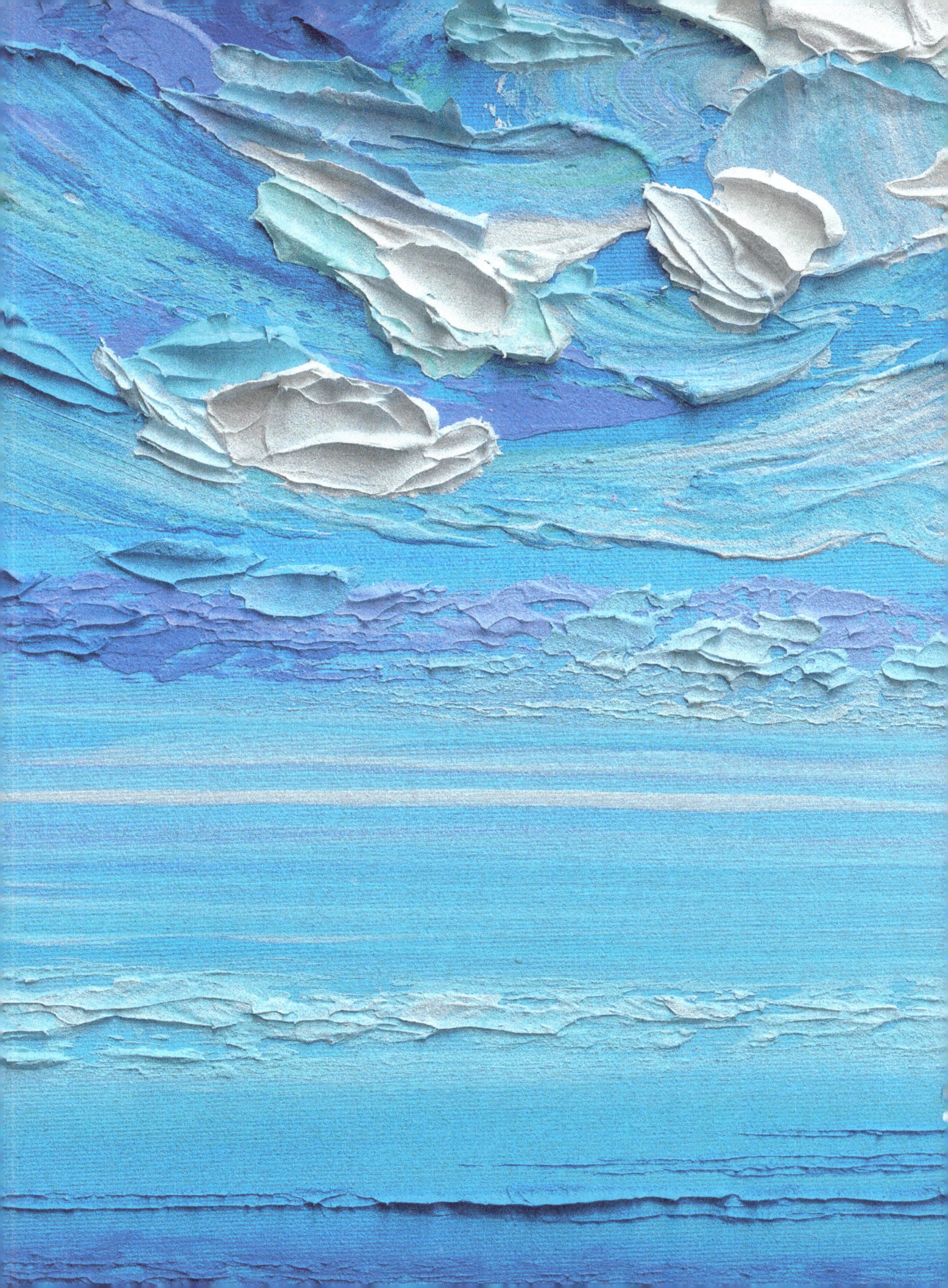

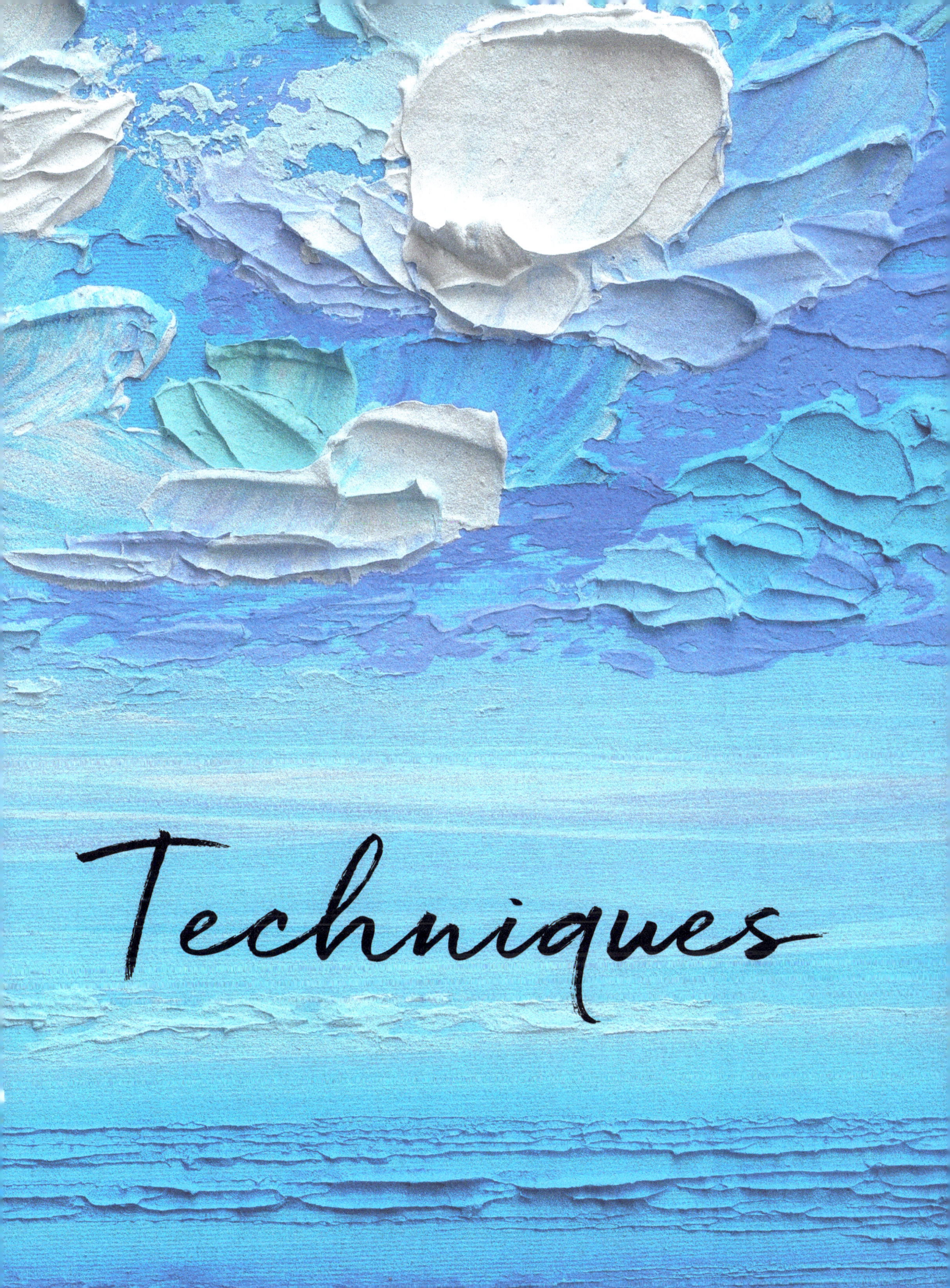

Techniques

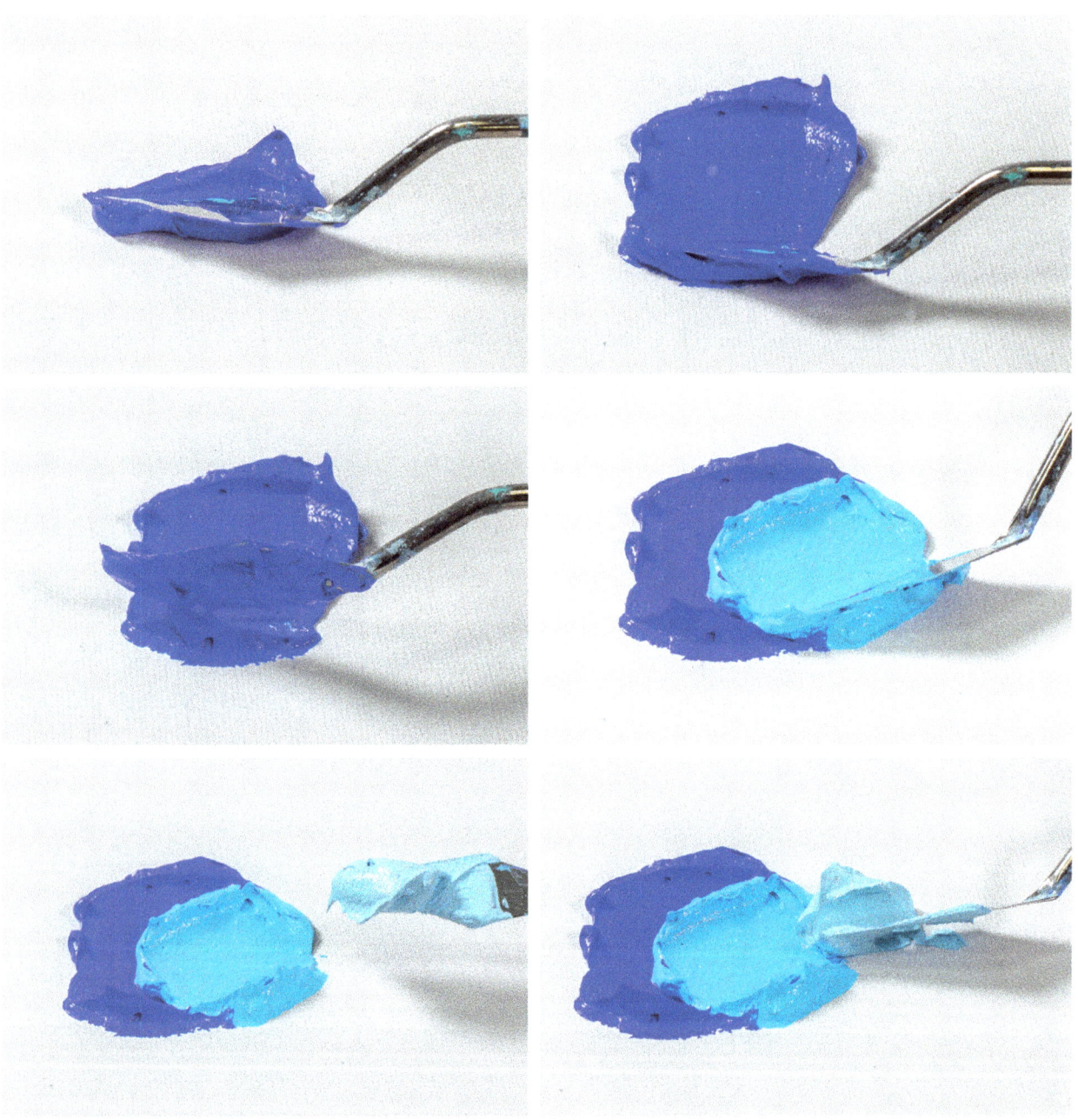

IMPASTO

Load the underside of your palette knife with a large amount of paint. Place it paint side down and lightly press down as you glide the knife across the surface until you've achieved the desired size. Gently lift your knife creating a raised edge. To create daubs, use the tip of your knife and apply a small amount of paint simply by touching the paint to the surface and lifting up. These daubs are used to create details in a number of the projects.

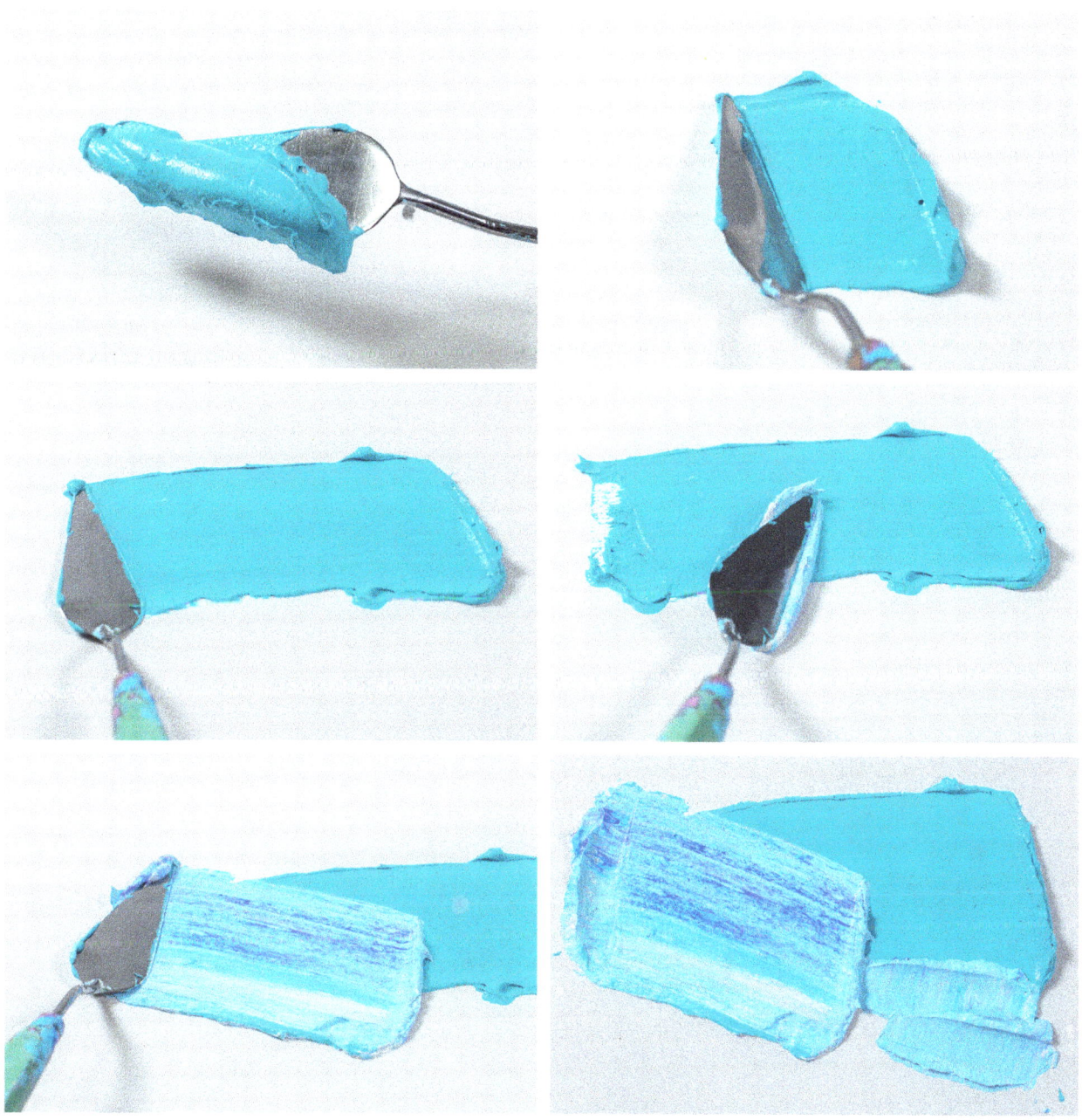

LONG SWATCHES

This is similar to the impasto technique but allow your knife to sweep across the surface creating a longer mark. This is great for creating clean passages of color and covering a large surface area, either with a solid color or multiple colors to create a blend. Use this for large clouds and sections of landscape.

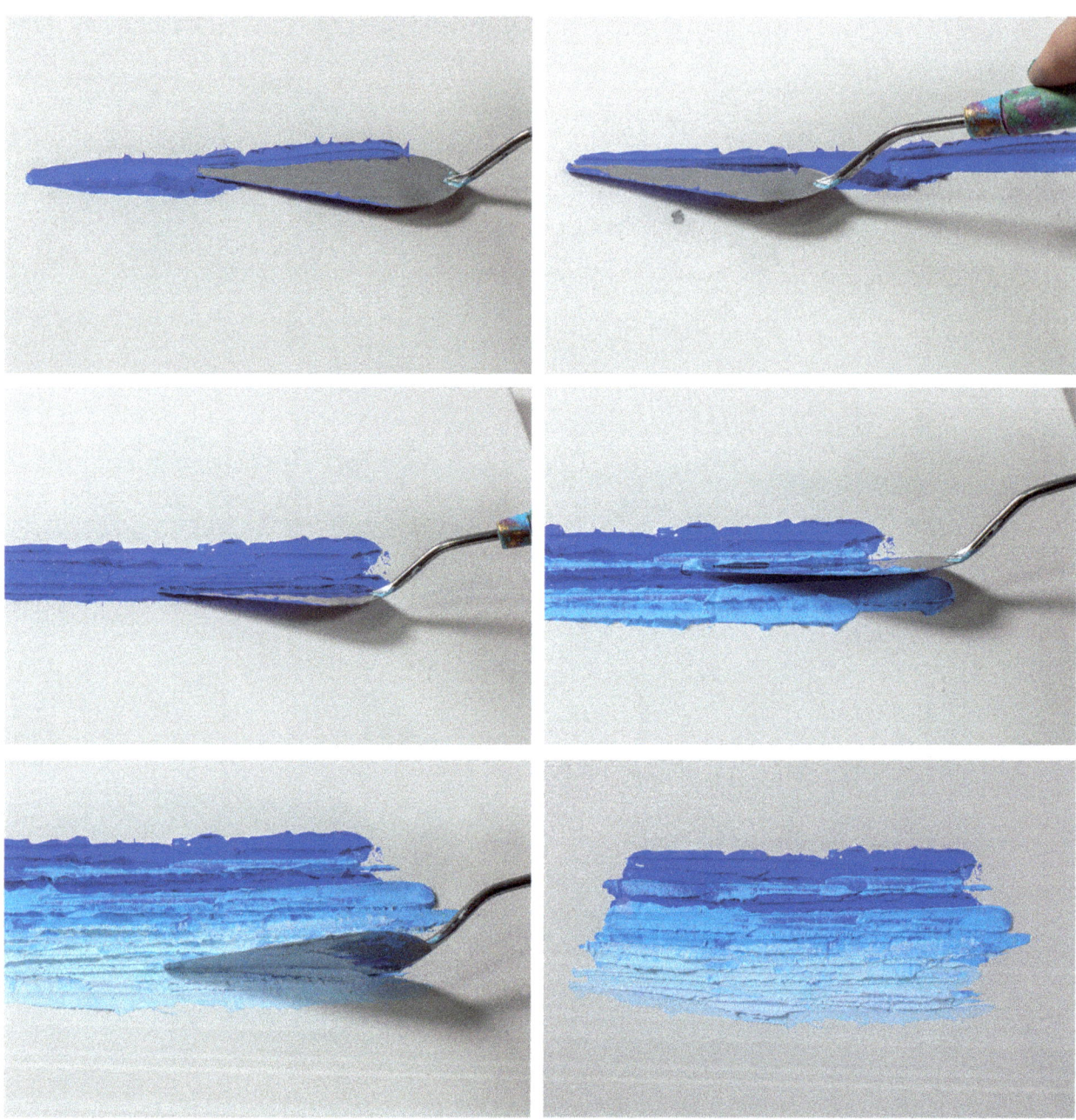

LINES

Load the underside of your palette knife with paint. Place the edge on the canvas and use a rotating wrist action to scoop the paint up and down creating a thin mark with raised edges. Use this for horizon clouds, small landscape fields, and ocean waves.

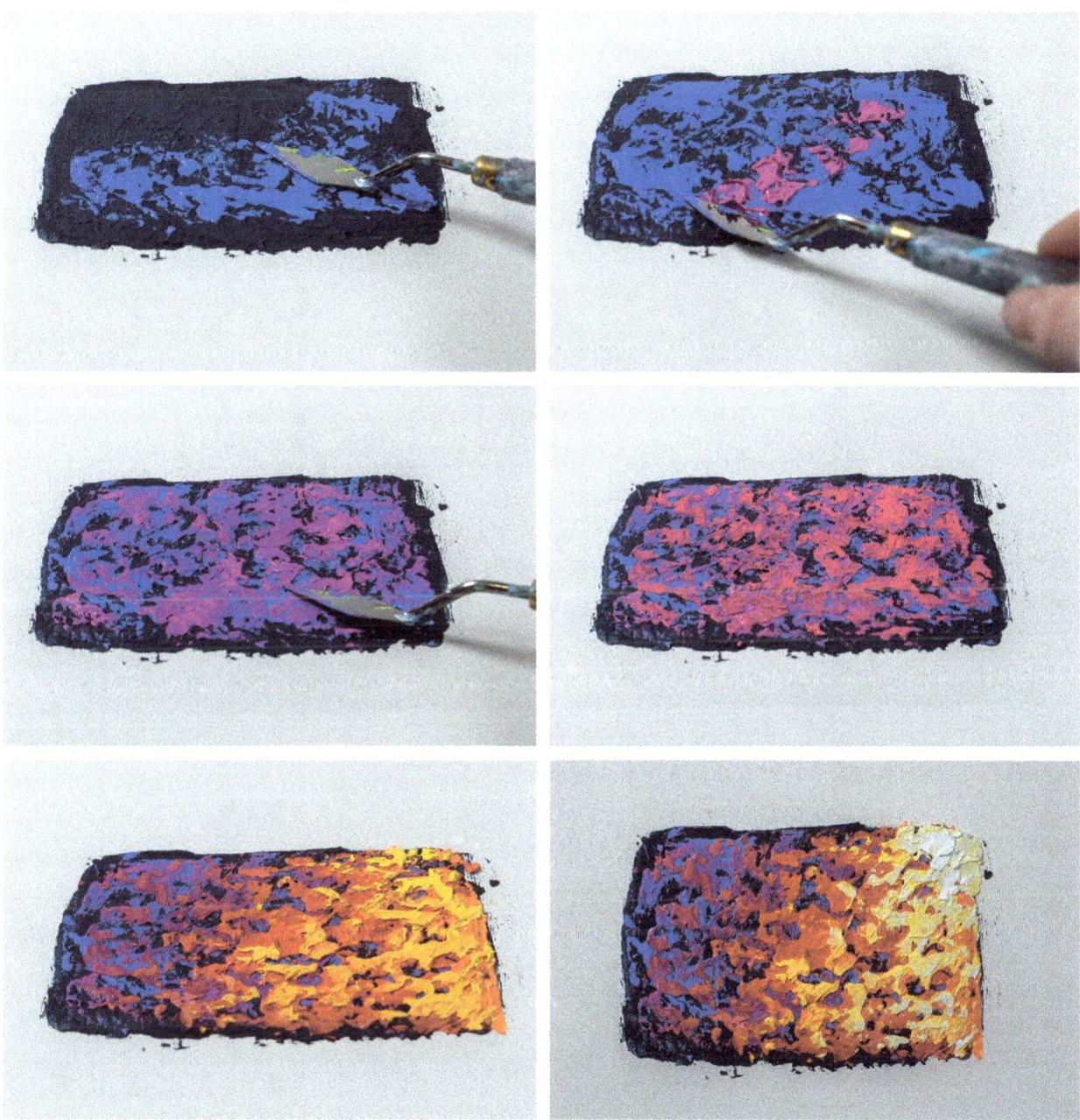

SCUMBLE

Load your palette knife and position it so the underside is parallel to the canvas. Apply light pressure and glide the knife across the surface allowing the paint to skip, creating an irregular textured surface. Allow the paint to dry and apply multiple layers to build more texture. Use this for backgrounds, landscapes, birch tree foliage, and clouds.

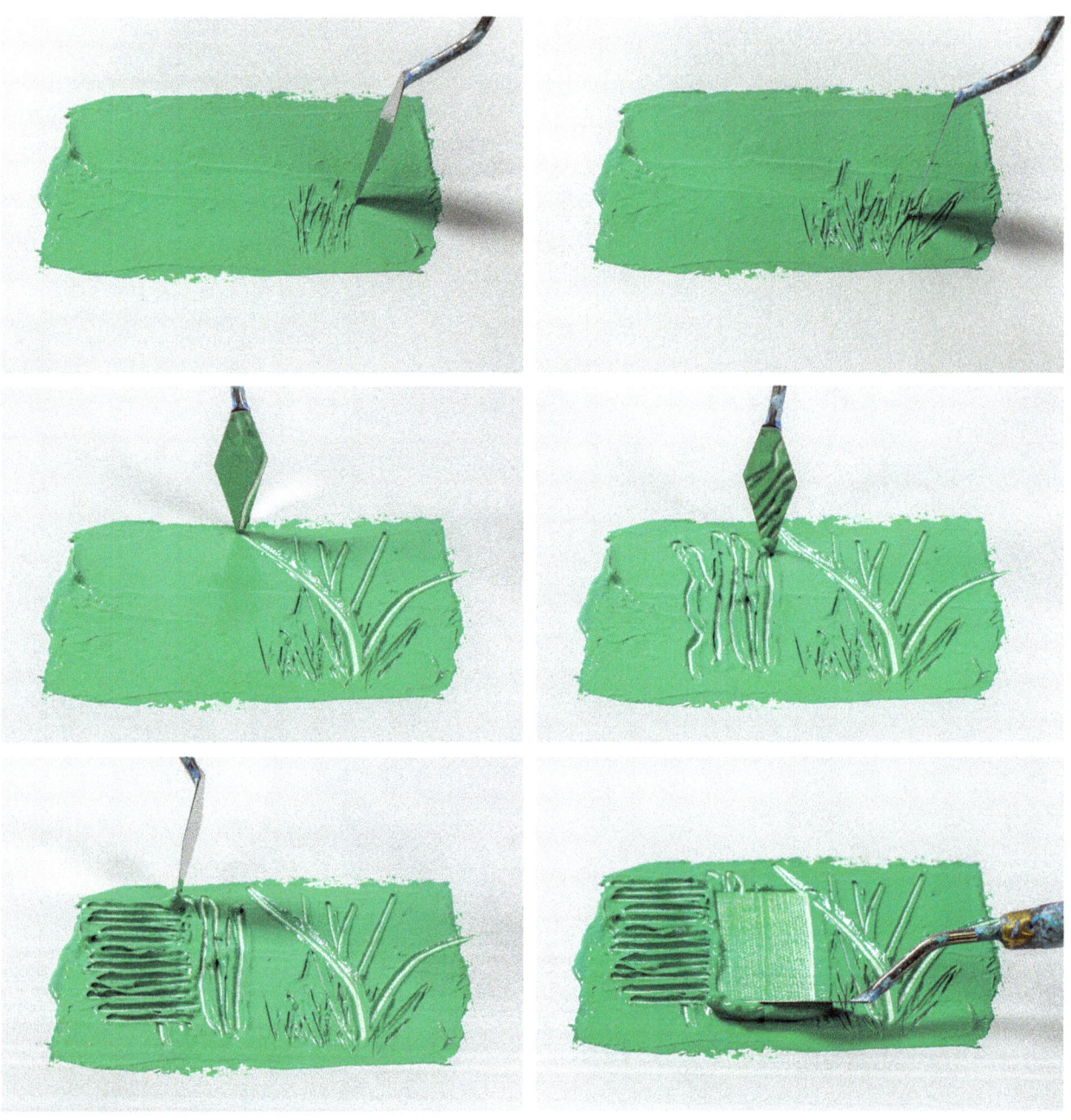

DRAWING IN WET PAINT

Coat the surface with a thick layer of paint. While it's still wet, use the tip of your palette knife or other tool to draw or scratch into the surface of the paint. Use this for stems, tree trunks, branches, grasses, or as a drawing tool to add details and added texture to abstract pieces.

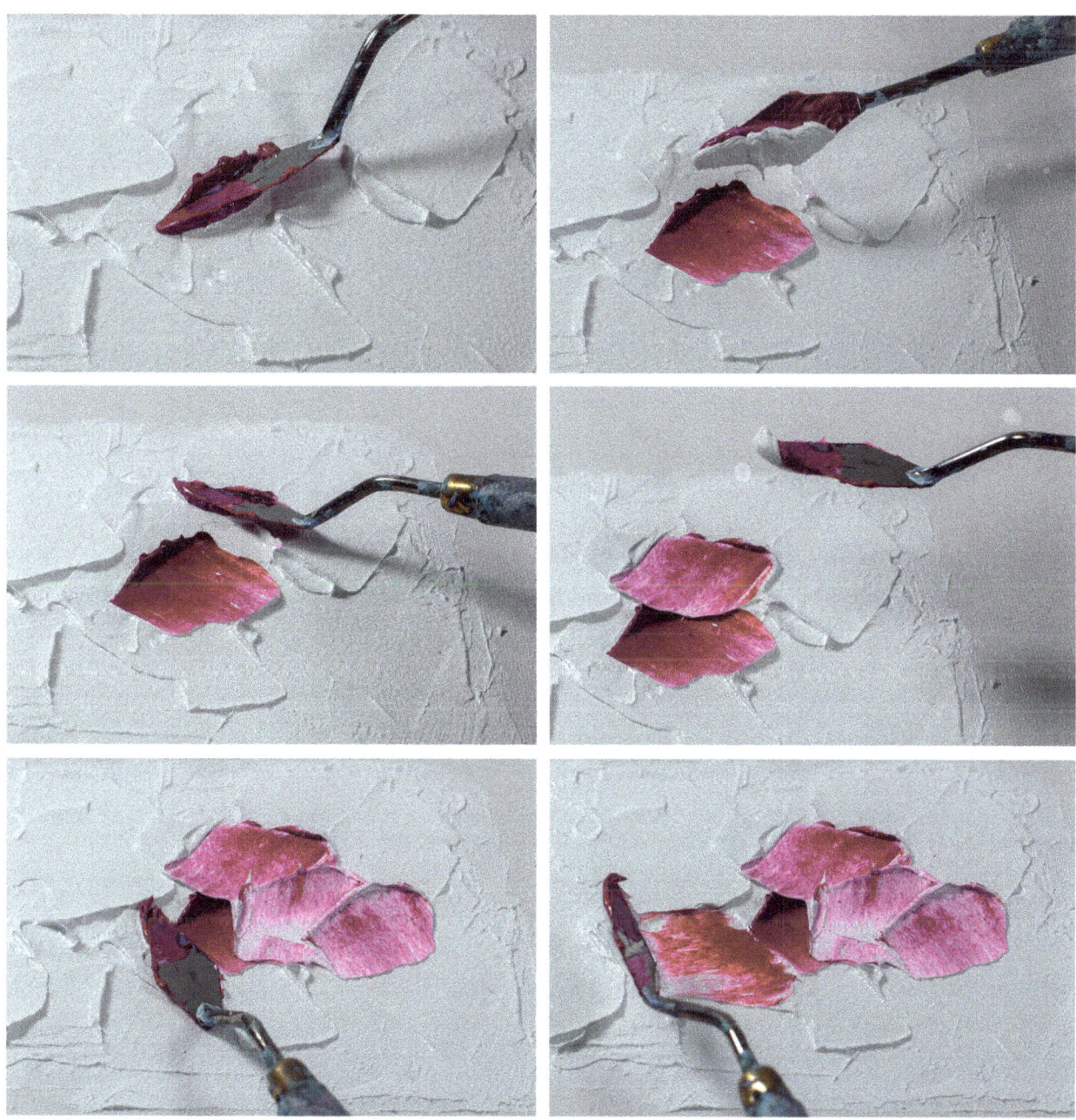

WET-ON-WET

This is the process of applying wet paint on top of wet paint. It's a great way to mix colors directly on the canvas, creating unique color blends and textures. When working wet-on-wet, it's important to work quickly and loosely. Allow the colors to blend slightly, leaving streaks of mottled color in the marks you make. But be careful, if you mix too much, you'll end up with a solid color of mud. Use this for petals and tree leaves.

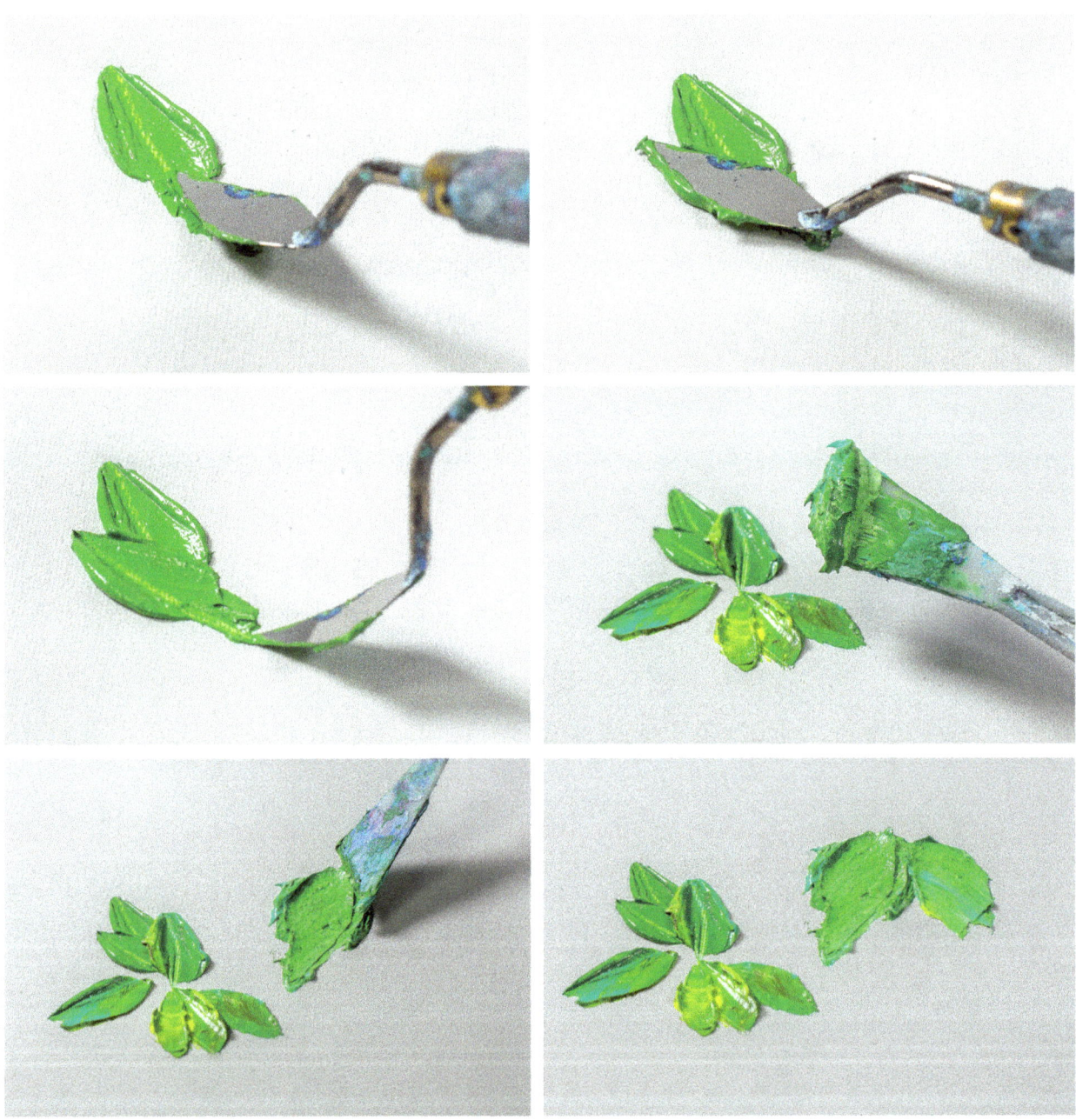

LEAVES

Load a spade-shaped palette knife with an even coat of paint. Apply pressure and pull your knife down, pressing the tip into the canvas to create a division in the center of the leaf. Another option is to load your angled straight-edged knife with paint and use the edge to apply it to the canvas. Re-load your knife and repeat using the other side of the knife to create a second leaf. Use this for both large and small leaves, solid color and blends.

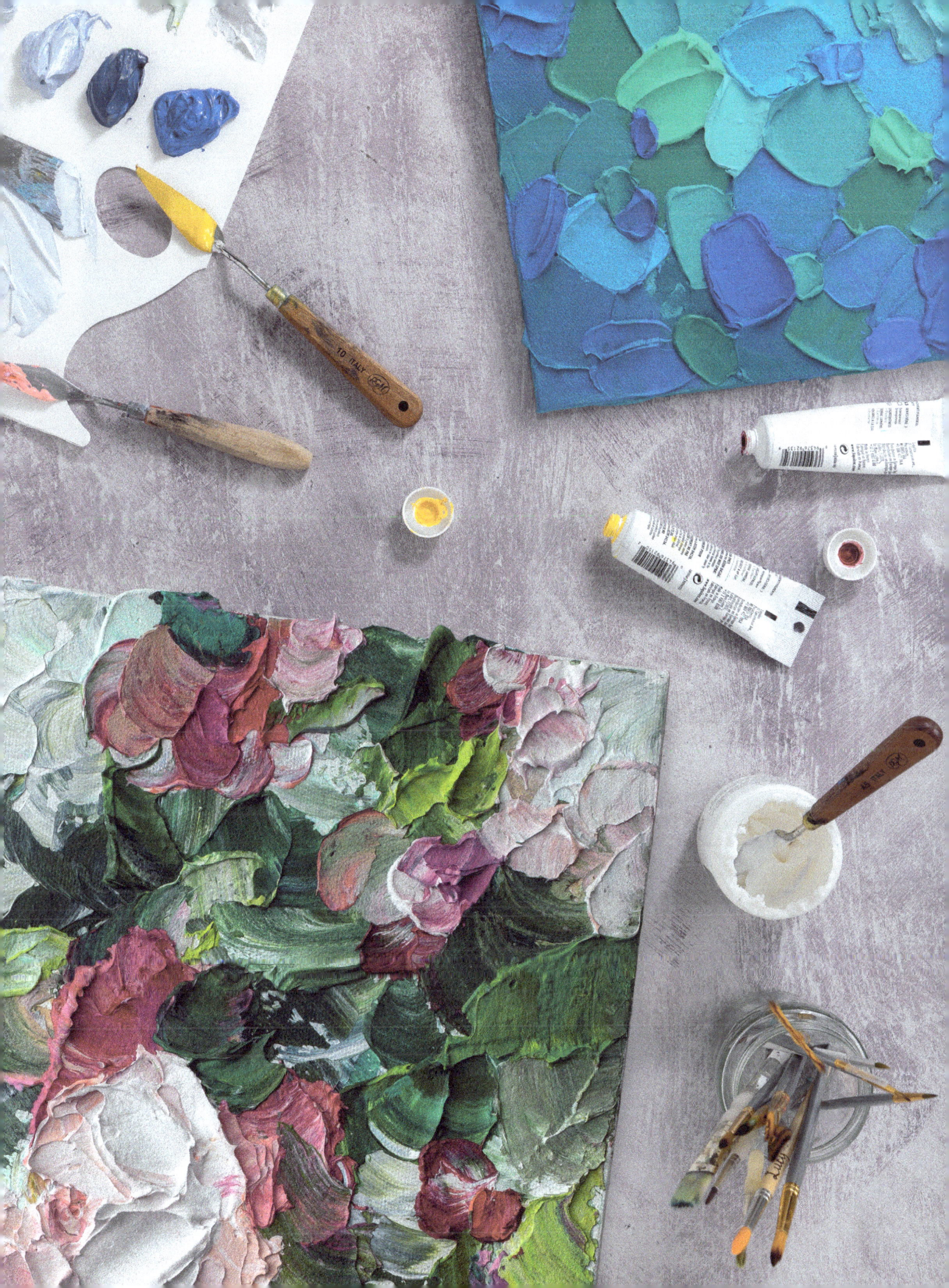

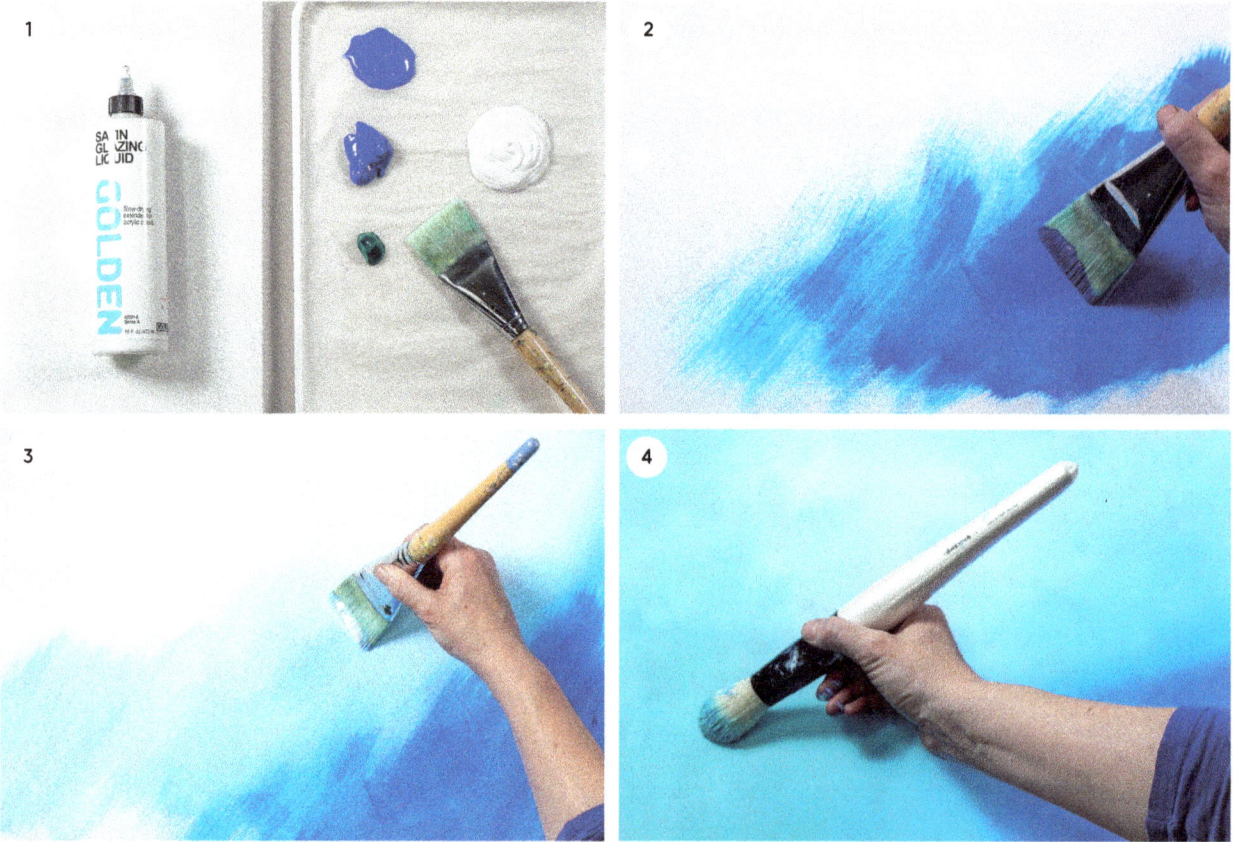

1

2

3

4

BLENDING WITH A BRUSH

Creating a background with a brush is one of the basic techniques that you will master as you work through these projects. Starting with a layer of color has two benefits: it provides a roadmap to follow of light and dark color on which to place your textured marks, and it provides a colored base to work on top of so that if any areas of canvas do show in between your palette knife strokes, the color will complement your painting.

COLOR PALETTE

Titanium white

Phthalocyanine blue (green shade)

Ultramarine blue

Phthalocyanine green

TOOLS AND MATERIALS

- Medium flat synthetic brush
- Large round natural bristle brush
- Glaze medium
- 16in x 20in (40.5cm x 51cm) canvas

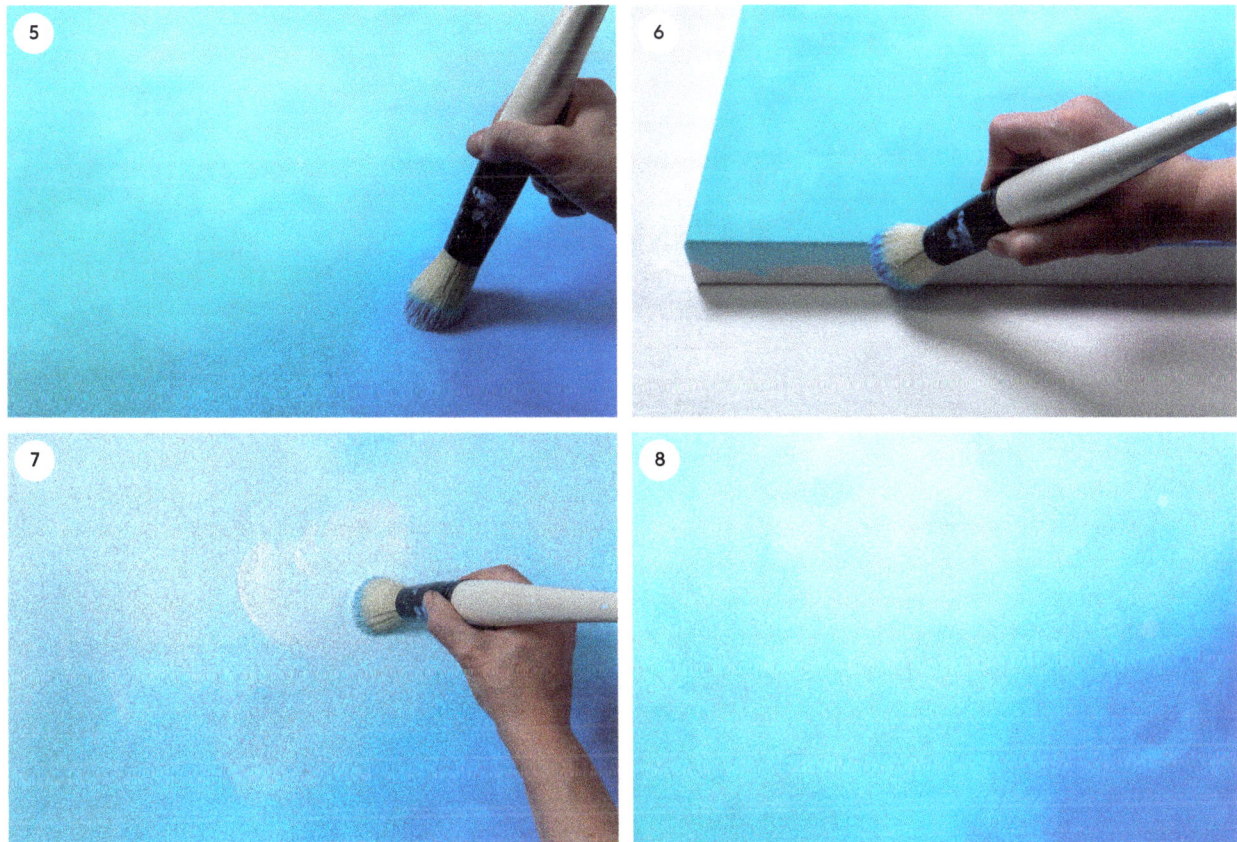

1. Before you begin, you can mix up to 25 percent glaze medium with your paint. This will slow the drying process and allow the paint to blend more easily.

2. Using a flat brush, start with phthalo blue in the bottom right-hand corner. Using broad strokes, slowly blend the color towards the center of the canvas.

3. Next, add a small amount of white and continue blending towards the left side of the canvas, allowing the color to become lighter as you go. The whole canvas should now be covered.

4. To alter the shade of blue, blend a small amount of phthalo green into the bottom left corner and blend into the wet paint below. You can continue to use the flat brush for a loose style, or for a smoother look, switch to a dry large round brush to blend the brushstrokes together.

5. Now alter the shade of blue on the right-hand side, but this time add small amounts of ultramarine blue.

6. Remember to take the paint over the edges of the canvas to blend in the sides.

7. As you move towards the top of the canvas, continue adding more and more white to blend with the various shades of blue.

8. This underpainting doesn't have to be perfect as most of it will be covered with texture when we use this actual canvas in Above the Clouds, and this technique in Dancing Clouds (see Projects).

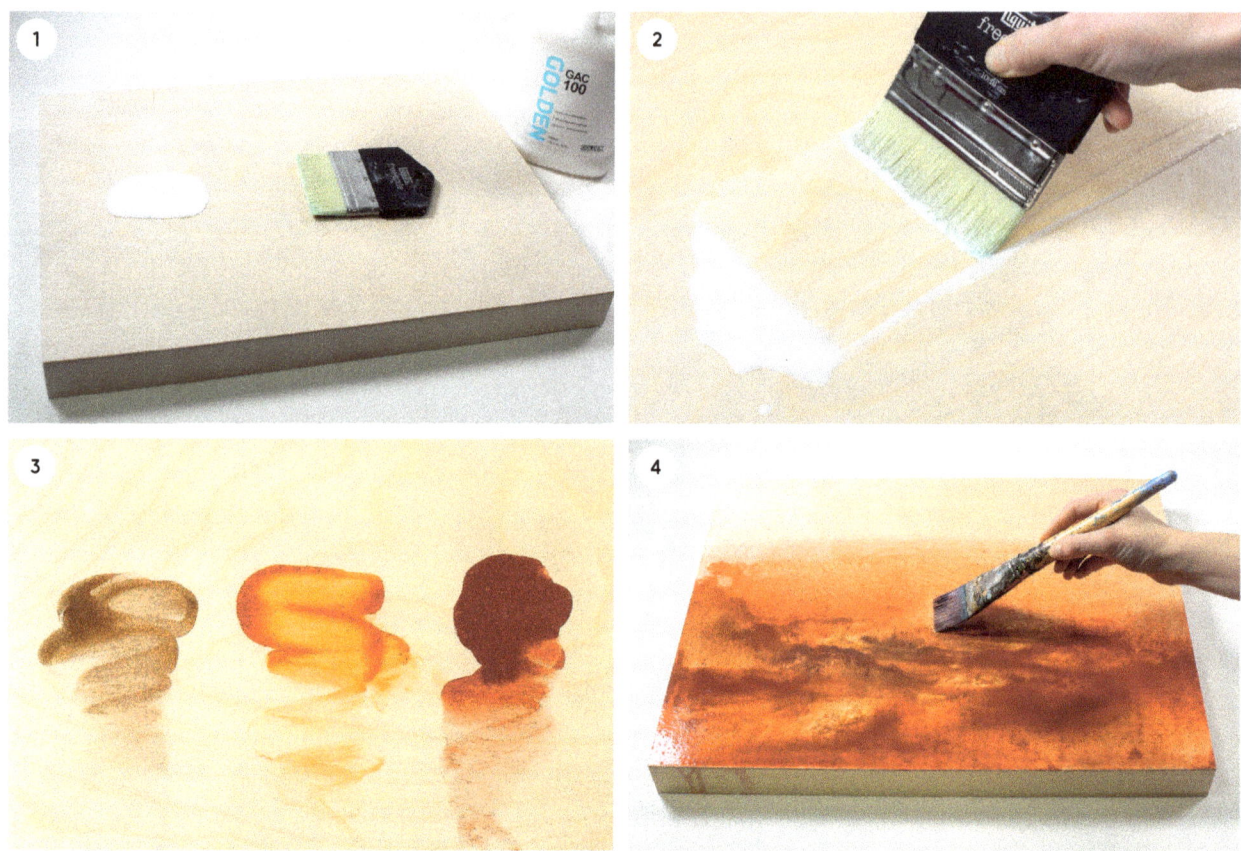

CREATING A TEXTURED BACKGROUND

For this exercise, we are going to use two of my favorite mediums, molding paste and crackle paste, to create a textured background to paint on. Molding paste creates an opaque matte absorbent surface with a rough texture, whereas crackle paste creates a similar surface but with deep cracks as it dries. The size and depth of the crackle pattern depends on the thickness of application and the environment during the drying process (such as the temperature and humidity). You can use these mediums alone and paint over the top or mix them with color before application to create a colored textured background. These mediums can be combined and layered with other acrylic products to create a variety of interesting effects.

COLOR PALETTE

Liquitex acrylic ink in iridescent rich bronze

Golden high flow acrylic in transparent red iron oxide

Daler-Rowney FW ink in red earth

TOOLS AND MATERIALS

- Medium flat synthetic brush
- Large flat synthetic brush
- Large spade-shaped knife
- Golden GAC 100, gloss medium, or clear liquid polymer
- Molding paste
- Crackle paste
- Liquid crackle paste
- Water in a spray bottle
- 16in x 20in (40.5cm x 51cm) wood panel

1. A strong rigid surface is required for this technique. I recommend a 1½in (38mm) cradled wood panel. Before painting, the wood panel needs to be sealed to prevent any discoloration from seeping up through the wood into the painting. It also makes the surface non-absorbent so the paint will sit on top of the panel rather than being absorbed into the wood, therefore requiring less product and preventing warping.

2. I'm using Golden GAC 100 to seal the panel but you can use gloss medium or clear liquid polymer. Use a large flat brush to coat the entire surface with a generous layer of polymer medium, and don't forget the sides. Let it dry completely and apply a second coat.

3. Next, I'm going to add a layer of color using fluid acrylic and ink. This step is optional but you can get interesting effects when you apply a layer of color underneath the crackle paste because once it dries the color will show through the cracks and in between the textures. I've chosen these colors because they are transparent and will allow the wood grain to show through. I added the iridescent rich bronze for a bit of sparkle to provide contrast with the matte surface of the mediums.

4. Apply the paint in random puddles to the bottom two-thirds of the panel. Use a medium flat brush to move the paint around in horizontal strokes, allowing each color to mix slightly with the next. Mist with water to increase flow and eliminate brush marks. You can tilt the panel from side to side to move the ink around in a natural fluid pattern. Once the panel is covered with color, leave it to dry. The fluid paint will continue to move and mix, creating interesting patterns as it dries.

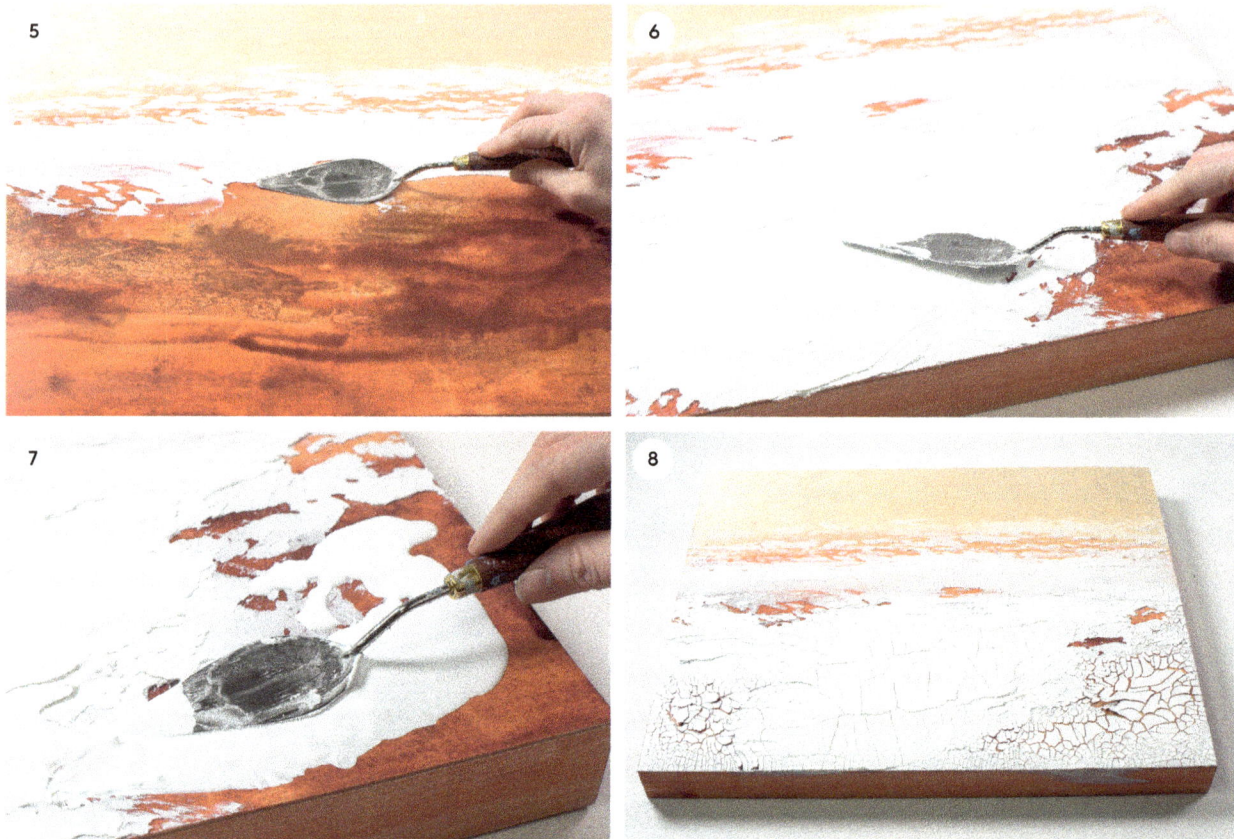

5. Starting with molding paste, use a large spade-shaped knife to apply a thick layer to the middle third of the canvas. Use sweeping strokes horizontally across the canvas to indicate clouds, mountains, or hills on the horizon.

6. Next, apply crackle paste ⅛in to ¼in (3mm to 6mm) thick to the bottom third of the canvas. How thick you apply the medium will determine the size and pattern of the cracks once it dries. Thicker layers usually equal bigger cracks.

7. Over the years, I've noticed that different brands of crackle paste will create different types of cracks, patterns, and surfaces. So, I'm going to add some crackle paste by Tri Art to show you the difference. This crackle paste comes in a liquid form so I'm going to pour it on the bottom corners of the panel and use the palette knife to gently move the fluid around. Let it dry for at least 24 to 48 hours.

8. Here's how it looks dry. Notice the different textures of all three mediums and how the underpainting shows through in some areas. We'll be using this panel for Under a Desert Sky (see Projects).

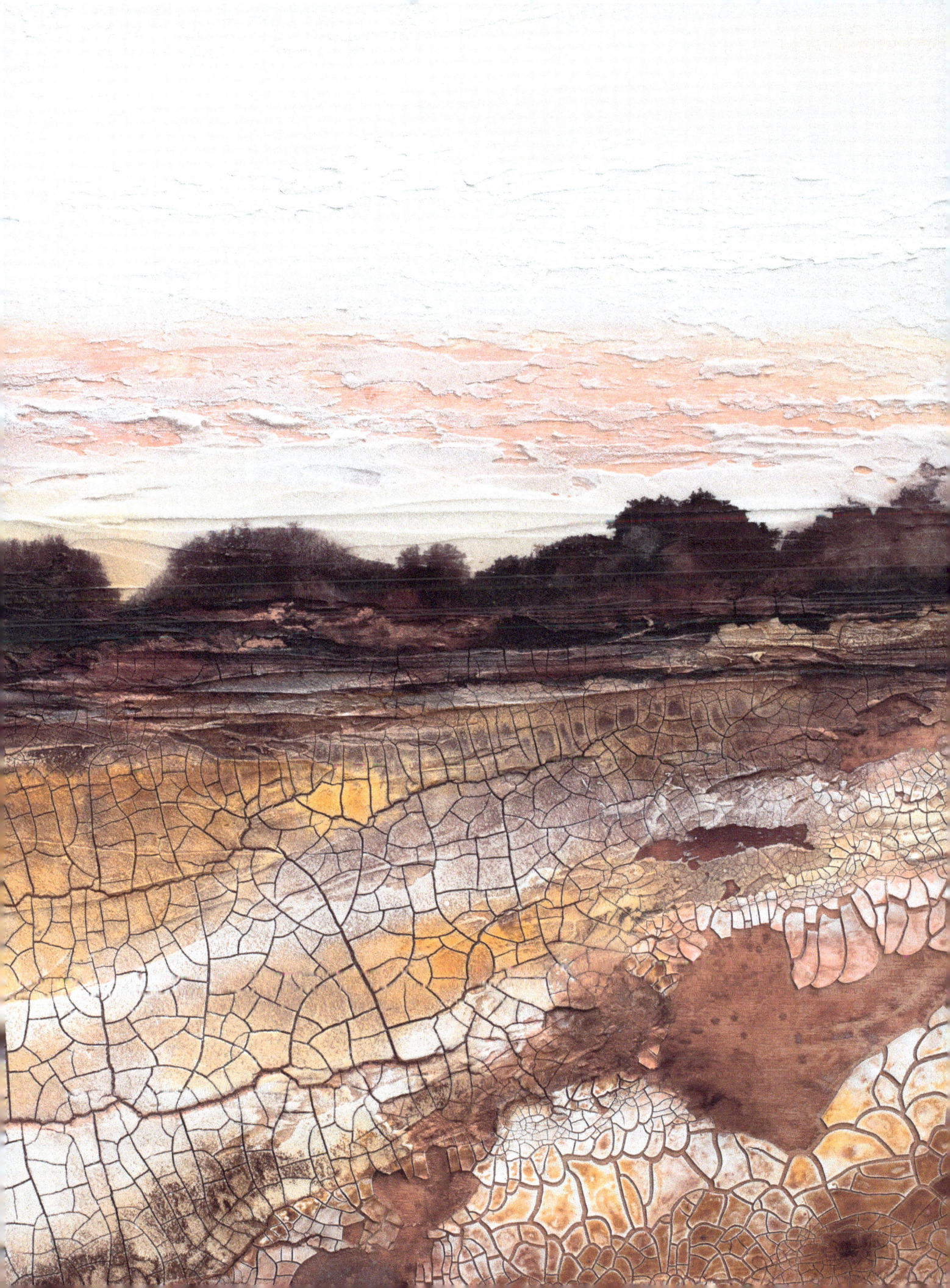

IMPRESSIONIST BRUSH WORK

For this technique, I'm going to show you how to use thick paint and a brush to create an impressionist style painting. We'll be applying the paint using broken strokes, so rather than blending the paint together, we are going to lay down each color in individual strokes, one by one, allowing some of the background to show in between. From a distance, the small, short strokes will merge together but up close, each stroke can be seen individually. Use your brush to mix colors directly on your palette. There is no need to clean your brush in between colors unless it has become a muddy mess. Start with one color and gradually add the next, allowing the colors to mix.

COLOR PALETTE

Titanium white

Cadmium yellow medium

Cadmium red medium

Quinacridone magenta

Fluorescent red (optional)

Phthalocyanine blue (green shade)

TOOLS AND MATERIALS

- Small flat synthetic brush
- Small round natural bristle brush
- 8.5in x 11in (21.5cm x 28cm) canvas paper
- Heavy body acrylic paint (see Mediums)

1. Using a flat brush, coat the entire surface with a layer of color that's bright or contrasts with the color palette. I'm using a mix of cad red medium and fluorescent red, making a warm red to contrast with the cool tones of magenta and phthalo blue. Most of this layer is going to be covered with paint strokes and only small areas of color will show through.

2. Starting with a dark phthalo blue (see Color Mixing), use the tip of a round brush to scoop up a dollop of paint.

3. Now we'll create a gradation of value (see Color Terminology). Starting at the top left corner of your paper, apply the paint in a short stroke, allowing it to glide off your brush. Do one stroke at a time and try not to disturb it. Continue adding strokes of blue across the top third of the page, changing the angle and direction. Some strokes can overlap but make sure to leave some of the background showing through. I'm using a simple cross-hatch pattern.

4. Use your brush to mix more white to your blue to create a mid-tone. Continue adding strokes next to the dark blue strokes.

5. Add a few strokes over the dark blue to create a transition of value. Notice how the two blues are starting to create a gradient.

6. Add more white to your mix and repeat the process.

7. Repeat the steps using a light blue.

8. This same technique can be used to transition from one color to another. Start by applying several strokes of the mid-tone blue to the left of the middle third of the paper.

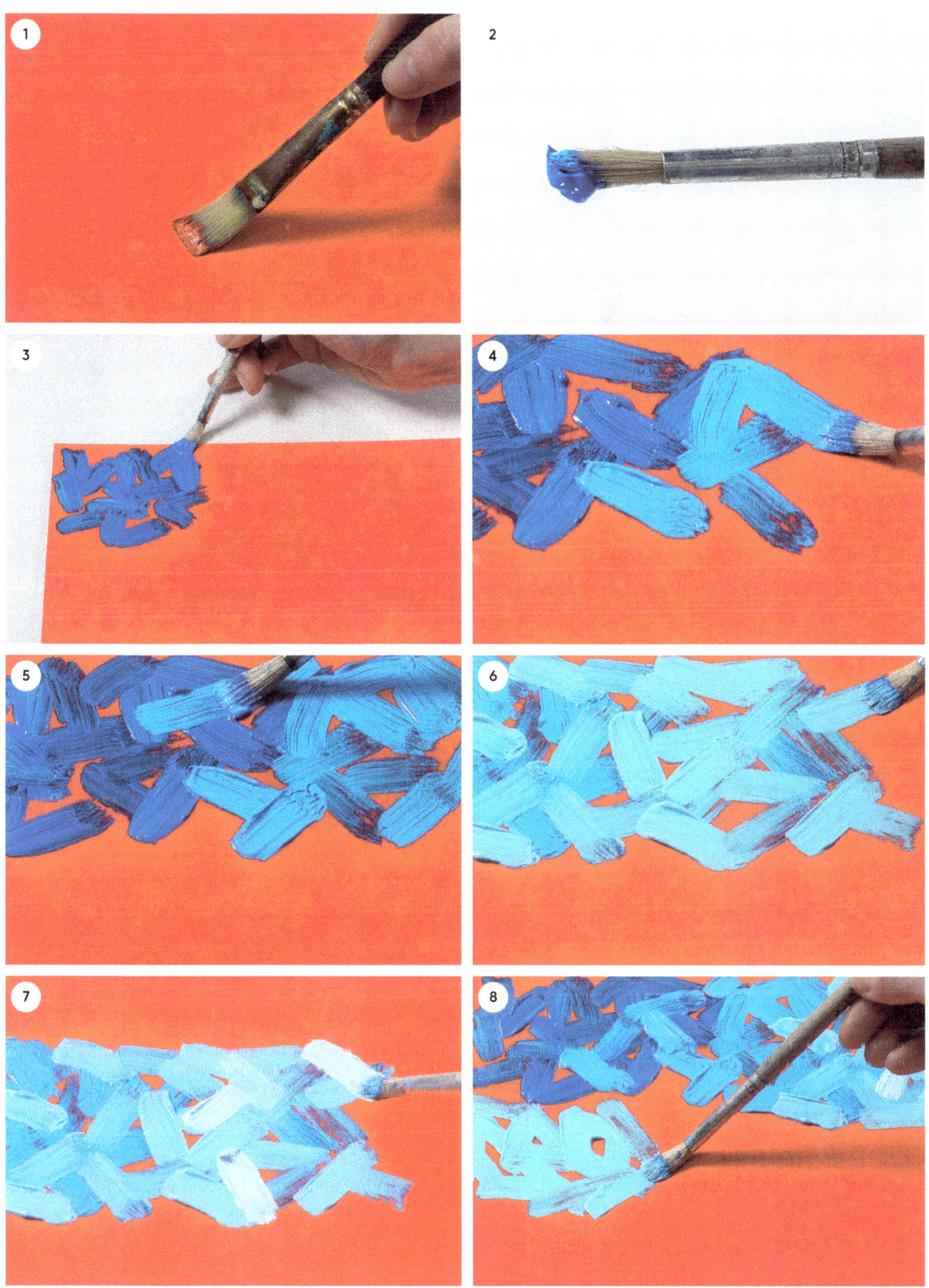

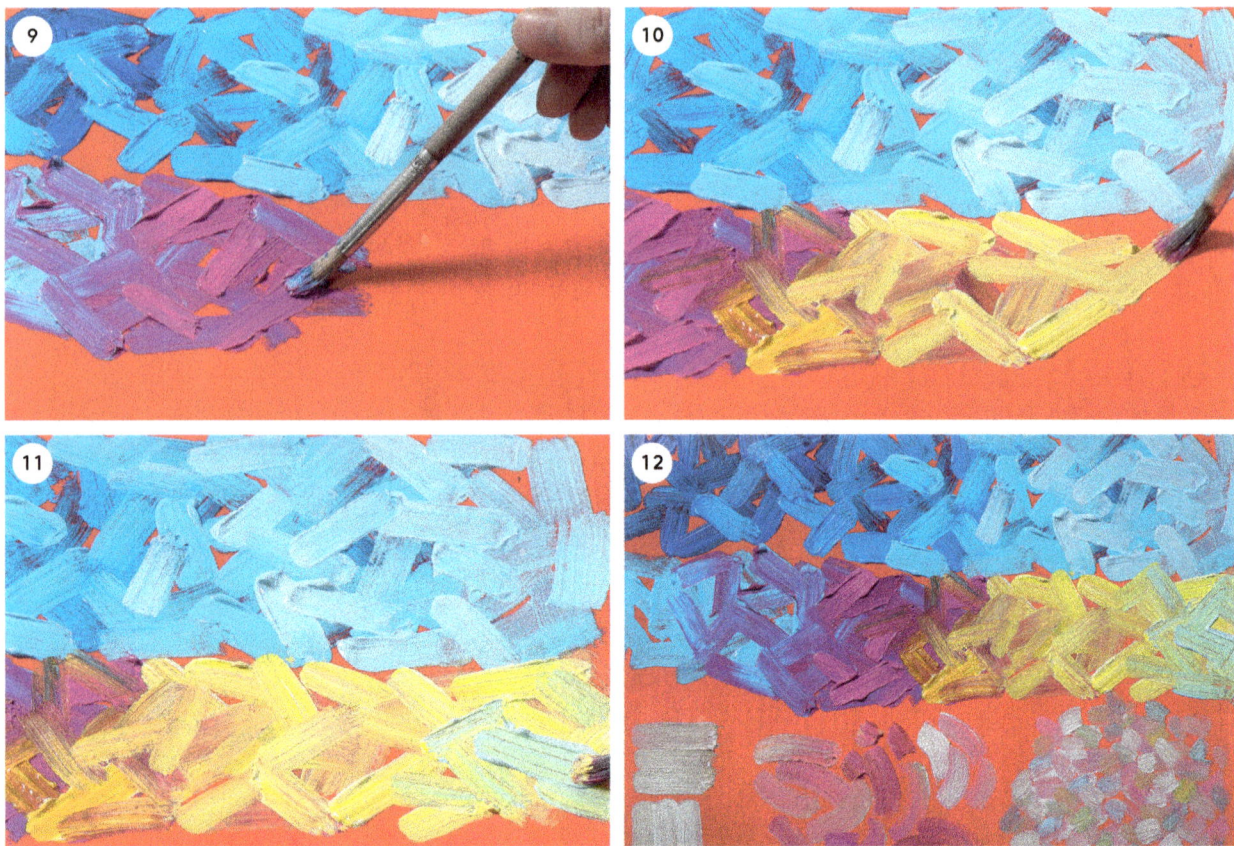

9. Mix a mid-tone magenta. Add strokes of this color and layer it over the top of the blue, allowing some of the color to mix together.

10. Repeat the process by adding cad yellow medium mixed with white to the gradient.

11. Lastly, add some of the light blue to see how it mixes with the yellow.

12. Experiment with different ways to apply brushstrokes to add interest and personality to your painting. In addition to cross hatch (top), try side-by-side, which is good for covering large areas of flat color (bottom left), or curved, following the direction of the shape you're painting (bottom middle). You can also use a dot pattern to apply your colors, known as pointillism (bottom right), or try loading your brush with multiple colors to create multi-colored strokes.

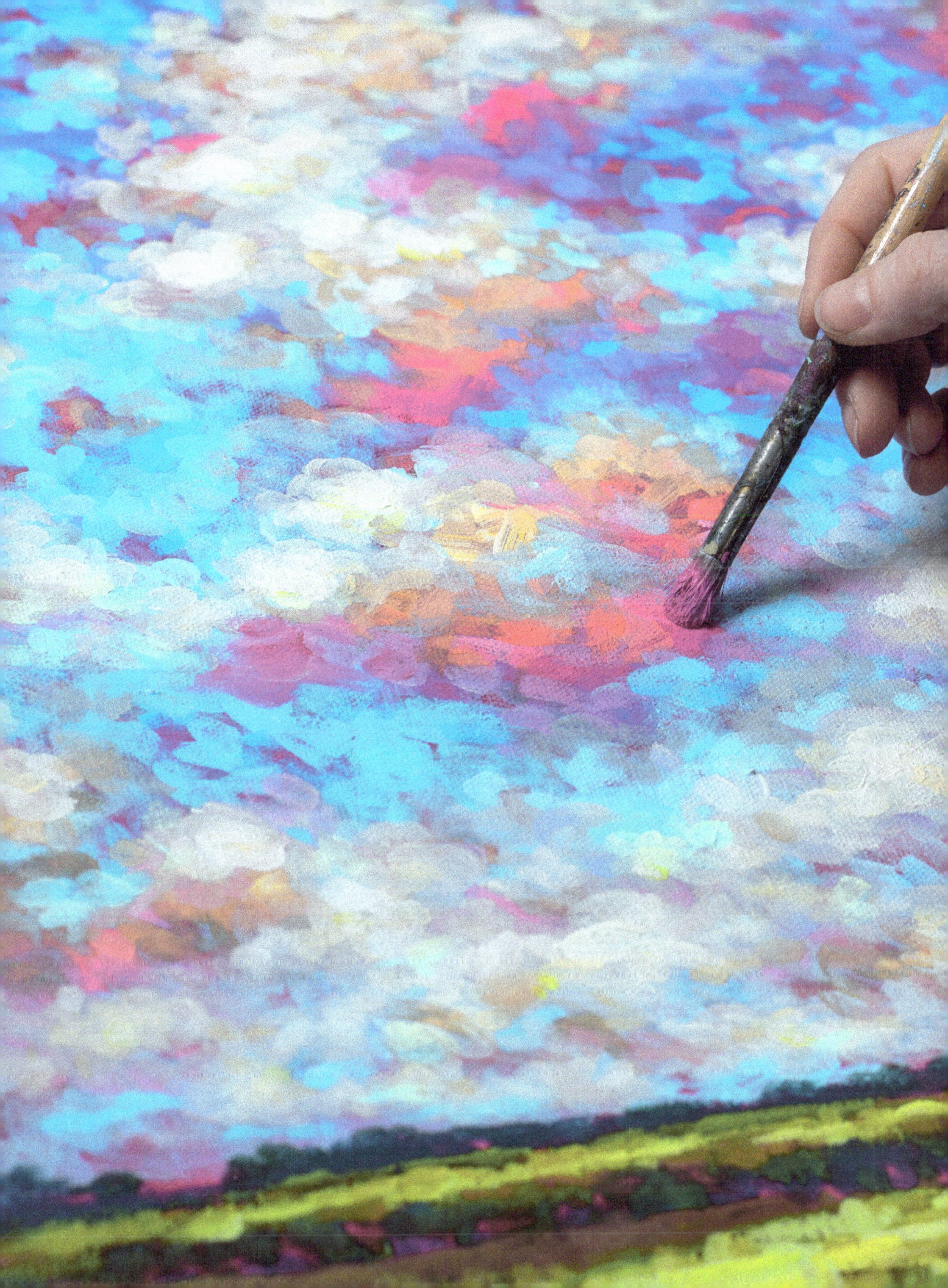

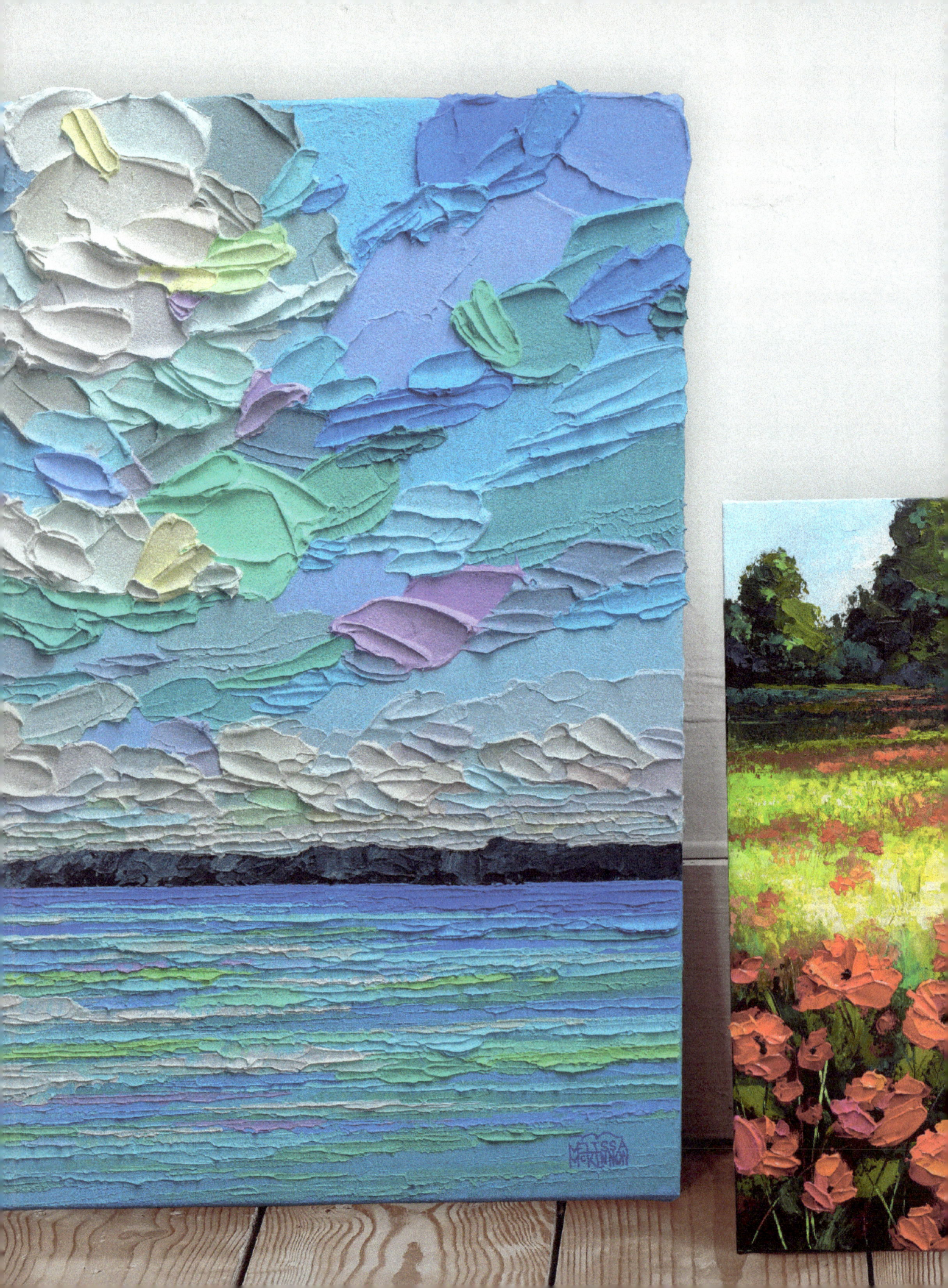

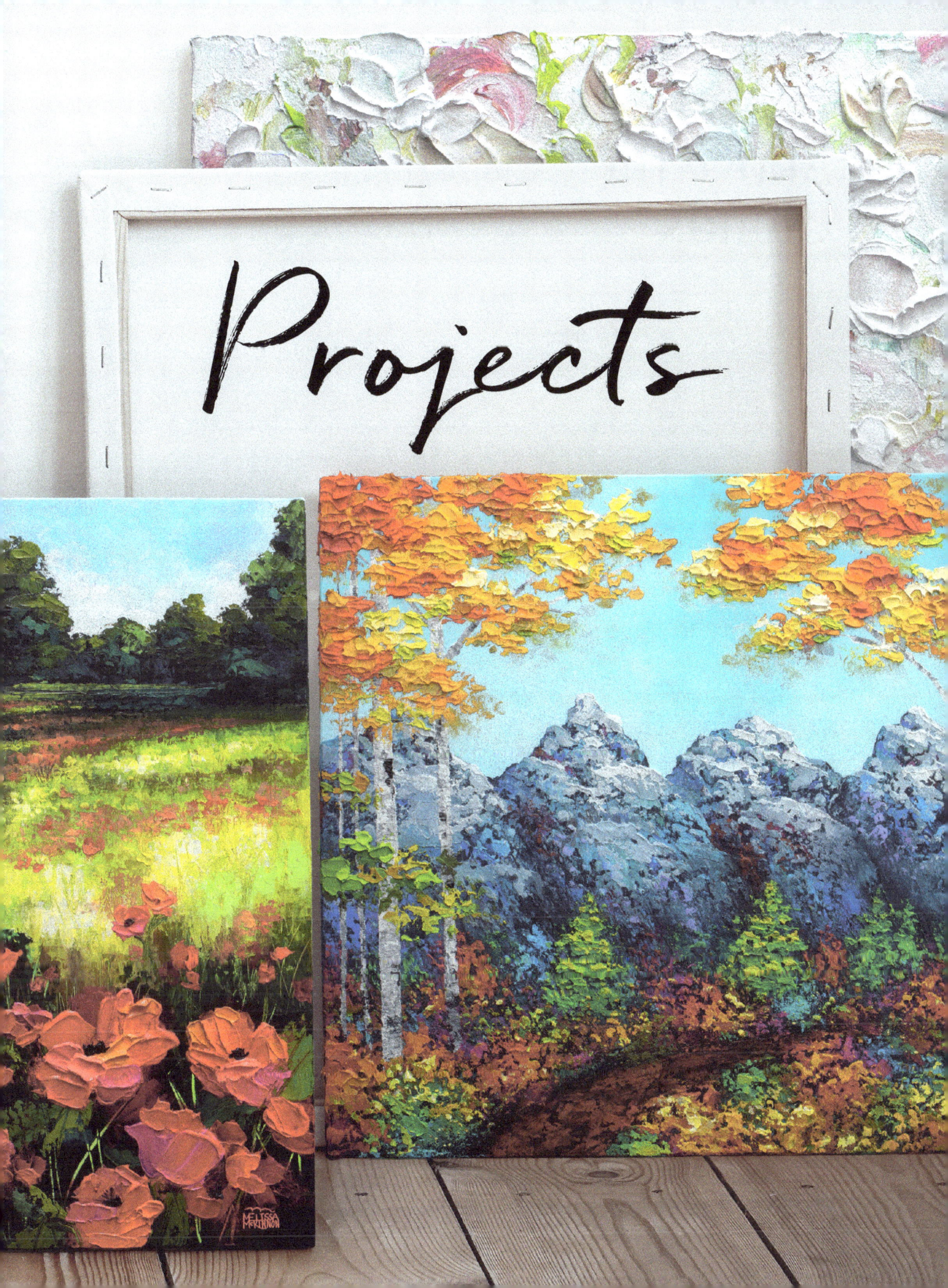

Projects

Above the Clouds

Much of my inspiration comes from the colors and textures found in nature. In my own practice, I've created a whole series of sky paintings that began life as an abstract interpretation of the sky, similar to this project. However, you don't need a specific subject matter to fall in love with abstract painting. Your creation can simply be inspired by color combinations, texture, mood, or emotion. Using the canvas we produced in the blending technique, we're going to add layers of impasto texture with a palette knife. Choose your favorite palette knife and method of mark making from your explorations earlier in the book.

Color palette

- Titanium white
- Cadmium yellow light
- Phthalocyanine blue (green shade)
- Ultramarine blue
- Phthalocyanine green

Tools and materials

- Angled straight-edged knife
- Medium spade-shaped knife
- Canvas from Blending with a Brush
- Molding paste or gel medium to thicken paint where needed (see Mediums)

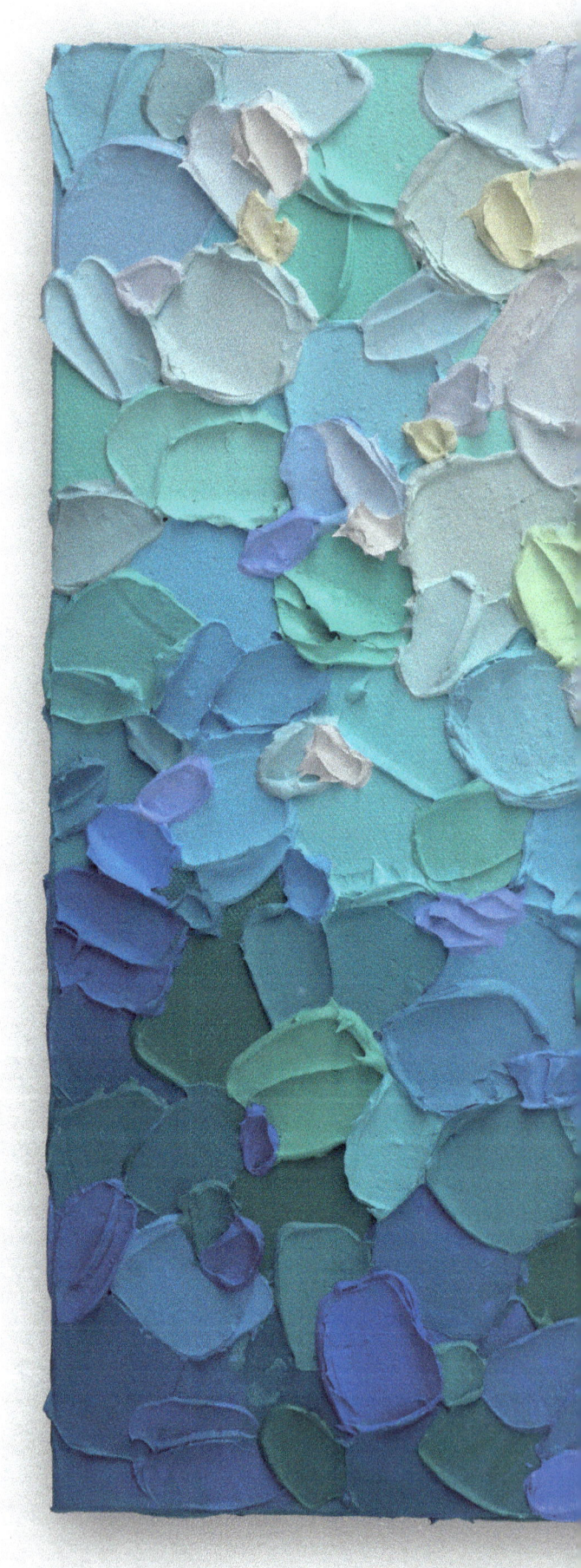

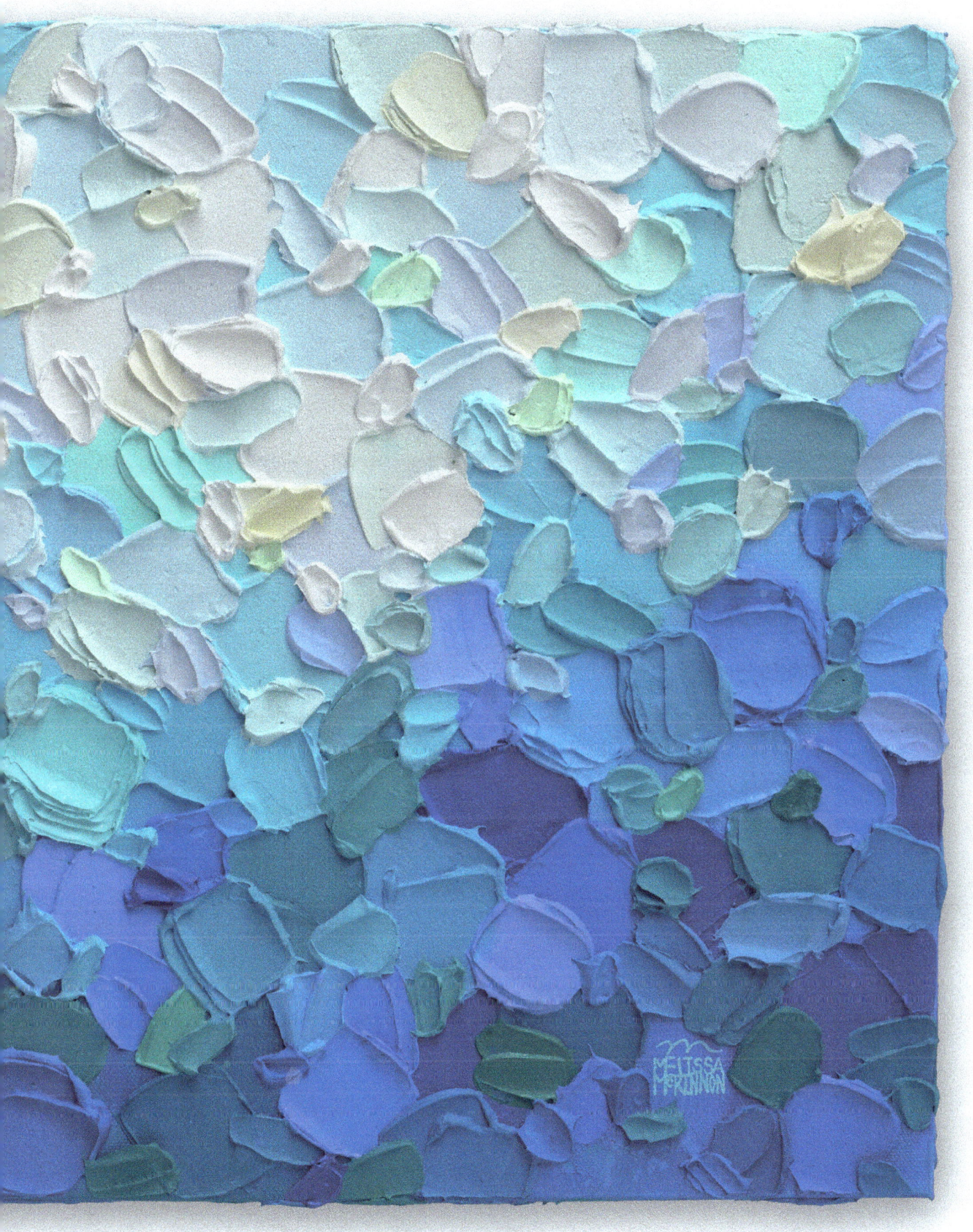

1. Starting with dark ultramarine blue (see Color Mixing), load a straight-edged knife with a large amount of paint.

2. Begin applying the paint in broad strokes onto the lower half of the canvas. To make the marks, place the knife paint side down and lightly press as you glide the knife across the surface until you've achieved the desired size.

3. Gently lift the knife creating a raised edge. Try to vary the direction and size of your strokes (see Impasto in Mark Making).

4. Next, repeat the process with dark phthalo blue, overlapping some of the ultramarine blue shapes. Repeat the process with the dark ultramarine blue and dark phthalo blue, varying the shades of blue by adding small amounts of white, phthalo green, or cad yellow light.

5. As you work your way up the canvas, start adding larger amounts of white to each color to create a gradient effect. I like to add my darker colors underneath and lighter colors on top to create depth in the painting.

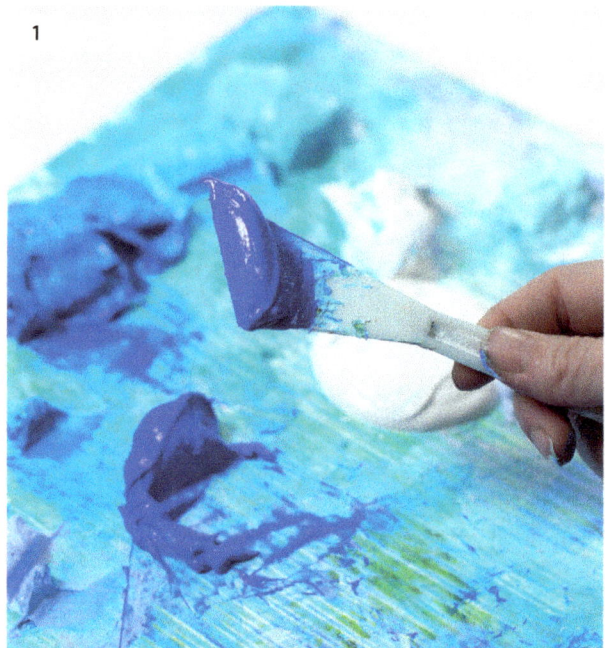

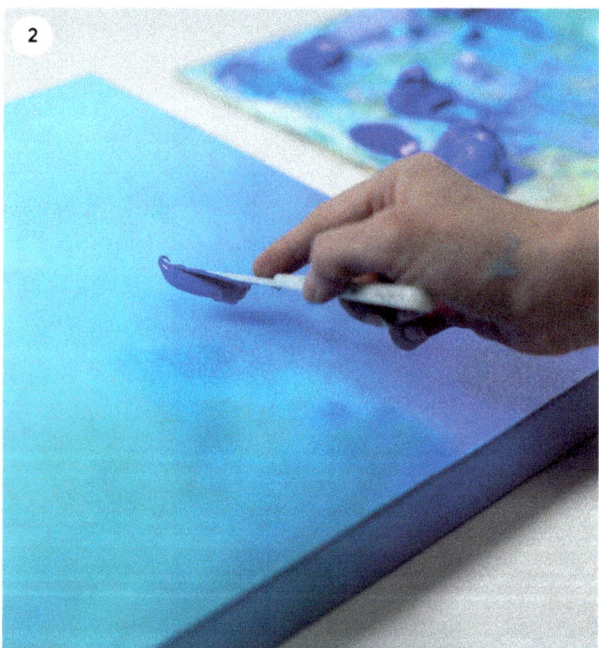

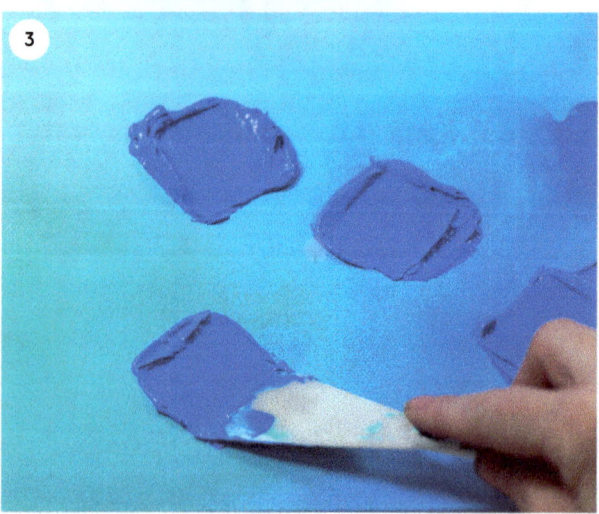

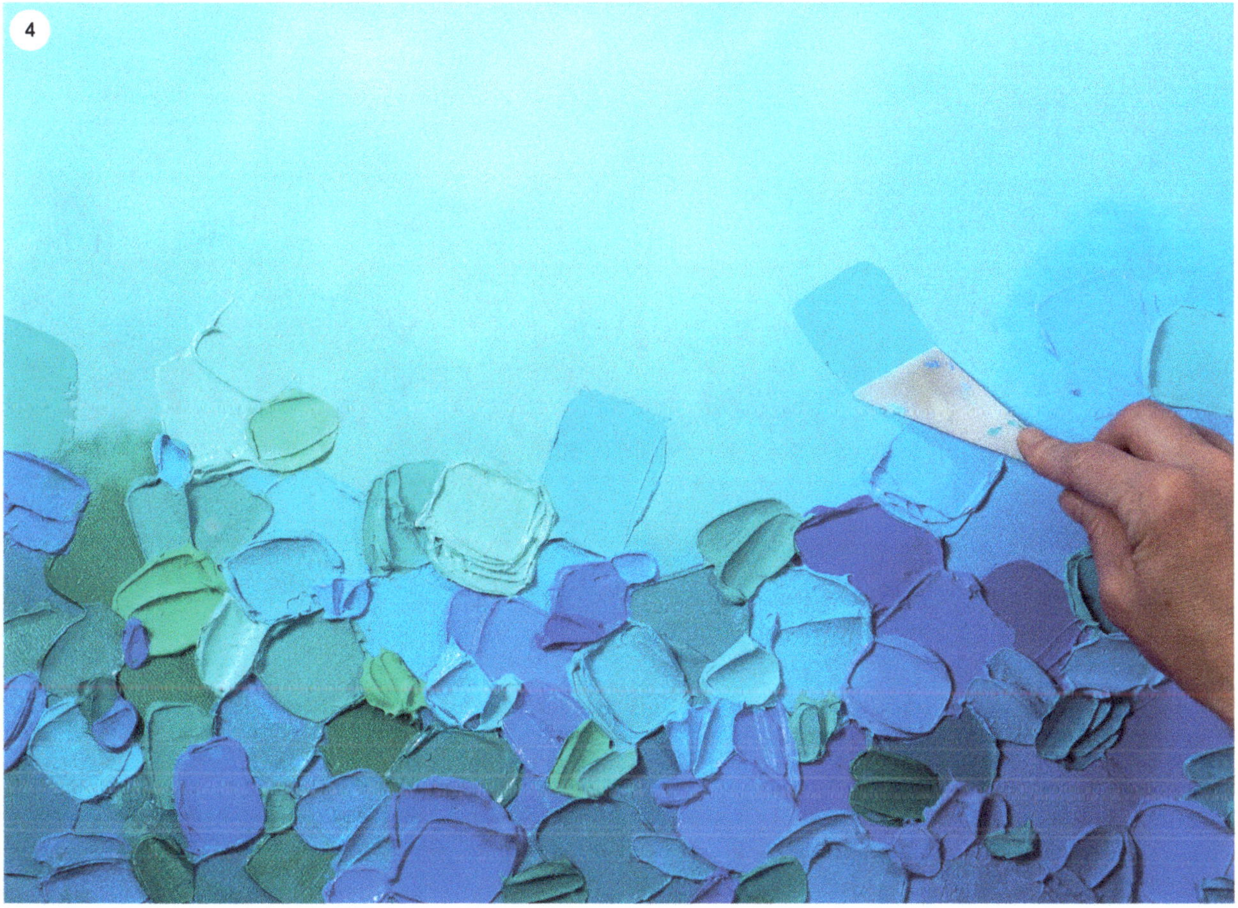

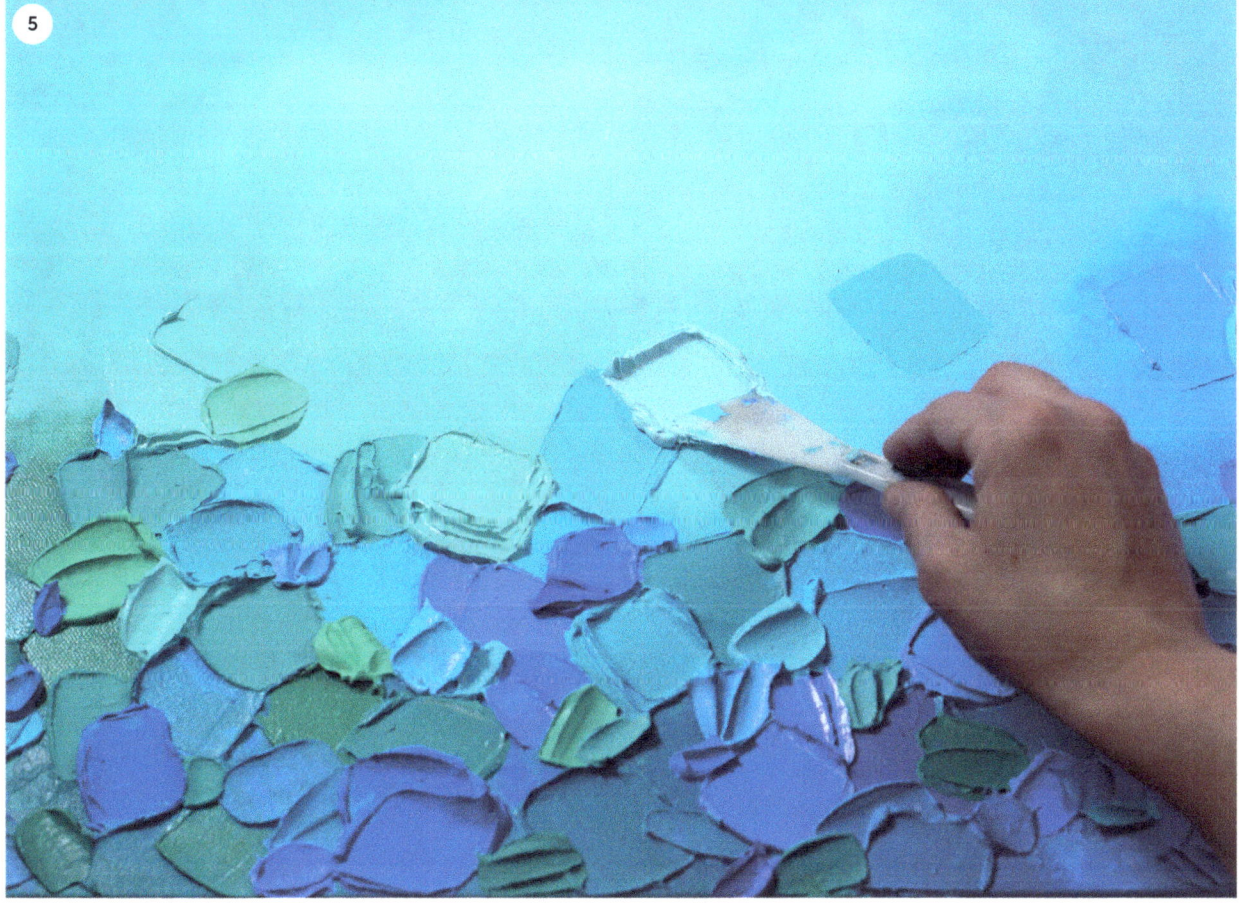

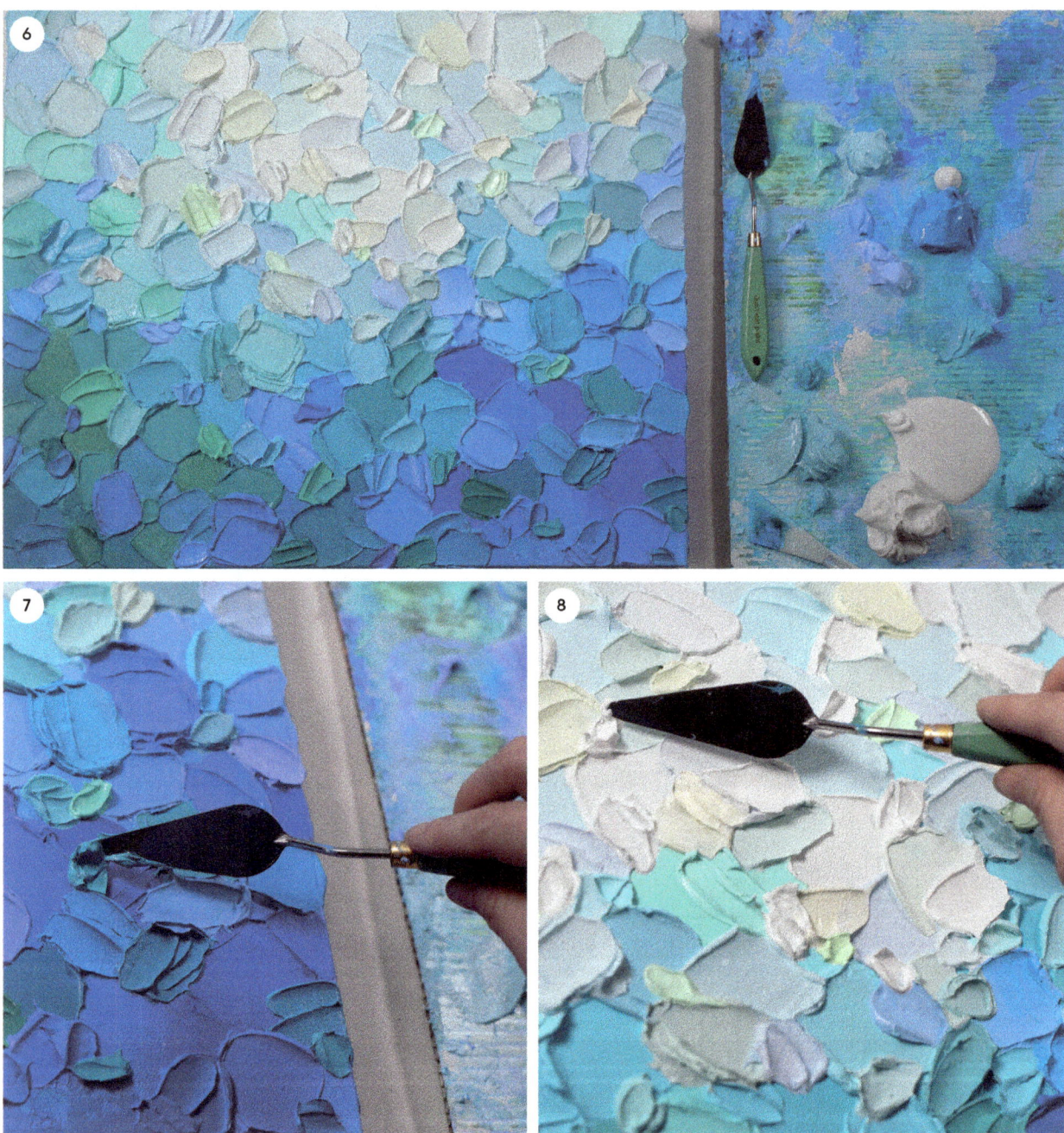

6. Once your canvas is covered, evaluate the colors and composition. Look for areas that need more interest or variety of color. Perhaps there's a mark that doesn't look great. You can layer color over the top to cover any areas that you want to change. Take time to look at the composition for flow in the painting.

7. I switch to a medium spade-shaped knife, which has a long, narrow point for adding smaller details and offers more control at the tip than the straight-edged knife.

8. Apply smaller details and contrasting colors to create dimension in the composition and draw the viewer's eye around the canvas.

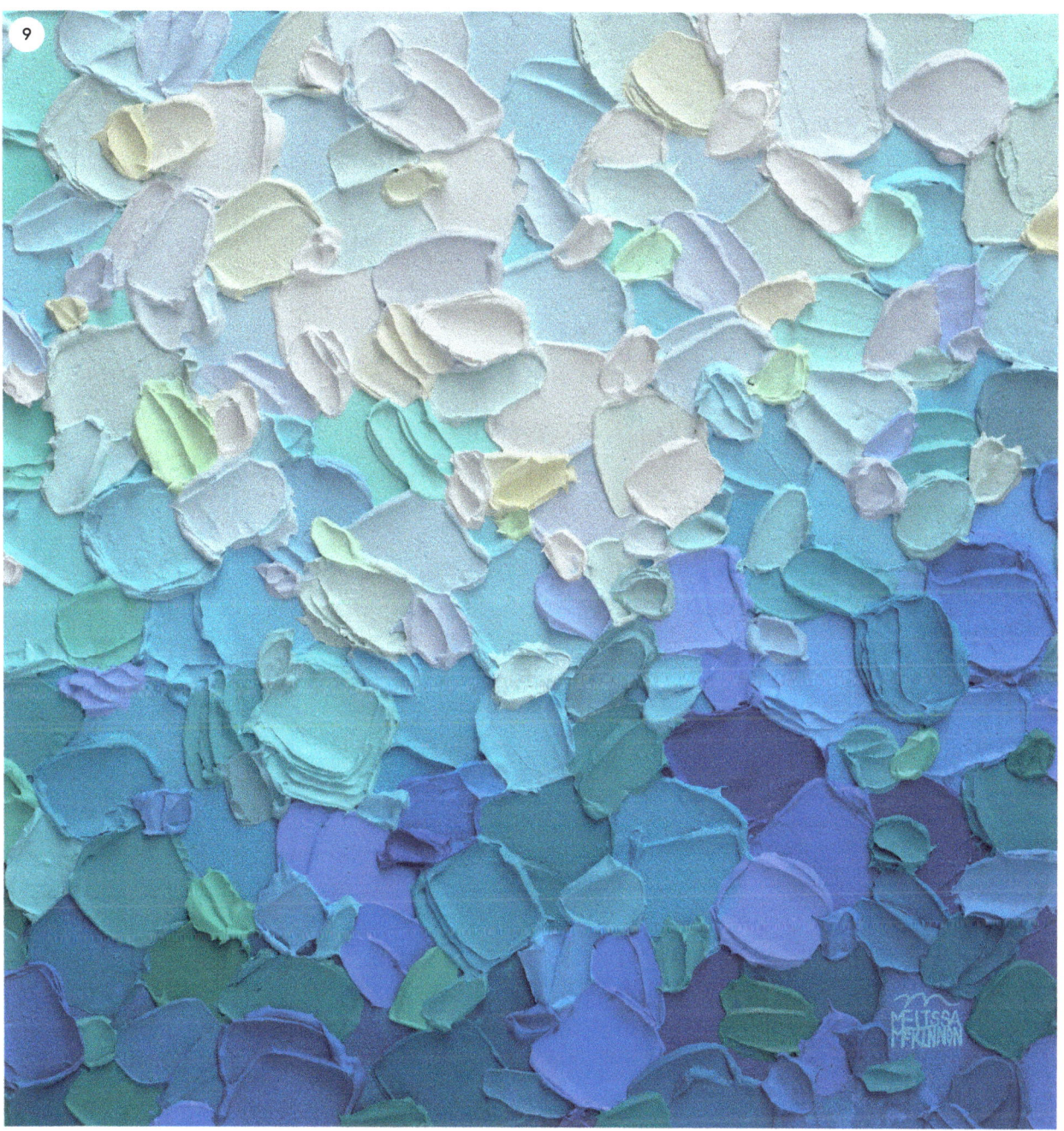

9. Using a shade of blue as the base color has kept all of the colors in the painting harmonious but the painting still has lots of variety and interest. This is because we created different values of blue versus just the two colors straight from the tube (see Color Mixing). Varying the size and direction of the marks has also added variety and interest.

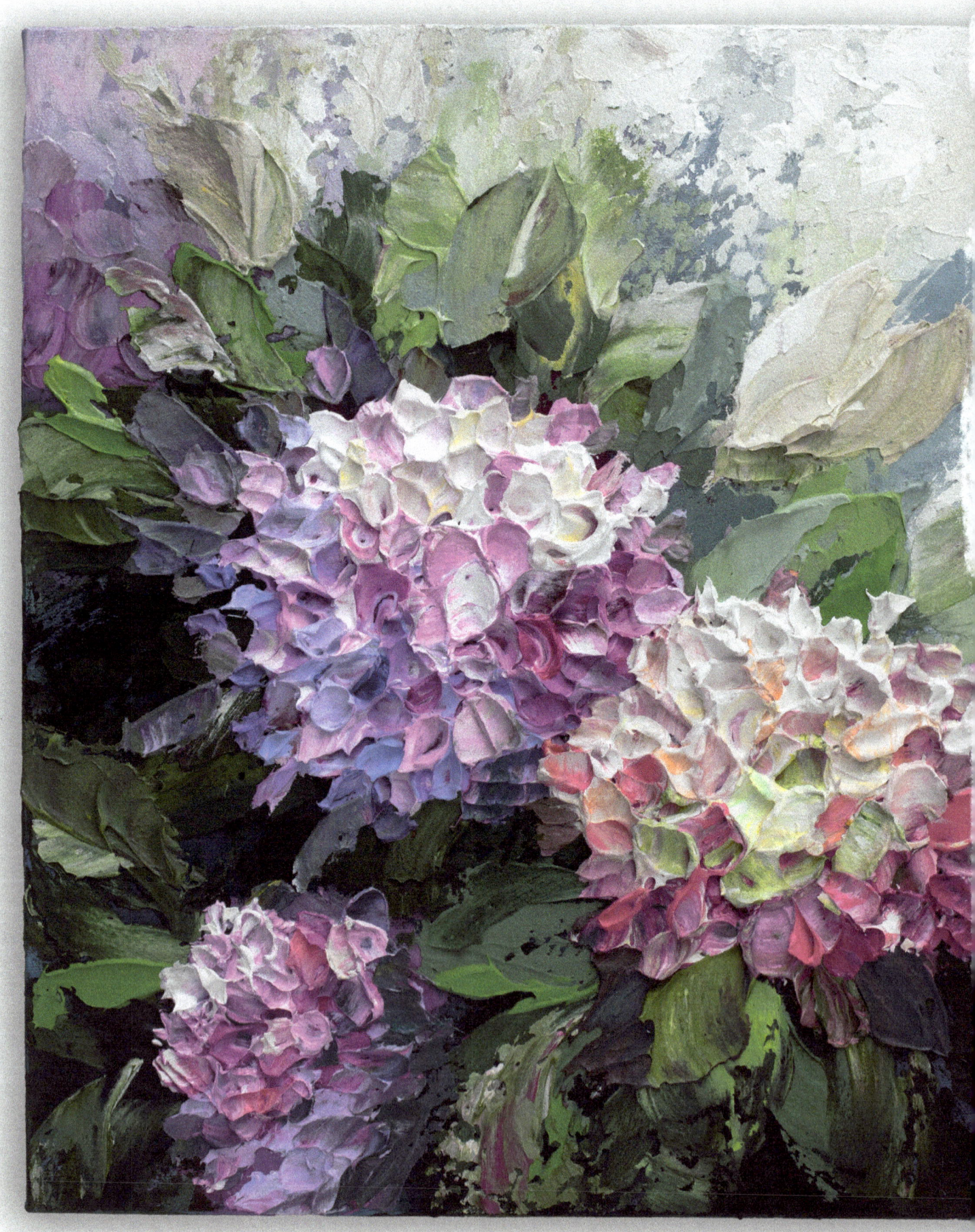

In Full Bloom

I love painting flowers. The variety of colors, textures, sizes, and shapes lend themselves perfectly to impasto painting. Here, I've used a palette knife to paint some hydrangeas – the three-dimensional texture really makes the blooms come to life. We will be working wet-on-wet and mixing colors directly on the canvas to create a multitude of colorful blends. We will also explore value using a full range of light and dark shades to bring realistic depth and volume to our abstract floral painting.

Color palette

- Titanium white
- Cadmium yellow medium
- Quinacridone red
- Quinacridone magenta
- Ultramarine blue
- Olive green, Hooker's green or deep green
- Chromatic gray or Payne's gray

Tools and materials

- Medium flat synthetic brush
- Large rounded knife
- Angled straight-edged knife
- Large spade-shaped knife
- Small oval-shaped knife
- Pen and paper for sketches
- 16in x 20in (40.5cm x 51cm) canvas
- Molding paste or gel medium to thicken paint where needed (see Mediums)

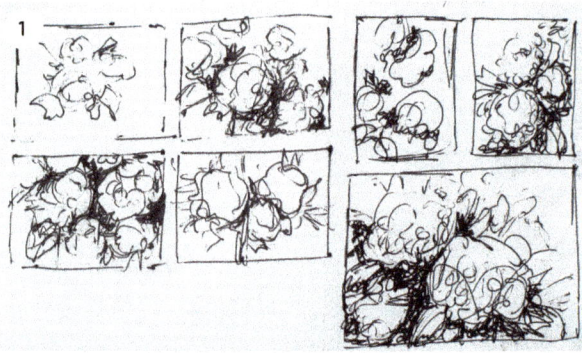

1. Using a pen and a piece of paper, create five to seven quick thumbnail sketches to work out the placement and size of your flower heads. Try not to place them directly in the middle of your canvas and vary the size of the flowers. An odd number is generally pleasing to the eye, so I used three and five flowers in my sketches. Choose a direction for your light source and fill in the shadow areas on the opposite side. Use this as a guide for your painting.

2. Mix a generous amount of dark gray (see Mixing Chromatic Black and Gray) with no medium, as we'll be blending the paint. Cover the entire surface of the canvas with gray using a medium flat brush, focusing on the darker shadow areas and adding small amounts of white to the lighter areas. This is an efficient way to establish the darks and lights in your painting and cover the dreaded blank canvas that can be intimidating. Apply the paint deliberately and with energy, and don't worry too much about how it looks as most of the surface will be covered by subsequent layers.

3. Mix a dark quin red and dark magenta (see Color Mixing) to create the darkest floral colors. Using a large rounded knife, loosely sketch the size and shape of the main hydrangea blooms with medium to large strokes. Mixing in small amounts of blue and green will help desaturate and cool the vibrant red color, making it look more natural. The color will recede into the shadows, adding depth and dimension to the blooms. I added three smaller blooms using magenta lightened with white that peek out from the background. At this point, evaluate your composition for balance and determine if there is anything you'd like to change before moving on. In my painting, I felt the bottom right bloom was too large. I mixed in some mid-tone olive green with the background color to loosely cover the flower with leaf shapes.

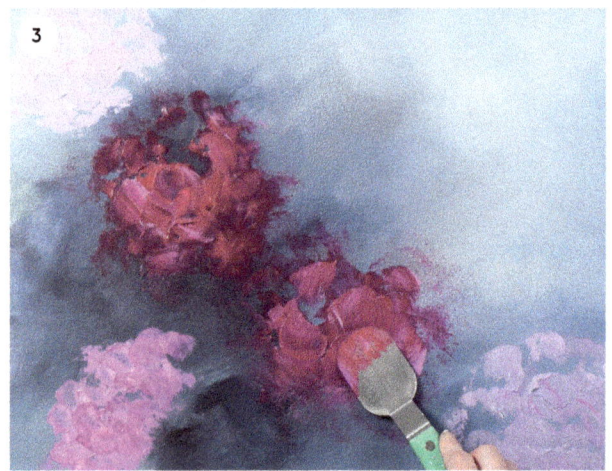

4. If you like the way your background looks, you can leave it smooth and blended. However, we can create a textured background that will give the painting depth, interest, and complement the thick texture of the hydrangea petals. Add white to the remaining chromatic gray used for the background to create a mid-tone gray. Apply a generous amount to the background with a straight-edged knife in a scumbling motion (see Techniques), leaving bits of the darker background showing through. I prefer to start in

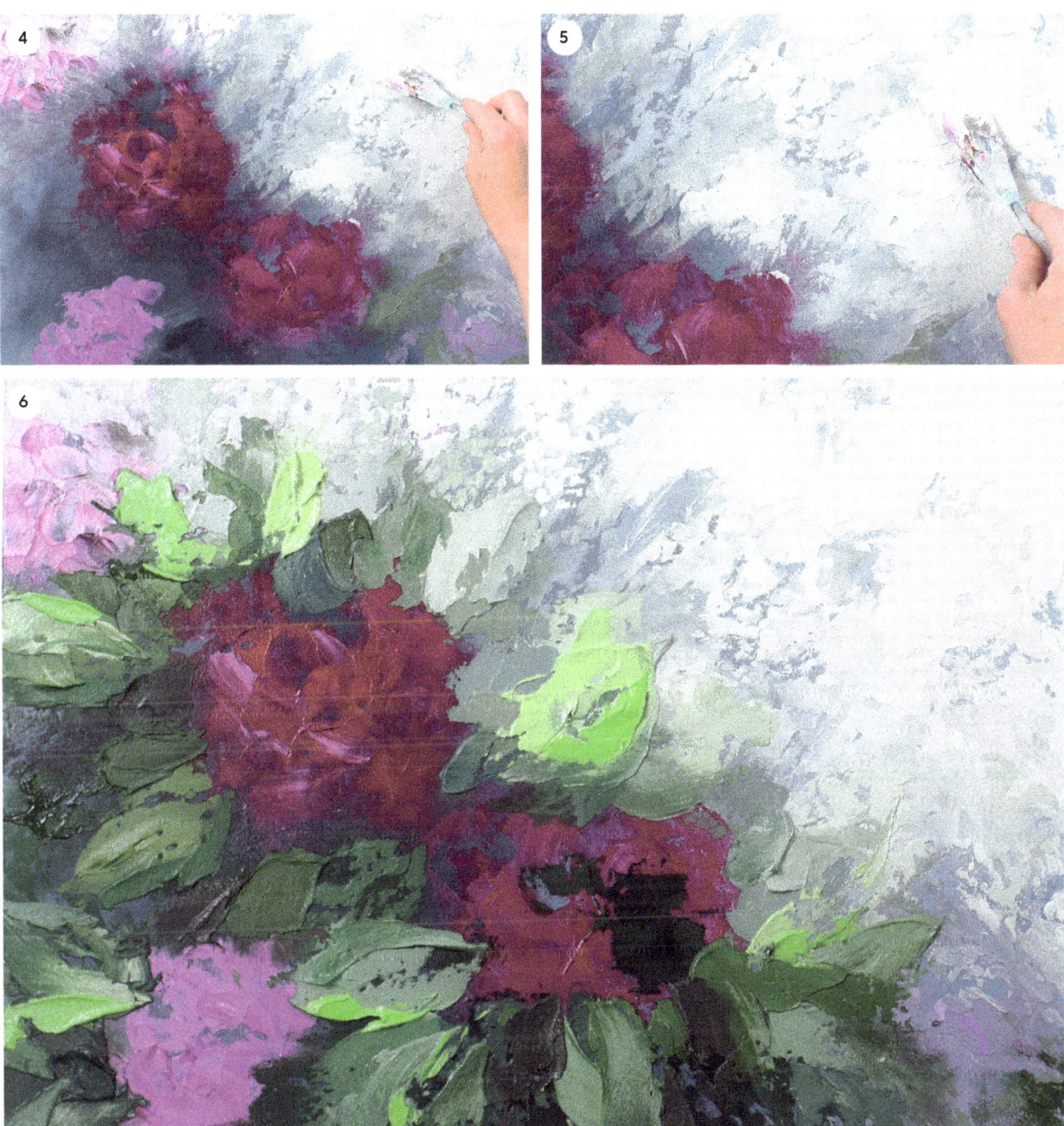

the upper right corner and work my way toward the flowers. Gradually add white with a hint of cad yellow medium to warm and lighten your background color to a soft cream.

5. Add another layer of soft cream, lightened again, over the top of the previous layer. Leave spaces around the flowers to indicate leaf shapes and other foliage. Lastly, scumble your lightest creamy white over the previous layers using your lightest touch. Go slowly at first and leave generous amounts of the under layers showing

through. It's easier to add more paint, if needed, but difficult to remove.

6. Add different values (see Color Terminology) of green to the gray background color to create a range of desaturated green colors. With a large spade-shaped knife, add loose leaf shapes and foliage behind the hydrangea blooms allowing them to fade into the background. This will create a soft and seamless transition from the flowers into the background.

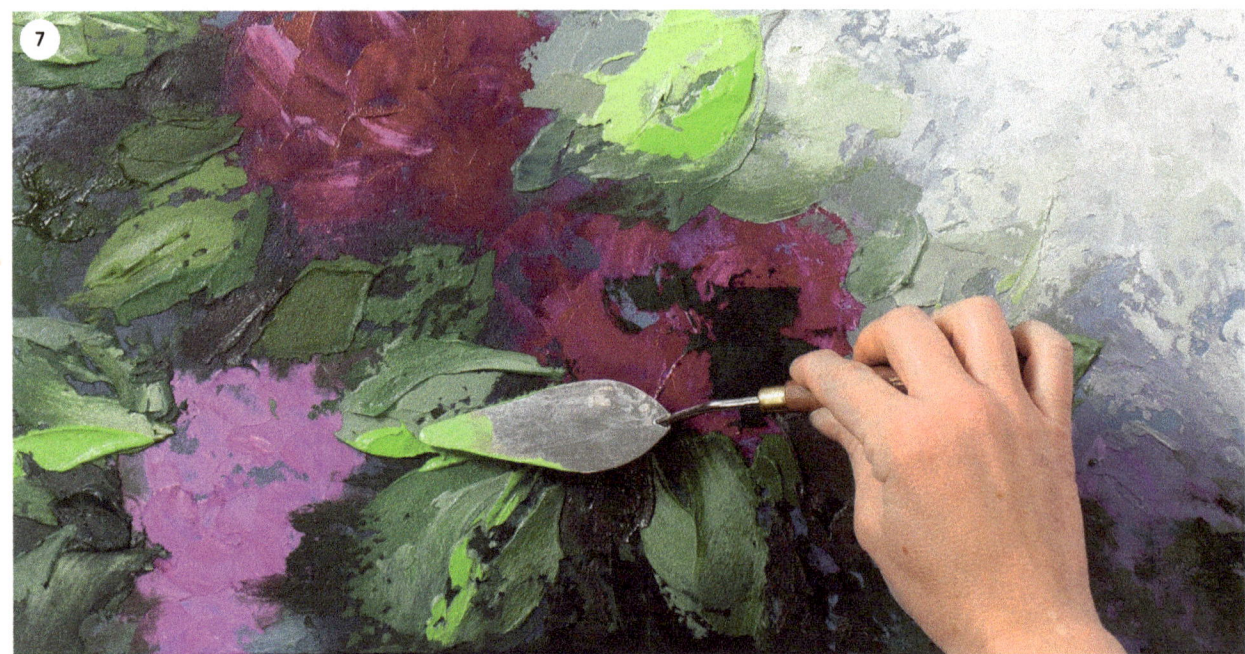

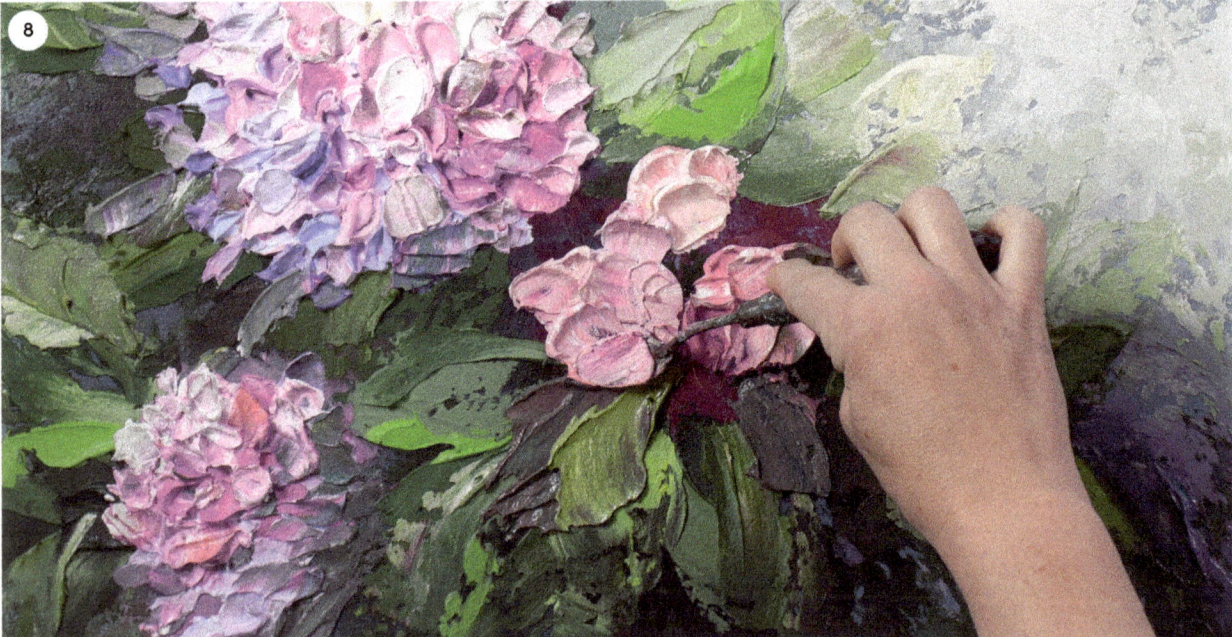

7. For the leaves, mix a dark, mid-tone, and light olive green on your palette (see Color Mixing). Start adding leaf shapes, extending out from the center of each bloom (see Techniques). Start with the darkest colored leaves and keep adding various sizes and shapes using lighter shades over the top. Add white to lighten, yellow to warm, and quin red to desaturate the color, if needed. This makes your painting look more realistic and adds interesting variations of green.

8. For the petals, mix three values each of quin red, magenta, and ultramarine blue, as well as a single pile of pale green and warm white. Starting with your darkest colors, use a small oval-shaped knife to apply daubs of paint (see Techniques) to the shadow side of the flower in overlapping clusters. There is no need to clean your knife in between strokes. Allow each new color to mix with previous marks, creating a multitude of purple and pink petals, each with unique blends of color. For the first two blooms, I started with cool

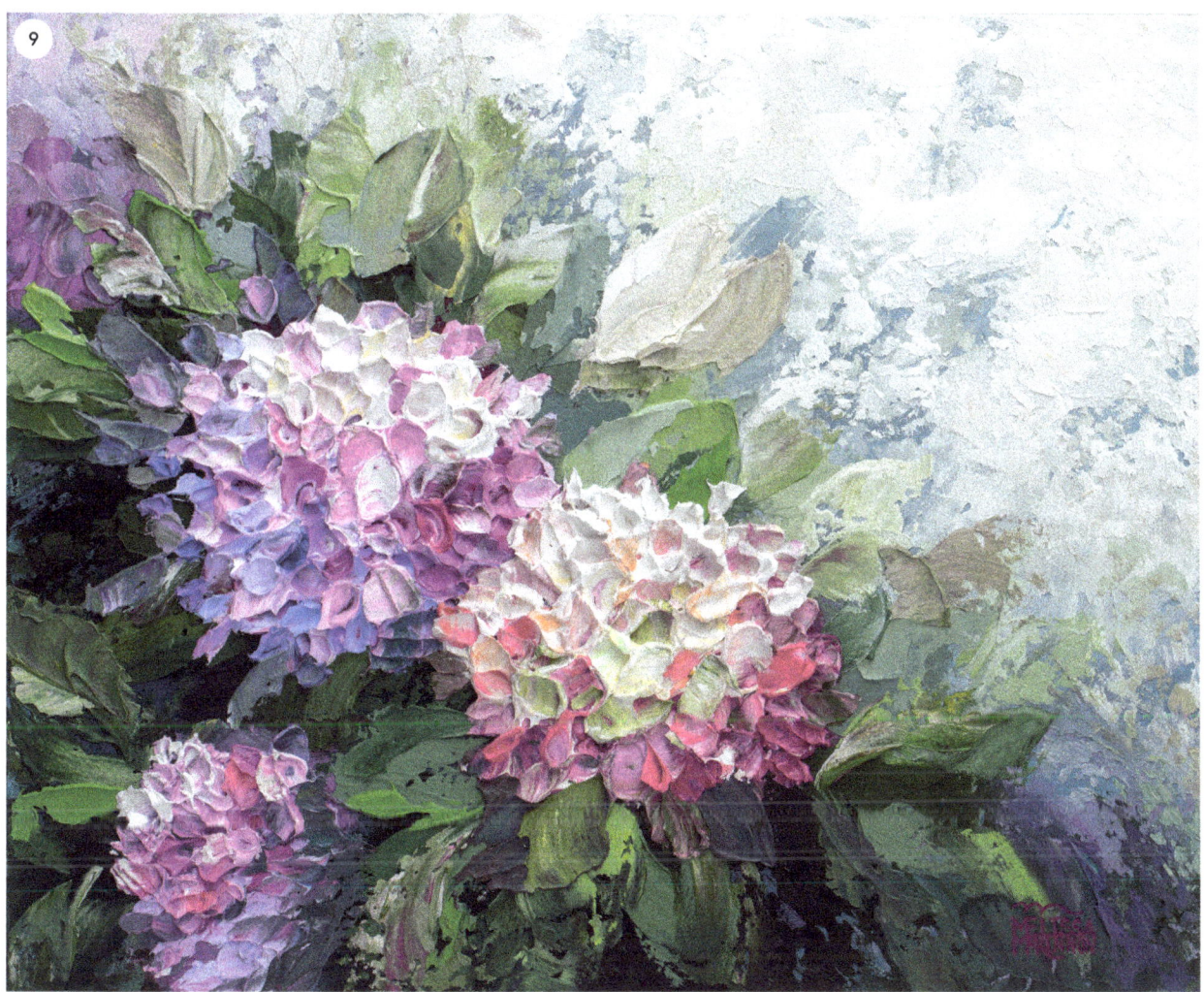

shades of purple and continuously added warmer, lighter tints of pink and white as I moved to the top of the bloom toward the light source. This gives the appearance of a rounded shape with volume. To add variety of color, repeat the process for the third bloom, this time using a range of pinks, pale green, and white for the petals.

9. Step back and evaluate your painting. Add additional details and highlights to the main blooms, leaves, and background in areas where you think they're needed.

Journey into Autumn

This painting is a fresh interpretation of a birch tree forest in autumn. I started this series almost ten years ago and continue to find endless inspiration in the vibrant colors contrasted with the black and white tree trunks. In this project, we will expand our color palette by incorporating both warm and cool colors to create a vibrant rainbow effect, and work quickly using loose strokes to bring energy into the painting. We will also work wet-on-wet to mix colors directly on the canvas and build layers of texture from thin to thick to create dimension and depth. This painting can be done using almost any palette knife, mark making method, or color palette, and I encourage you to explore the possibilities.

Color palette

- Titanium white
- Cadmium yellow light
- Cadmium yellow medium
- Quinacridone red
- Cadmium red medium
- Phthalocyanine blue (green shade)
- Ultramarine blue
- Permanent green light
- Phthalocyanine green
- Raw sienna
- Chromatic gray or Payne's gray
- Chromatic black or ivory black

Tools and materials

- Medium flat synthetic brush
- Small diamond-shaped knife
- Chalk
- 16in x 20in (40.5cm x 51cm) canvas
- Molding paste or gel medium to thicken paint where needed (see Mediums)

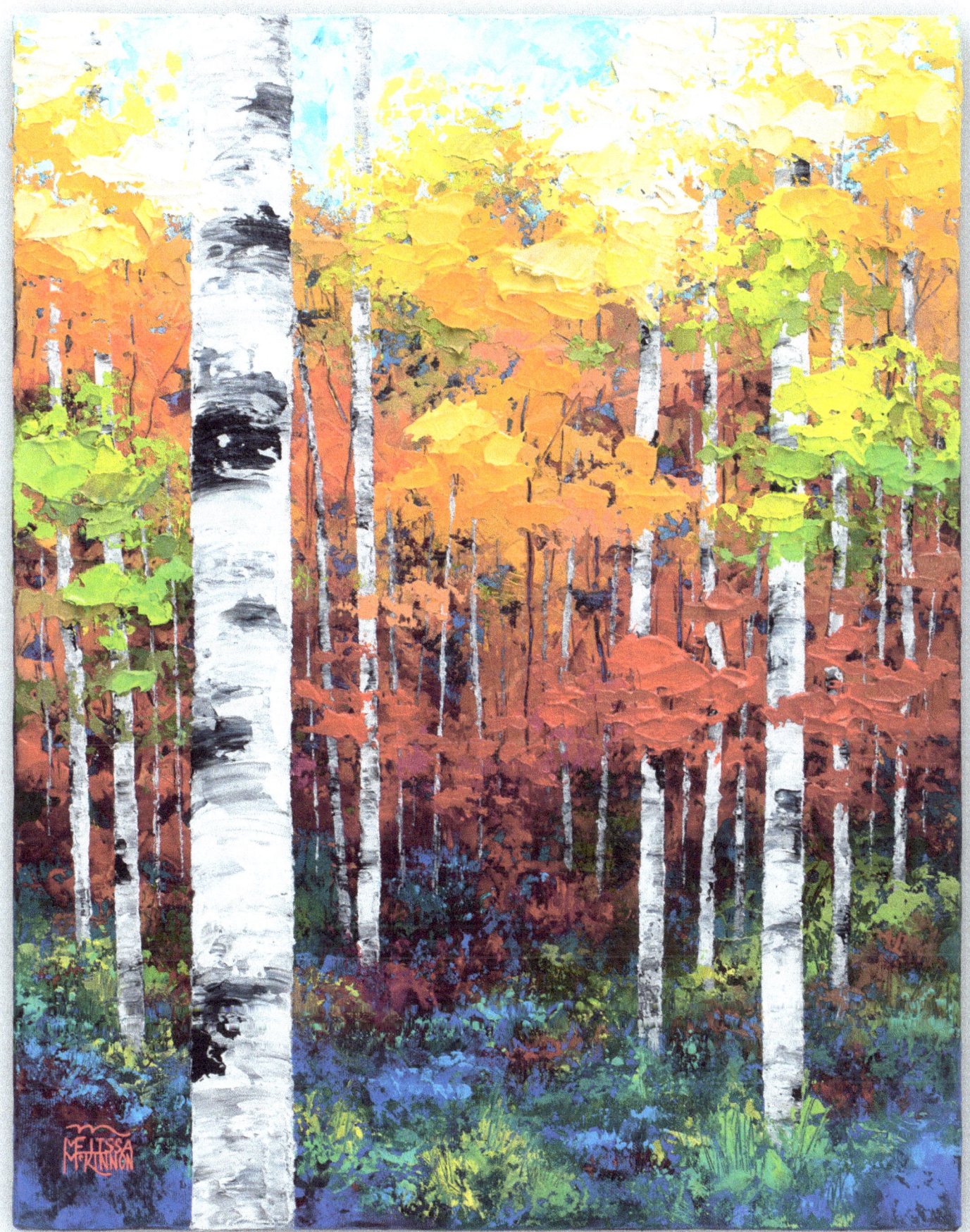

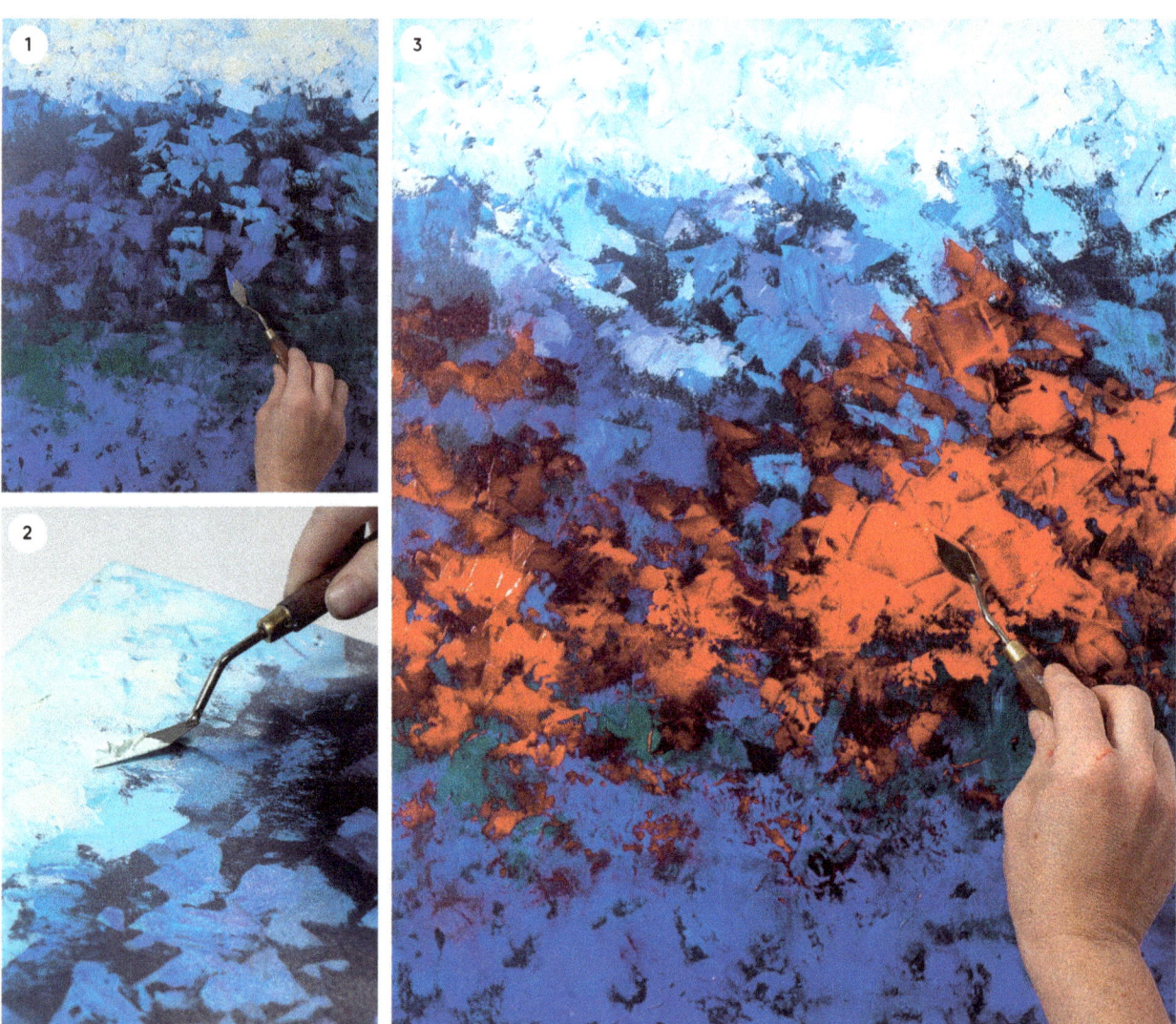

1. Using a medium flat brush, coat the entire canvas with a base layer of dark gray with no medium (see Mixing Chromatic Black and Gray). To create the background layer of the forest, use a small diamond-shaped knife and scumble (see Techniques) dark ultramarine blue (see Color Mixing) across the bottom of the canvas, keeping the paint quite thin. We don't want too much texture until after the tree trunks have been added. Add dark values of phthalo blue and phthalo green (see Color Mixing), and loosely blend into the blue horizontally, moving upwards, covering the bottom third of the canvas. Leave space between strokes to allow small portions of the gray to show through. Wipe off any excess paint from your knife onto the middle of the canvas – these little bits of color will become shadows in the background.

2. Use phthalo blue mixed with increasing amounts of white to indicate a patchy section of sky on the upper third of the canvas. Add white mixed with a touch of cad yellow light to indicate sunlit clouds against the cool blue sky.

3. Apply a thin layer of dark quin red overlapping (and mixing with) some of the blue and green, and work your way up the canvas. Add cad red medium in patches throughout the middle of the canvas, allowing it to blend into the layers below in some areas. This will indicate leaves and foliage in the distance. Allow some areas of the gray and blue background to show through the red as shadow areas.

4. Mix at least three versions of yellow using raw sienna, cad yellow med, cad yellow light, and white to lighten. Starting with the darkest yellows, apply

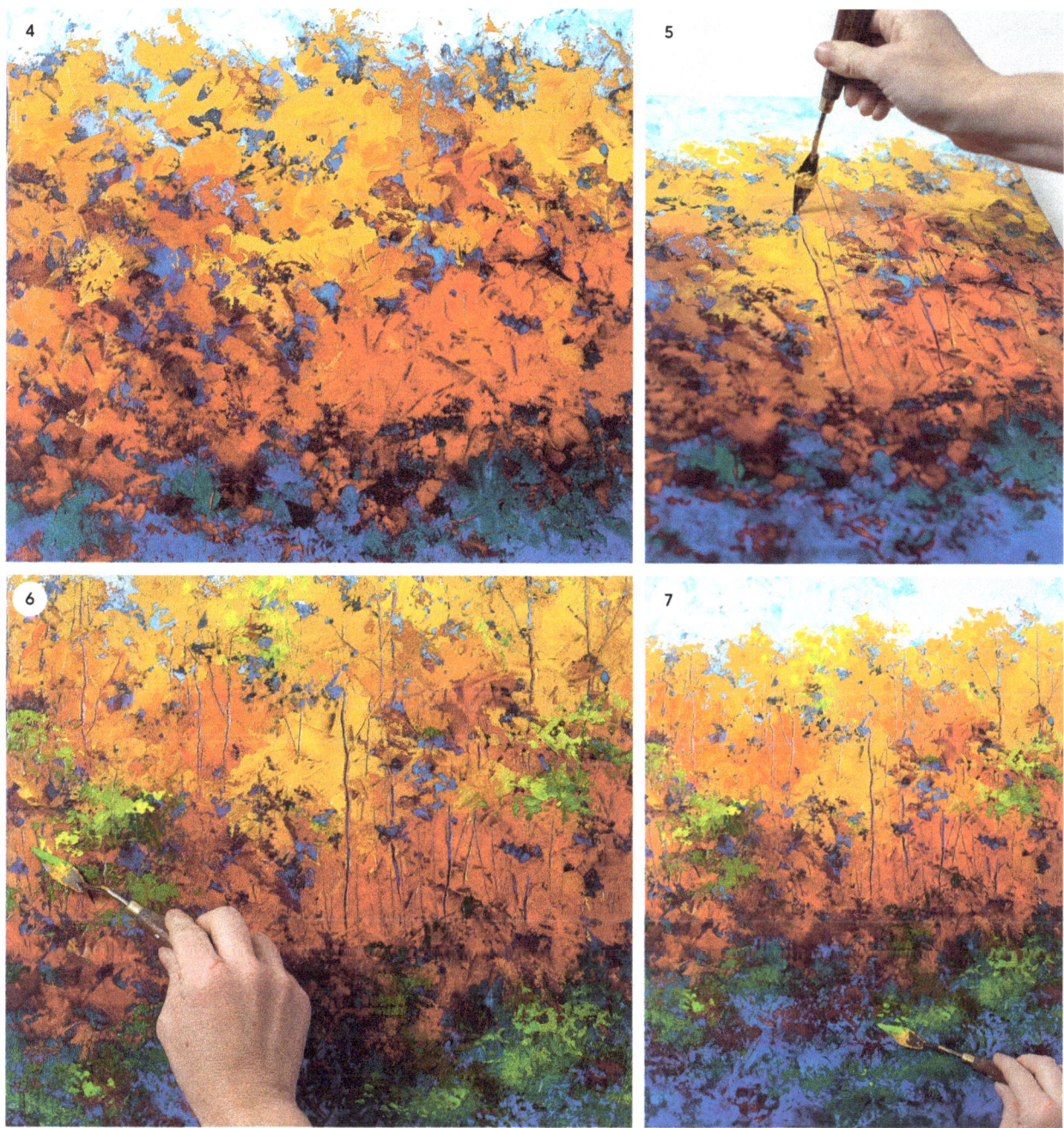

in patches just below the skyline, working your way down over the red. Allow the colors to mix to create new shades of yellow and orange. Repeat this, layering yellows from dark to light. Next, add smaller areas of cad yellow light in places where the sunlight would hit the tops of the trees in the distance.

5. Using the tip of your knife, cut through the wet paint to indicate tree trunks and branches in the distance.

6. Add a few areas of foliage (using permanent green light plus raw sienna, and cad yellow med) in the trees that will sit over the top of some of the distant tree trunks once blocked in.

7. For continuity, add some of the tree colors (reds, greens, and yellows) to the foreground to indicate bushes and fallen foliage on the forest floor. Once you are happy with the range of colors, mark making, and tree trunks, allow the painting to dry completely.

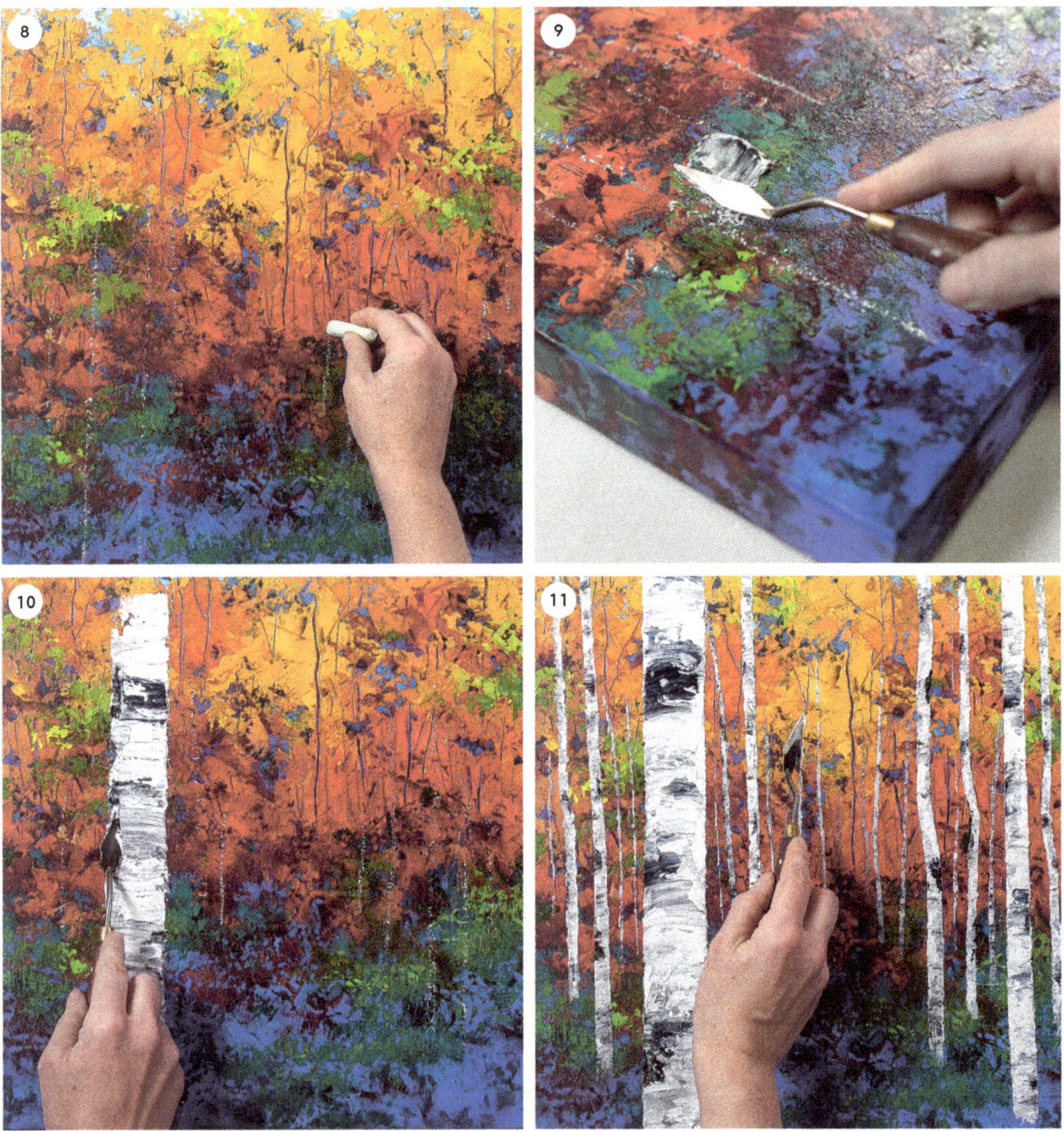

8. Once the painting is dry, add in the main aspen and birch tree trunks in the foreground. You can paint the trunks freehand or use a piece of chalk to draw an outline first. If you want to change the size or shape of the trees, use a damp cloth to wipe away the chalk and start again. Alternatively, creating a sketch first will help you visualize the size and placement of the tree trunks and determine whether your composition is successful or not before you commit to adding paint.

9. The largest trees in the composition will appear closer to the viewer, while the smaller tree trunks will recede into the background. Paint the tree trunks with a loosely mixed white and black paint to create a marble effect on the knife. Starting from the edge of the tree trunk, line up the straight edge of the knife with the outer edge of the trunk, place your knife down and sweep toward the center. Do this on both sides until your trunk is filled in.

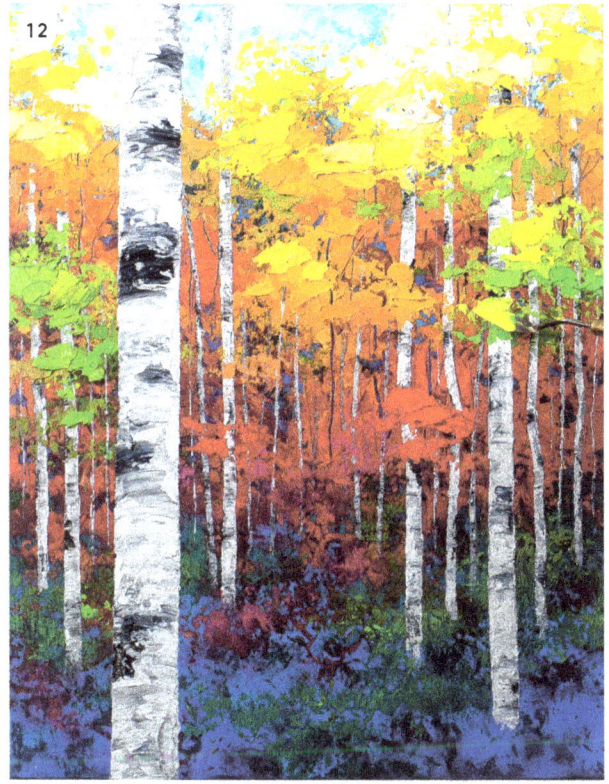

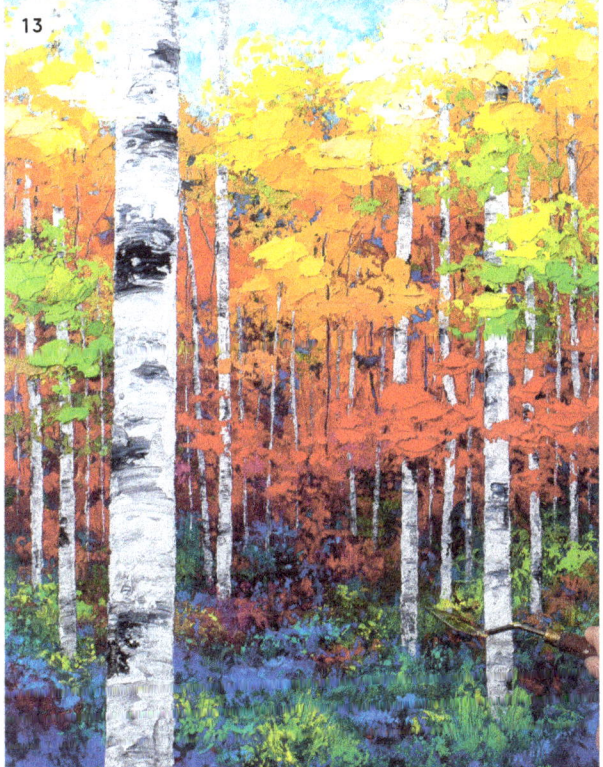

10. Once you have a base layer of paint, go back over the top with lighter shades of gray, black, and white in selected areas to create the iconic black pattern of birch trees. Using lots of paint and working wet-on-wet (see Techniques) allows the knife to glide over the top of the paint, creating beautiful blends and texture. You can make your tree trunks as thickly textured as you wish, just keep adding more layers of paint until you are happy. Aspen and birch tree trunks are imperfect by nature, so don't get too caught up in making them perfectly straight. Give them personality!

11. For the tiny trees in the distance, use only the thin edge of the knife dipped in paint. Lightly tap on the surface of the painting to indicate the impression of a tree trunk in the distance. Add as many of these as you wish to fill out the forest.

12. To push some of the tree trunks farther into the distance and add depth to the forest, lighten your leftover foliage colors with cad yellow light and white. Using lots of paint, add another thick layer of leaves and foliage in a pattern that pleases you.

13. Lastly, add lighter highlights and details to the foreground foliage. Use the tip of the knife to scratch into the paint (see Techniques) to indicate grasses and shrubs near the base of the tree trunks. I like to add these grasses and shrubs to ensure the trees are firmly planted in the ground.

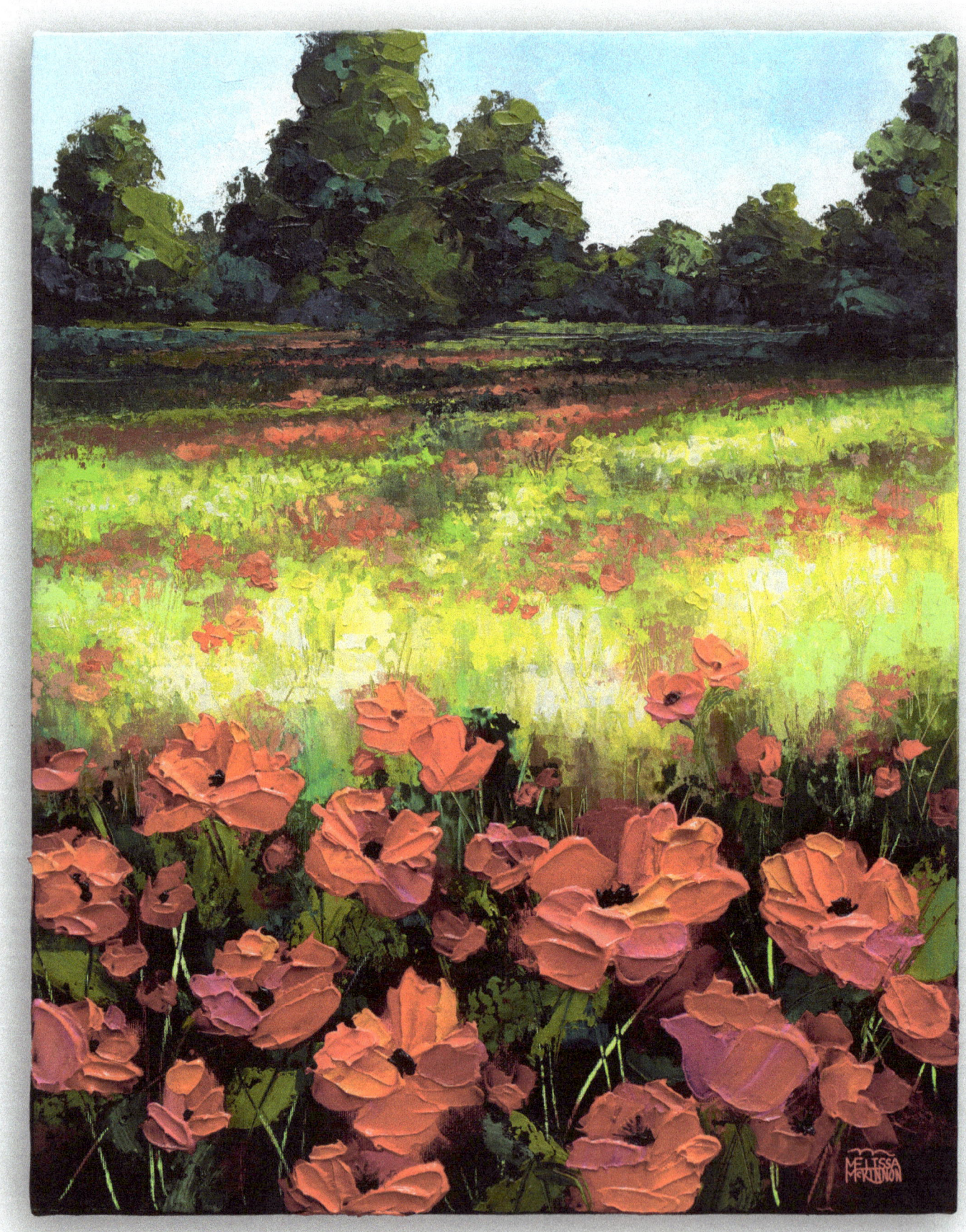

Wild Poppies of Tuscany

I fell in love with poppies one summer in Italy. In Tuscany, they grow wild and carpet the landscape in a field of delicate red blooms as far as the eye can see. Their thin petals blow in the wind, creating a myriad of interesting shapes that are a delight to paint with a palette knife. Working on these textured blooms will help us create depth in our landscape by using perspective, scale, and saturation. We will also work with value and complementary colors to create contrast and drama.

Color palette

- Titanium white
- Cadmium yellow light
- Cadmium yellow medium
- Cadmium red medium
- Quinacridone red
- Phthalocyanine blue (green shade)
- Ultramarine blue
- Permanent green light
- Phthalocyanine green
- Chromatic black or Payne's gray

Tools and materials

- Medium spade-shaped knife
- Small oval-shaped knife
- Small diamond-shaped knife
- Pencil or chalk
- 16in x 20in (10.5cm x 51cm) canvas
- Molding paste or gel medium to thicken paint where needed (see Mediums)

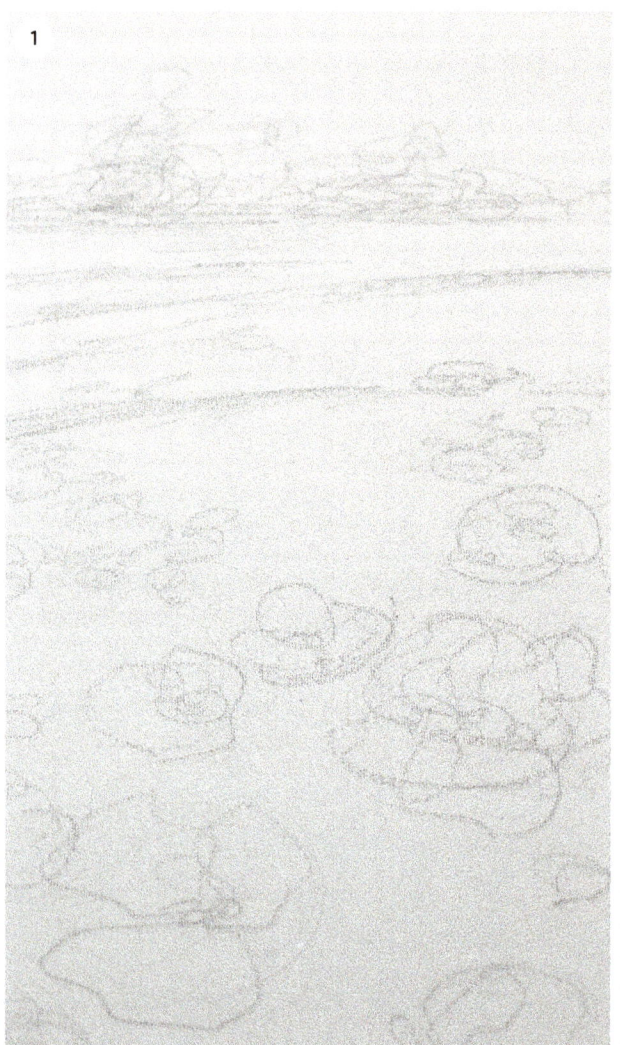

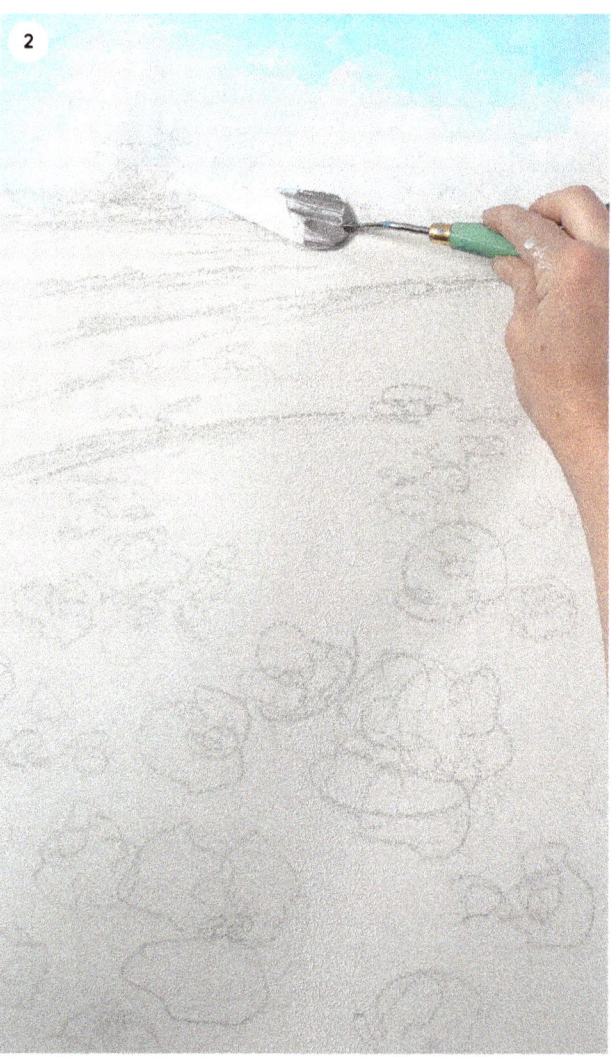

1. Begin with a quick sketch using pencil or chalk directly on the canvas to establish the composition and perspective (see Composition).

2. Starting at the top of the canvas, use a medium spade-shaped knife loaded with light phthalo blue (see Color Mixing) and block in the sky. Then, using short, loose strokes, apply warm white (white plus cad yellow light), to indicate fluffy clouds near the horizon.

3. Mix a dark black with a green tone (see Mixing Chromatic Black and Gray). Use a small oval-shaped knife to block in the tree shapes along the horizon. Soften the edges of the trees by allowing the paint to mix with the wet sky for a

more realistic look. I added small amounts of ultramarine blue and phthalo green to the shadow areas. Continue adding layers of progressively lighter and warmer shades of green (permanent green light mixed with yellow and white) to give the trees shape and volume. For a more natural green, add red to desaturate it. Layer your colors dark to light and cool to warm. Allow each layer to mix with the wet colors underneath creating a variety of new green shades. In this painting, the light source is coming from the right, so I've placed my lightest colors and highlights on the right-hand side of the trees. The highlights should be lighter and warmer than the shadow side.

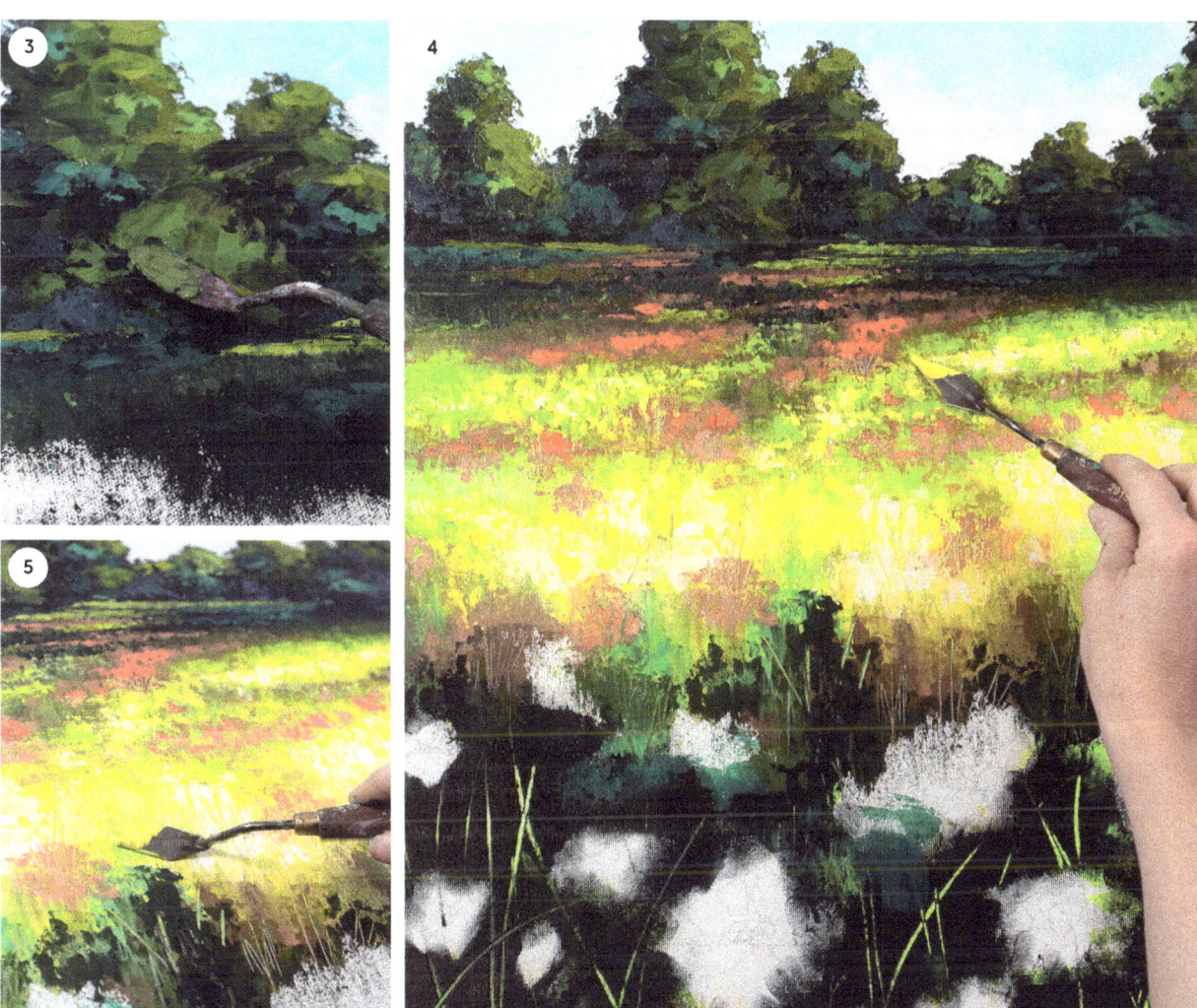

4. Using a small diamond-shaped knife, begin applying the distant fields in horizontal lines of color just below the tree line. Alternate areas of shadow colors with patches of brighter green in areas where the sun might hit the fields. Add increasing amounts of cad red medium to your green to suggest groupings of poppy flowers in the distance. I placed my fields on a slight diagonal to create a sense of perspective as the fields fade away toward the top right of the painting. This helps draw the eye down from the horizon line (and zigzag through the composition) towards the focal point at the bottom. Continue adding larger areas of light greens to fill the middle third of the painting. Lastly, cover the lower third of the canvas with your left-over black and dark greens leaving the flower shapes blank.

5. Using a scumbling motion (see Techniques), continue to add layers of bright green to the center of the painting, adding increasing amounts of yellow and white to lighten your colors as you go. This strong contrast in value creates depth and drama in the painting. Add details by using the tip of the knife to scratch through the wet paint for grasses and stems.

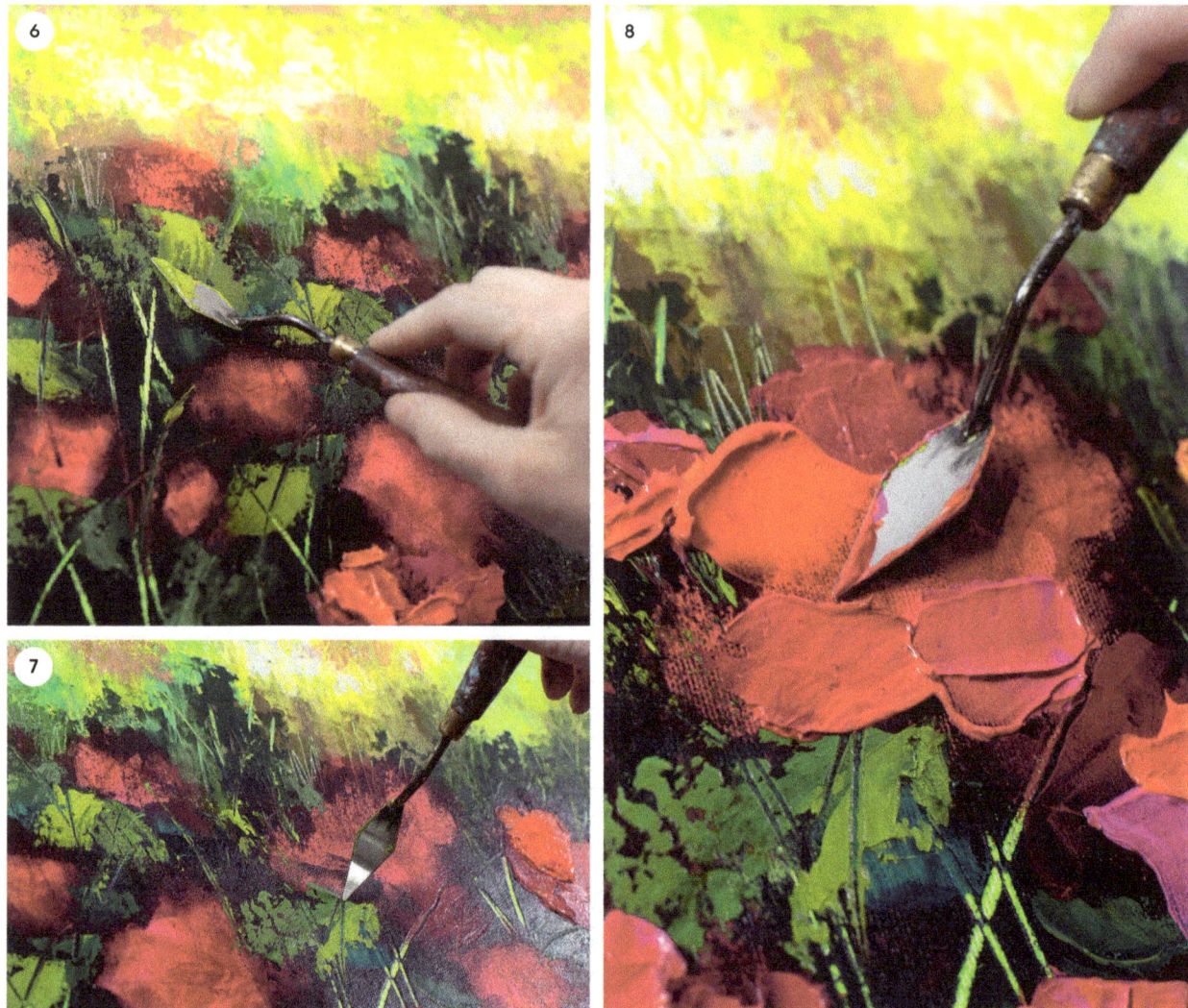

6. Moving to the bottom third of the painting, apply a thin layer of quin red on top of the main flower shapes and surrounding areas of dark paint, suggesting petals in the background. Next, add in any leaf shapes and stems (see Techniques) that you'd like to see in the background of your flowers.

7. Use the tip of the knife to scratch through some of the leaf and petal shapes to suggest stems and grasses, adding more interest and texture to the background.

8. Mix a dark and a mid-tone red of both quin red and cad red medium (see Color Mixing) to make four shades. Mix in small amounts of cad yellow medium and white to lighten and warm the colors. Load your knife with a large amount of dark red and apply two to three large petals to each of your flowers.

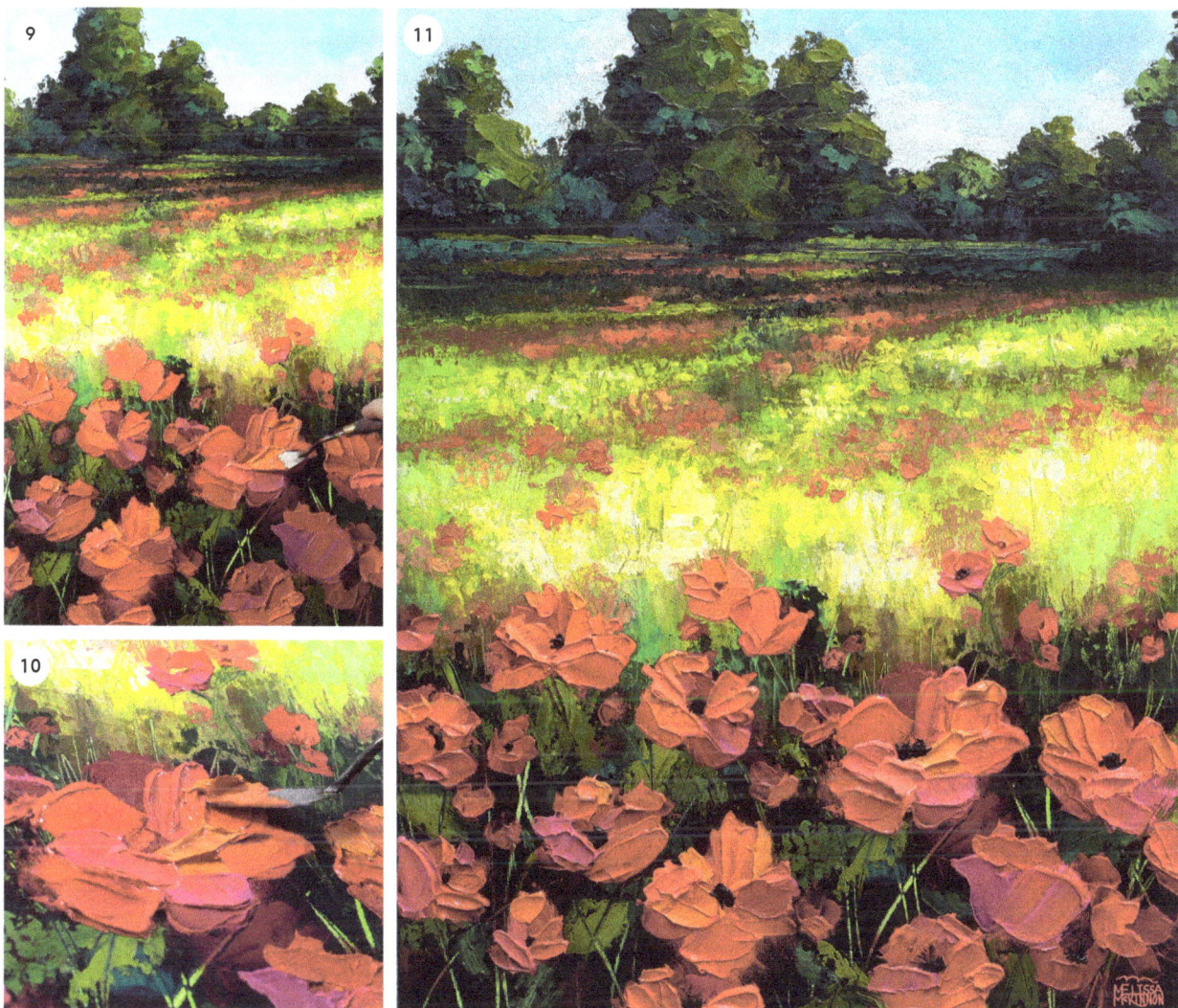

9. Next, use the mid-tone reds to sculpt in the next layer of petals. Poppies have large thin petals that twist and turn in a variety of shapes and patterns, so try to reflect that by varying the size, shape, and direction of your petals. Use the tip of the knife to apply small amounts of red to the patches of greenish red in the fields above to create small clusters of flowers and suggest individual blooms as they fade into the distance.

10. Use your lightest red colors to add highlights and extra petals for variety and detail.

11. Lastly, add a dollop of black to the center of each open flower. Keep in mind that some of the flowers may be closed or pointing away from you so won't require a center.

Spring Blossom

Nothing says spring like the tightly packed clusters of fragrant pink and white blossoms on orchard trees. The anticipation of the first bloom after a cold, colorless winter... the burst of beauty as a bud opens to life... the exhilaration of stopping to see a field of color against a clear blue sky. Relax and have fun with this painting. Focus more on creating interesting abstract shapes and textures rather than realistic flowers. Keep your palette knife loose and allow it to dance the color around the canvas. We'll be creating a textured background for our painting, and using a knife to carve through wet paint, creating lines and unique texture. We'll also be making lush blossoms using a palette knife and lots of layers.

Color palette

- Titanium white
- Cadmium yellow medium
- Quinacridone red
- Quinacridone magenta
- Ultramarine blue
- Hooker's green or olive green
- Chromatic gray or Payne's gray

Tools and materials

- Medium flat synthetic brush
- Angled straight-edged knife
- Small diamond-shaped knife
- 16in x 20in (40.5cm x 51cm) canvas
- Molding paste or gel medium to thicken paint where needed (see Mediums)

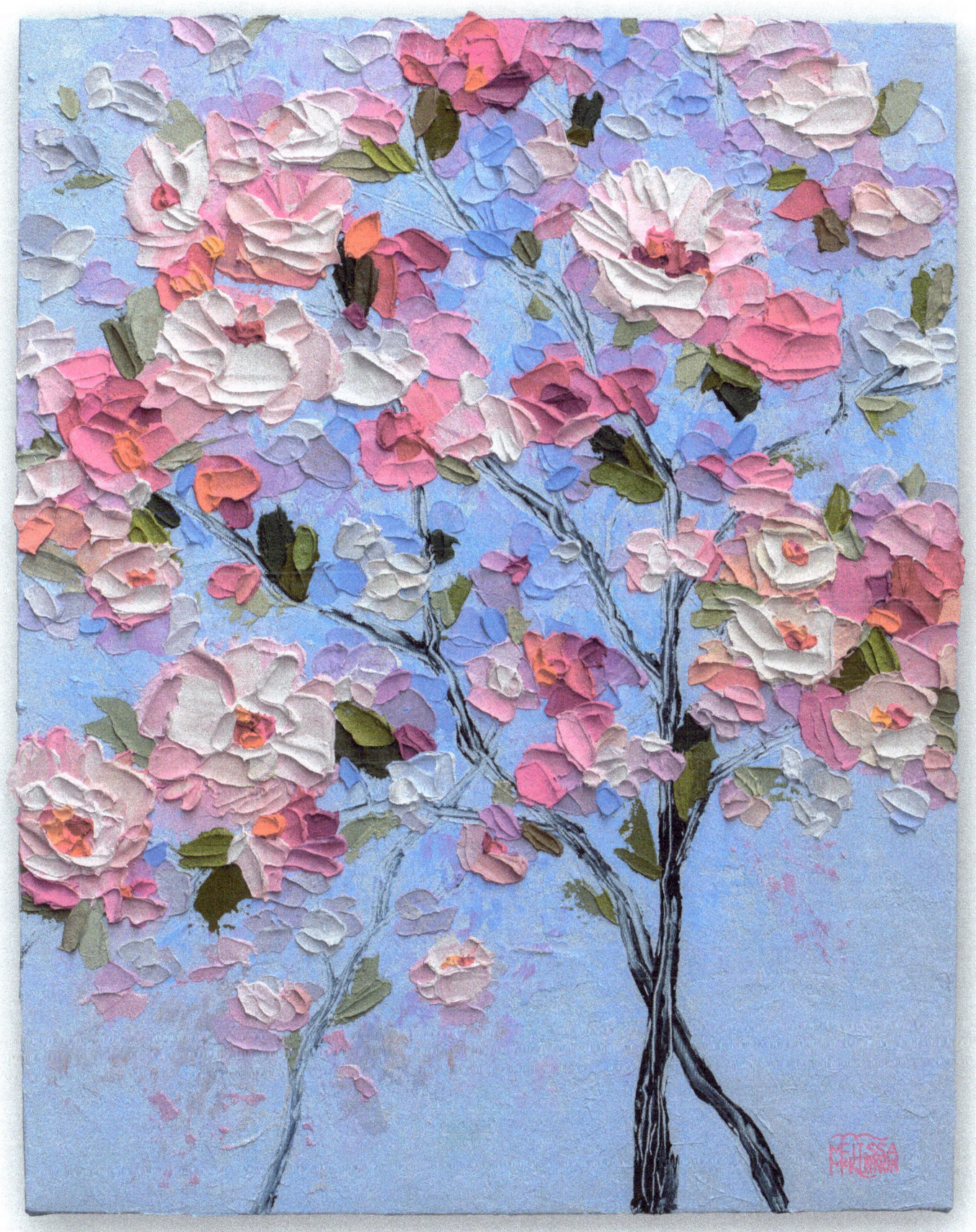

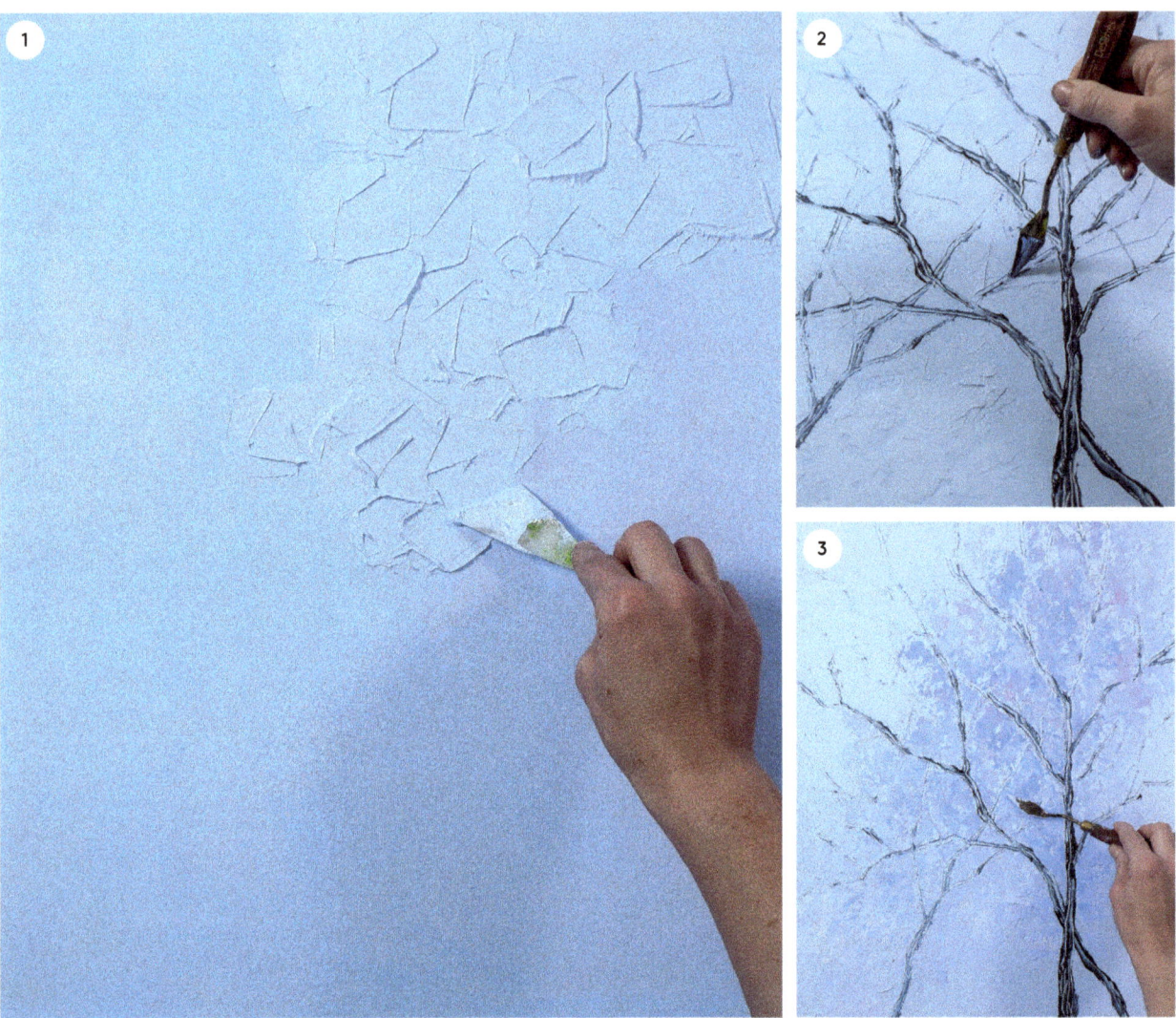

1. Mix a large amount of light ultramarine blue (see Color Mixing). With a medium flat brush, paint the entire canvas and sides. Then add gel medium or molding paste to the paint mix and loosely cover the surface in short strokes using a straight-edged knife, allowing the texture to build.

2. While the paint is still wet, use the tip of a small diamond-shaped knife loaded with dark gray (see Mixing Chromatic Black and Gray) to carve irregular branch shapes into the paint (see Techniques). Allow the drawn lines of the palette knife to create texture and dimension in the tree trunks. You can go over the branches several times until you are happy with the texture and pattern you have created. I always start from the bottom and work my way to the outer branches. You can see the concentration of paint is thicker at the bottom and is almost nonexistent at the tips where the branches are thinnest.

3. Next mix three shades of ultramarine blue: one slightly darker than your base color, one lighter, and one with a hint of magenta. Use the knife to scumble (see Techniques) the dark blue over the background in between the branches to create another layer of texture and some shadow areas. Next, add a layer of the light blue, allowing the colors to blend on the canvas as you coat the surface. Allow the texture to build up in areas while leaving some of the background to show through. Lastly, add the blue mixed with magenta in some areas for a variety of color.

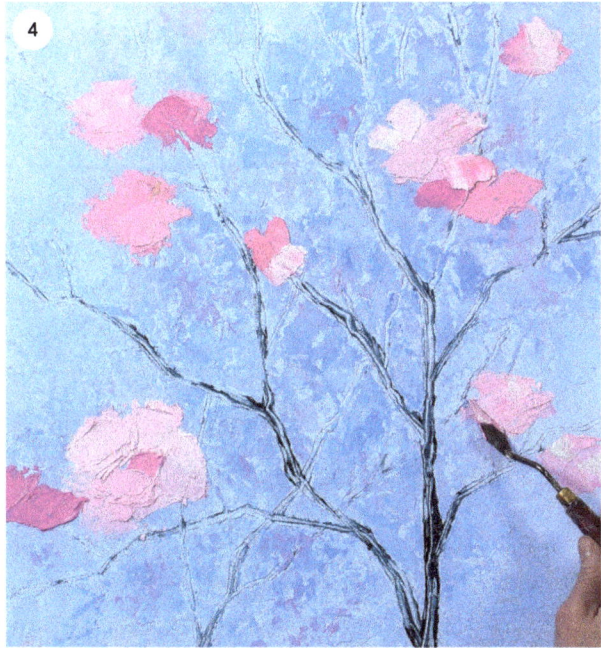

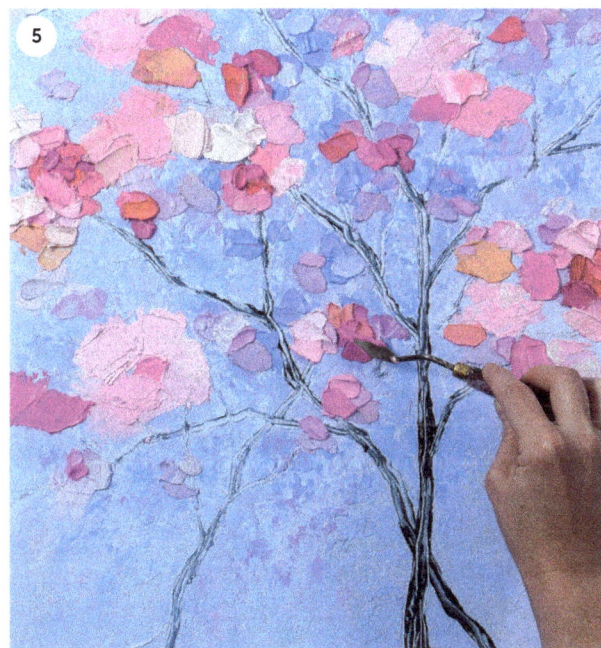

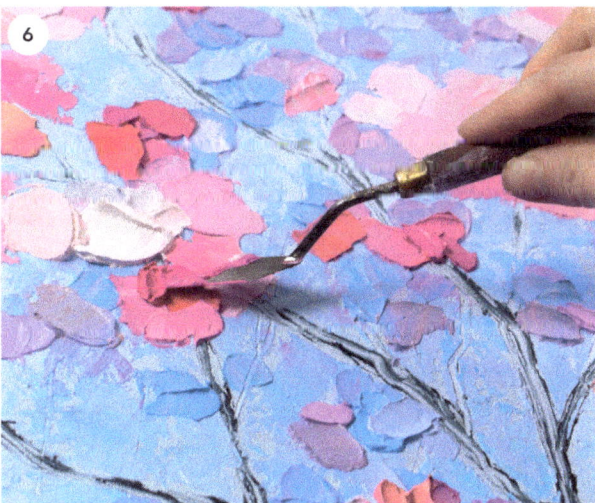

4. Mix six shades of pink: a dark, mid-tone, and light magenta, and the same again of quin red (see Color Mixing). Select the mid-tone pinks and loosely block in your largest blooms. Don't worry about being precise, we are going to add several layers of petals on top. For now, these shapes will help plan our composition and establish where our main flowers will be. Continue adding more pink tones to create the petal shapes.

5. For the smaller clusters of petals, add some of the background blue to cool and desaturate the pinks and/or add yellow to brighten and warm the colors. Use the back of your knife to apply the new colors in small petal shapes in between the flowers. These marks give an impression of petals in the distant shadows and allow our big, light blooms to stand out against the darker background. Continue this process while adding increasing amounts of pink to your mix to create a variety of purple and pink petals.

6. I approach this stage in a loose and abstract manner. I choose my darkest pinks and apply them in several areas around the canvas. I modify the color a little bit with each stroke by adding more pink or white and place that color next to my first marks, then repeat this process over and over, while changing the color, saturation, and value in small increments as I go. To avoid complete randomness and chaos, try to place your petal shapes together in small clusters around your main blooms. As you can see, I haven't made any actual flower shapes yet, just textured marks. I feel that this approach allows your mind to be free. It's an exercise in abstraction, looseness, and color. Try to vary the size, shape, and direction of your marks.

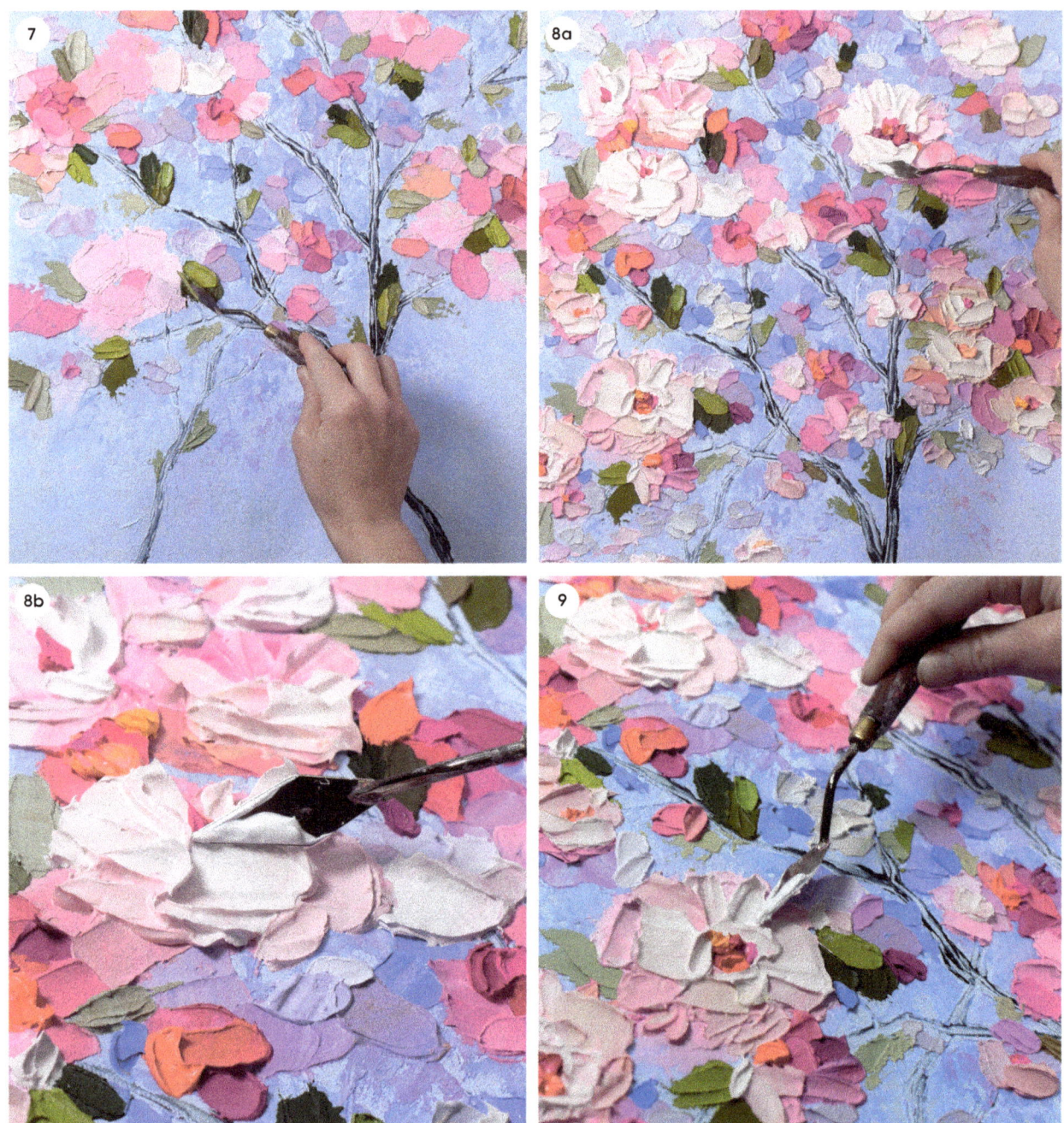

7. Mix a dark, mid-tone, and light green for the leaves. You can add small amounts of yellow, pink, or background blue mix to alter the hue and saturation of your greens to create variety and interest. Apply the paint in leaf shapes (see Techniques) around the composition, overlapping shapes for added dimension. Keep adding layers of color until you are happy with how the background looks.

8. Next, we are going to create the main flower blossoms by adding multiple layers of individual petals to the areas of pink we've already blocked in. Starting with a mid-tone to light pink, load a large amount of paint onto your knife and sweep the edge of it across the canvas. Start with the largest petals first, leaving some of the base layer to show from behind. I like to alternate strokes working from the center outward and from the outside in.

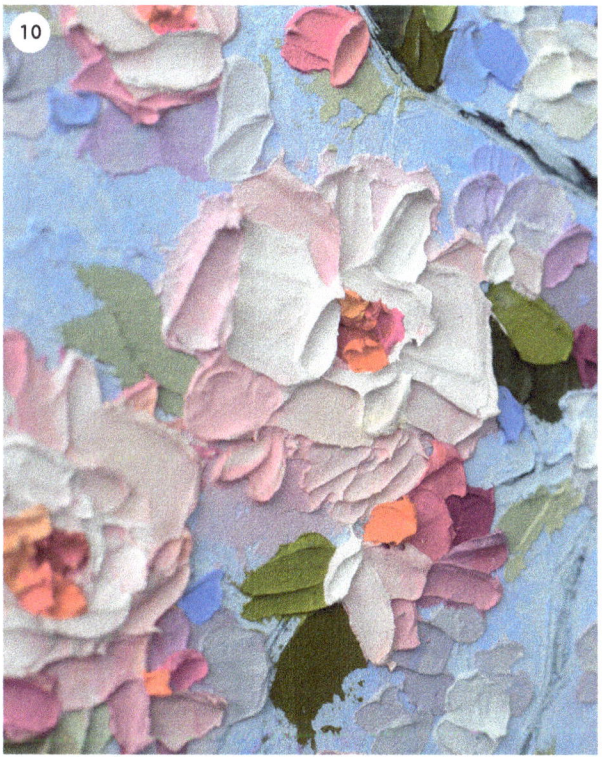

9. Continue adding layers of petals to each flower. Slightly change the color, size, shape, and direction of each stroke, allowing some of the previous layers to show underneath. Work from dark to light colors and large to small petals. You can also use different amounts of pressure with your strokes. More pressure will allow you to pick up some of the color underneath creating a blend of color on your petal. A lighter touch will allow you to layer a solid color over another.

10. Once you have the majority of your flower forms created, load the tip of your knife with paint and apply it to the center of your blooms. I've chosen a vibrant dark magenta (magenta, quin red, and cad yellow light) and pops of bright tangerine (quin red and cad yellow med) and orange for interest. I've also used some of these vibrant colors to add smaller flowers and petal shapes around the main blooms. The dark saturated color adds contrast to the pale tones of the background and main flowers.

11. Assess your composition for value and how your eye moves around the canvas. Add any additional details to help with flow or interest. I added extra petals and smaller flowers to fill in empty spaces to add more texture and balance the composition.

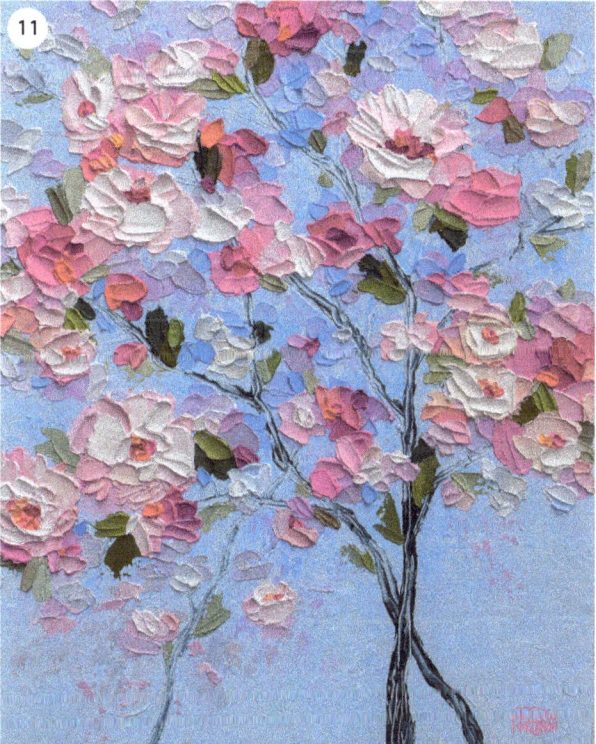

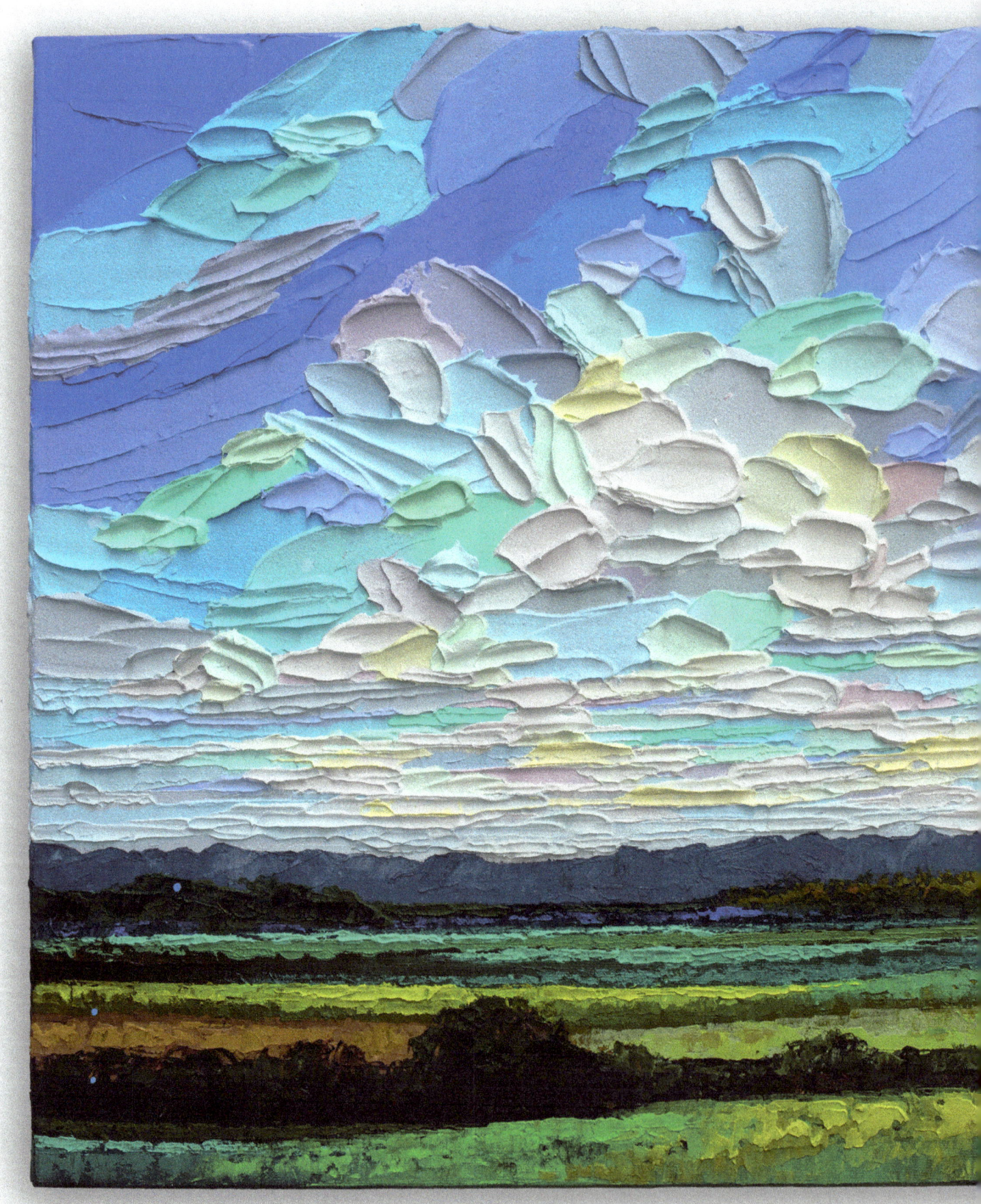

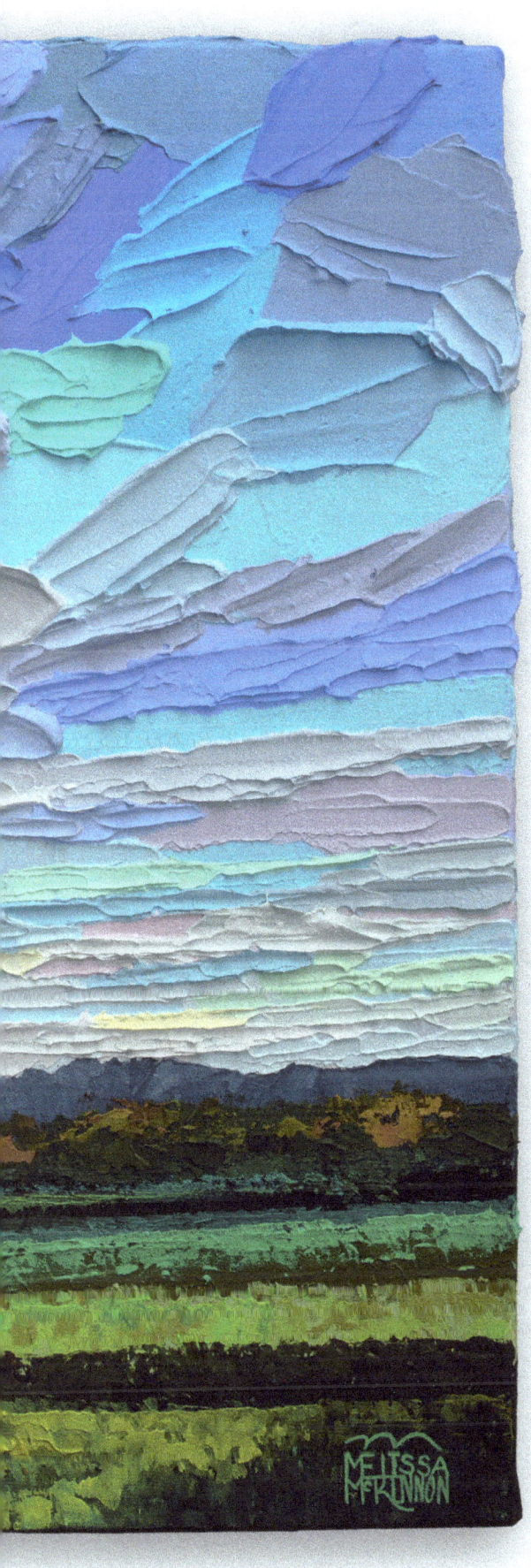

Break of Day

I feel lucky to live in one of the most beautiful places in the world. My home in western Canada is nestled in the foothills between the Rocky Mountains and golden prairies. With its four seasons and unique chinook weather patterns, our big beautiful sky is constantly changing and provides endless inspiration. It can be calm and peaceful or energetic and swirly, so for this painting, play with the size and composition of the sky. We'll use the impasto technique to create a simple landscape with a big impact. We'll work with color, perspective, and pattern for this design. This painting will develop your mark making skills as you will need to change the size and shape of your knife, the size, shape, and direction of your strokes, and the amount of paint you apply.

Color palette

- Titanium white
- Cadmium yellow light
- Quinacridone magenta
- Phthalocyanine blue (green shade)
- Ultramarine blue
- Phthalocyanine green
- Permanent green light
- Raw sienna
- Burnt sienna
- Chromatic black or Payne's gray

Tools and materials

- Medium flat synthetic brush
- Medium spade-shaped knife
- Small diamond-shaped knife
- 16in x 20in (40.5cm x 51cm) canvas
- Molding paste or gel medium to thicken paint where needed (see Mediums)

1. Roughly divide your canvas into thirds horizontally and decide on the ratio of sky to land (see Composition). My horizon line is between the middle and bottom thirds to create a large, dramatic sky. Using a medium flat brush, cover the top two-thirds of the canvas with a mid-tone ultramarine blue (see Color Mixing), most of which will be covered by subsequent layers. Mix two large piles of dark blue paint, one of ultramarine and another of phthalo blue. Then create smaller piles in a range of values from dark to light. If you do this before painting, it will save you time and make color mixing easier. Using a medium spade-shaped knife, begin applying the paint in long, sweeping strokes (see Techniques) across the canvas, starting with your darkest color.

2. Work from the top down, overlapping colors in layers and working from dark to light, large to small, cool to warm. Add small amounts of magenta and cad yellow light to alter the color slightly as you go. Adding both will desaturate the blue creating beautiful chromatic gray tones.

3. In this painting, I'm simplifying the landscape into long linear shapes contrasted with thick rounded daubs of color to create focal points in the sky and foreground. Using colors already on your palette, apply large shapes first to establish the composition. Then, use a diamond-shaped knife to add multiple layers of smaller cloud shapes on top to add dimension, variations of shape, size, and color, as well as to cover any rough edges.

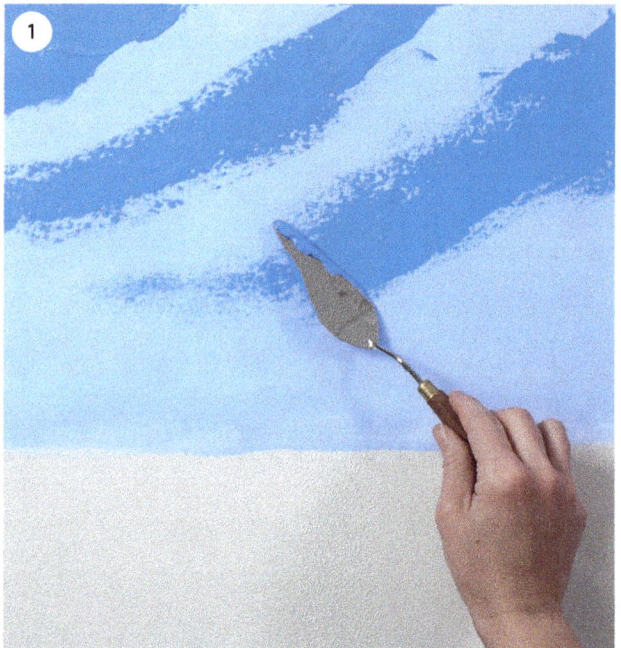

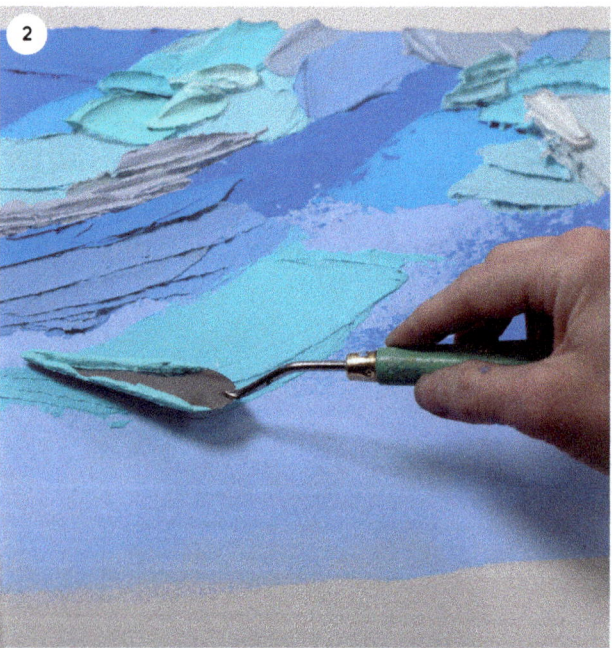

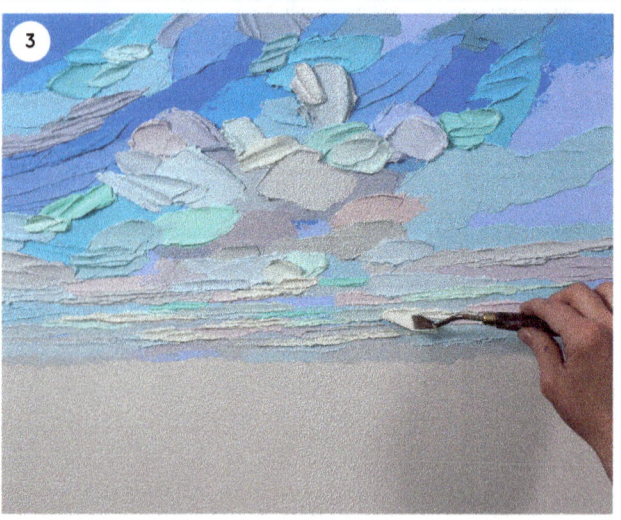

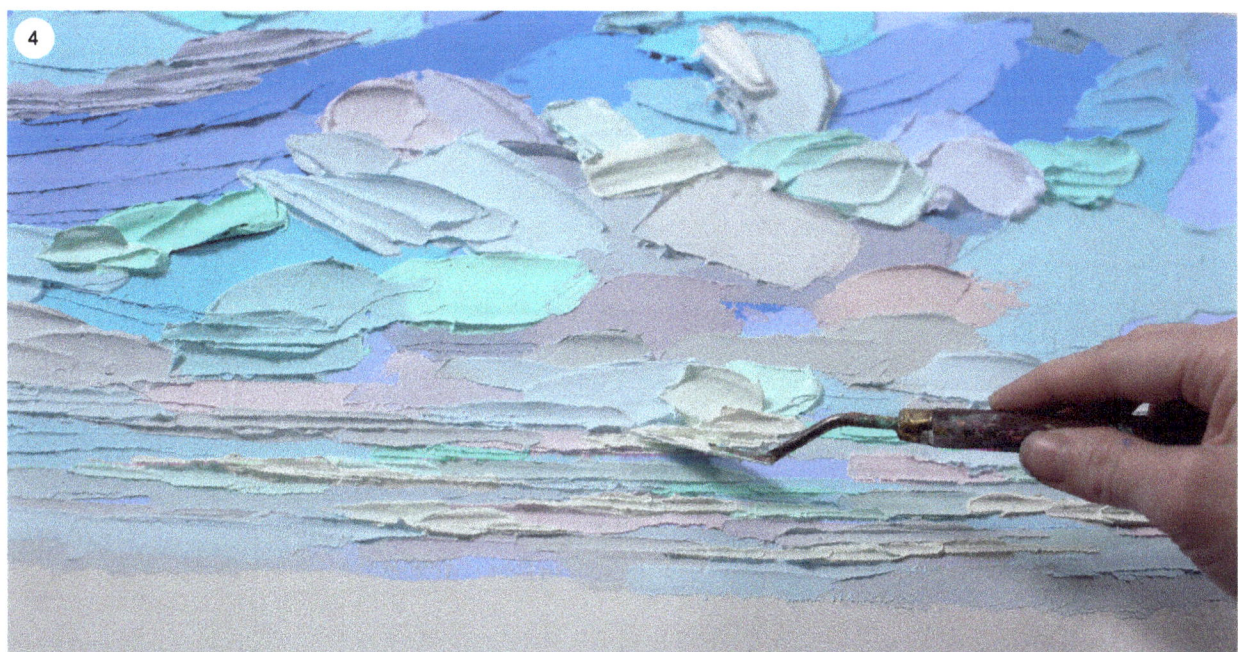

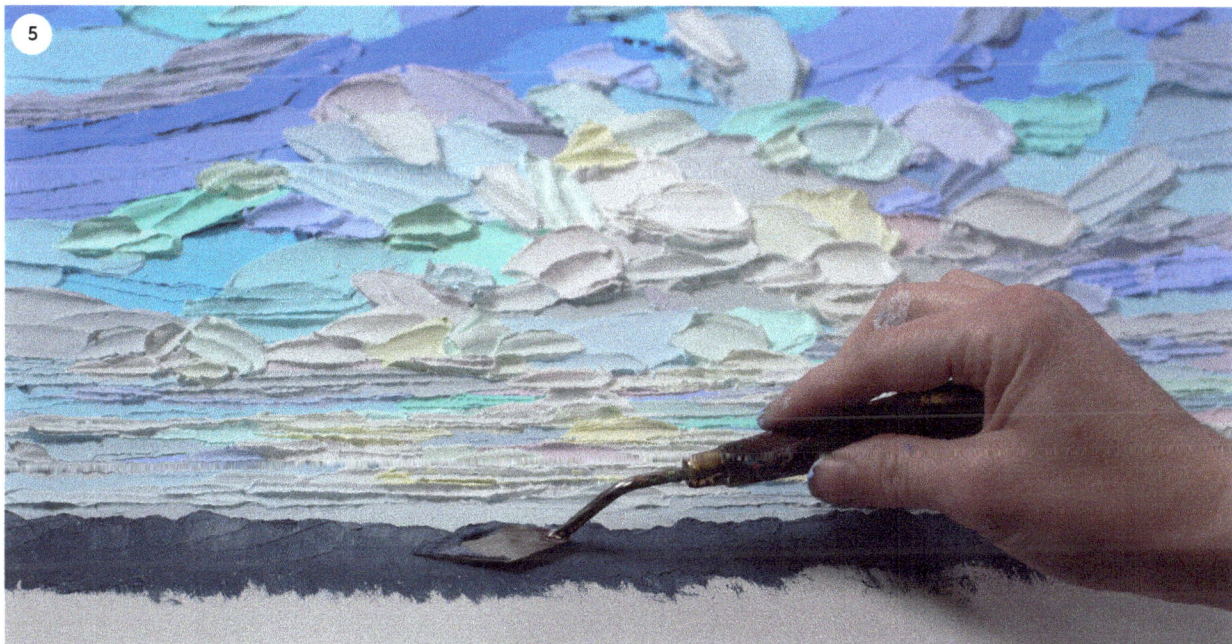

4. As the clouds move further away toward the horizon, use the edge of your knife to apply lighter colors in small elongated shapes in horizontal rows across the canvas. To mix these light colors, use white and the following: a small amount of cad yellow light for a pale yellow, magenta for pink, phthalo blue and yellow for a beautiful aqua color, and of course the blues and grays you have already mixed on your palette.

5. Mix a cool-tone chromatic black (see Mixing Chromatic Black and Gray), divide it in half and add a small amount of white to one pile to lighten the value slightly. Apply the black with the flat of your knife to block in a row of mountains along the horizon line. Scumble (see Techniques) the lighter black over the top to add variation. Utilize the straight edge and tip of your palette knife to create the peaks and ridges of the mountains.

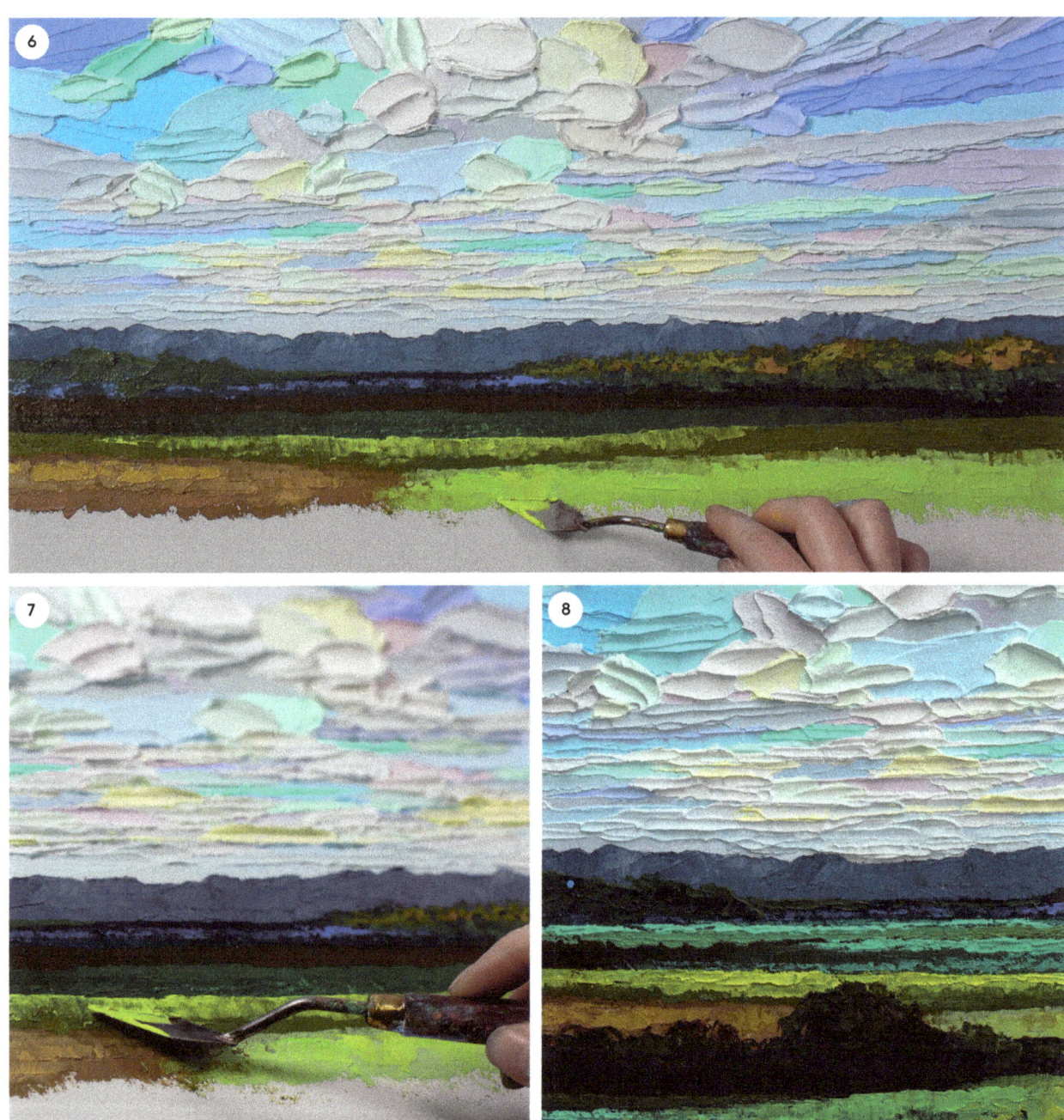

6. Next add distant foliage and fields of color. Starting with a layer of chromatic black placed below the mountains, block in the suggestion of a tree line in the distance. Mix a dark green color using permanent green light and ultramarine blue, and layer it over the top of the gray, allowing some of the color to mix on the canvas. Alter the green slightly by adding cad yellow light, burnt sienna, and/or raw sienna to create lighter and warmer shades of green. Scumble over the trees leaving areas of dark showing through to suggest leaves on the trees.

7. Layer dark to mid-tone shades of green and brown in alternating horizontal layers working your way down the canvas. I've also added a thin line of ultramarine blue to incorporate some of the sky color into the landscape. Keep in mind that fields in the distance will appear cooler in color and more narrow. Fields in the foreground, closer to the bottom of the canvas, will be larger in size and warmer in color. Next, mix a variety of bright saturated greens using cad yellow light and a touch of phthalo blue, phthalo green or

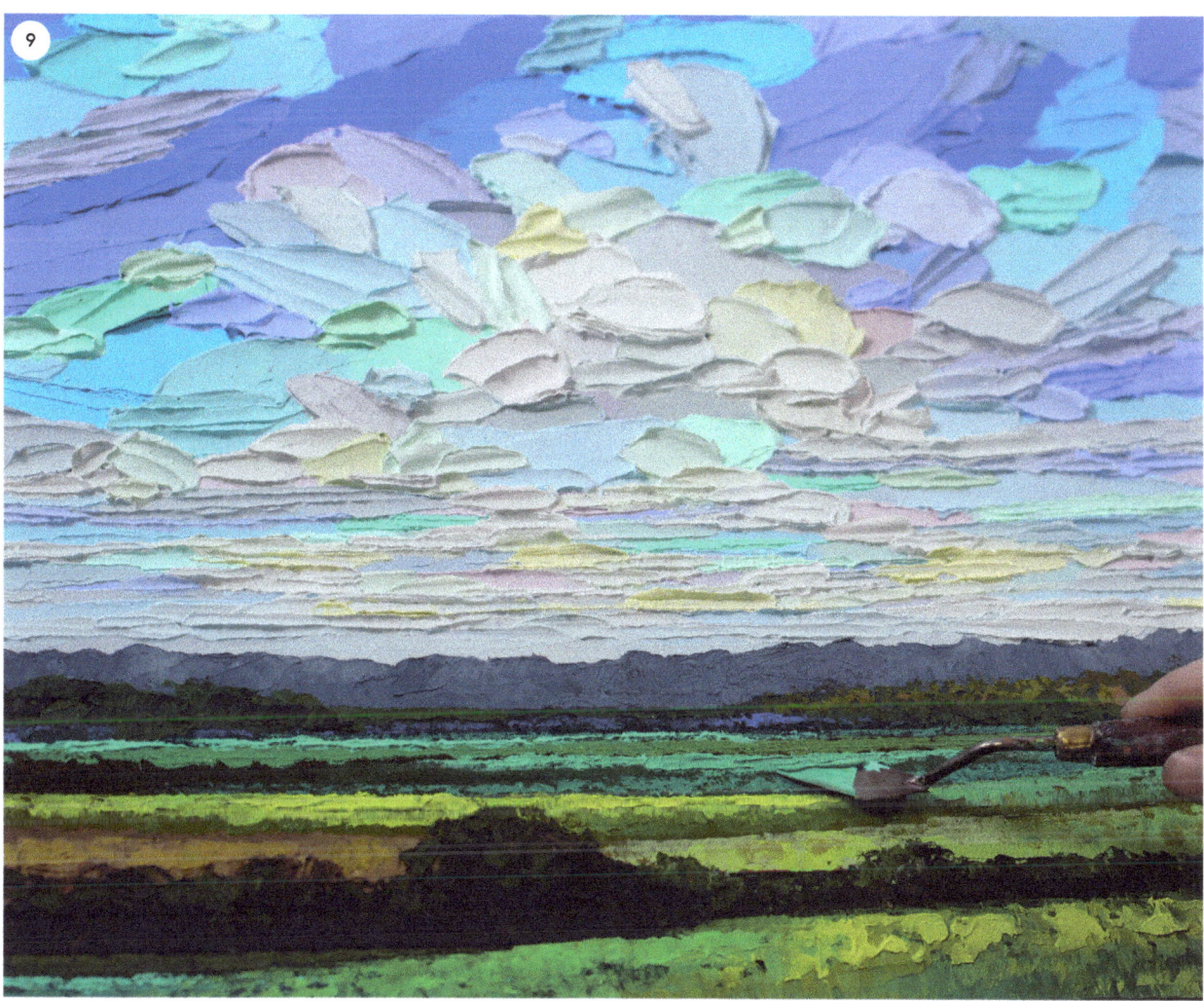

permanent green light, adding a small amount of white to lighten, if needed. Layer them on the canvas, allowing some areas to mix with the wet paint creating new colors and values.

8. For contrast, add another row of dark trees in the foreground approximately twice the size of the tree line in the distance, using the same techniques as before, as well as another grassy plane that transitions from a dark cool green to a warm light green. Allow them to mix on the canvas to create a gradation of color from one to the next.

9. Lastly, add thin lines of phthalo green as a finishing detail. Assess your painting and continue adding smaller details of color to help draw the viewer's eye around the canvas until you are happy with your composition.

At the Water's Edge

Water has always captured my imagination and made me reflect. The grandeur of the sky set against the sea has a way of soothing us and washing away our everyday troubles. When I look out onto the vast beauty of the ocean, I can't help but want to paint what I feel: serenity, freedom, and total surrender. Exploring the landscape theme further, I'm going to show you how to translate the impasto skills you've already learned into a seascape. We'll practice a new mark making technique and use different palette knife skills. We'll experiment with composition, as well as explore one color to gain confidence mixing a variety of blues.

Color palette

- Titanium white
- Cadmium yellow light
- Quinacridone magenta
- Phthalocyanine turquoise
- Phthalocyanine blue (green shade)
- Ultramarine blue
- Chromatic black or Payne's gray

Tools and materials

- Medium spade-shaped knife
- Large spade-shaped knife
- Small diamond-shaped knife
- Measuring tape or ruler
- Masking tape
- Pencil
- 16in x 20in (40.5cm x 51cm) canvas
- Molding paste or gel medium to thicken paint where needed (see Mediums)

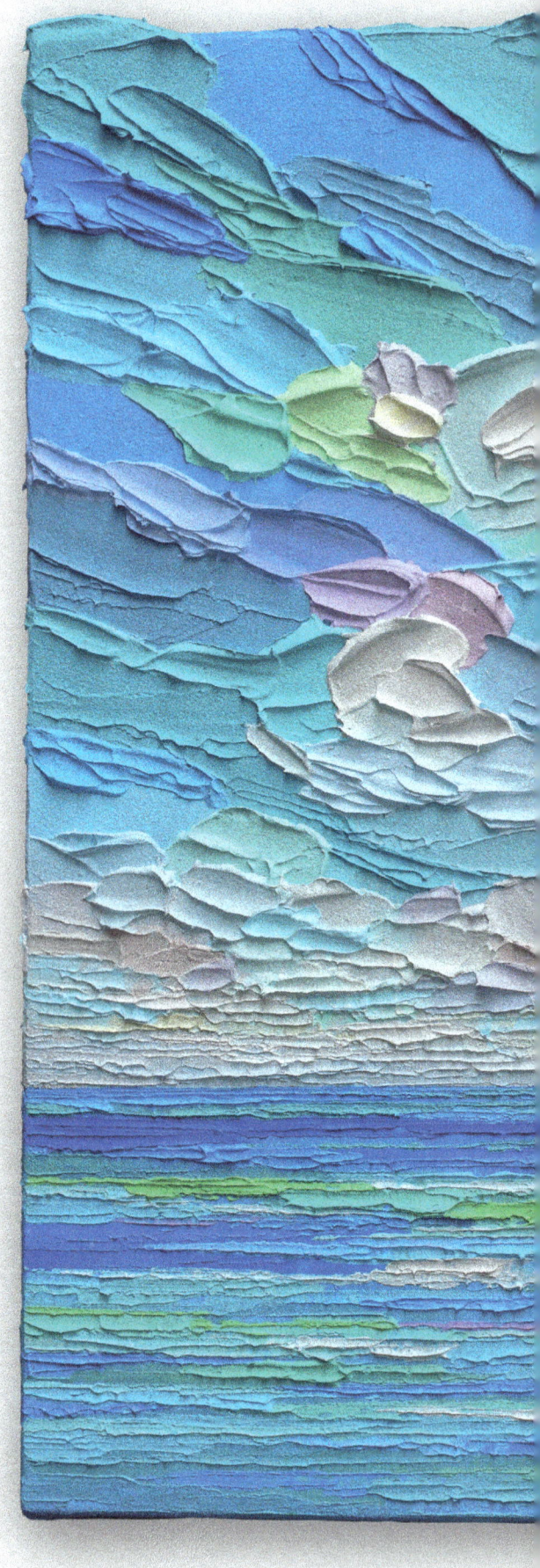

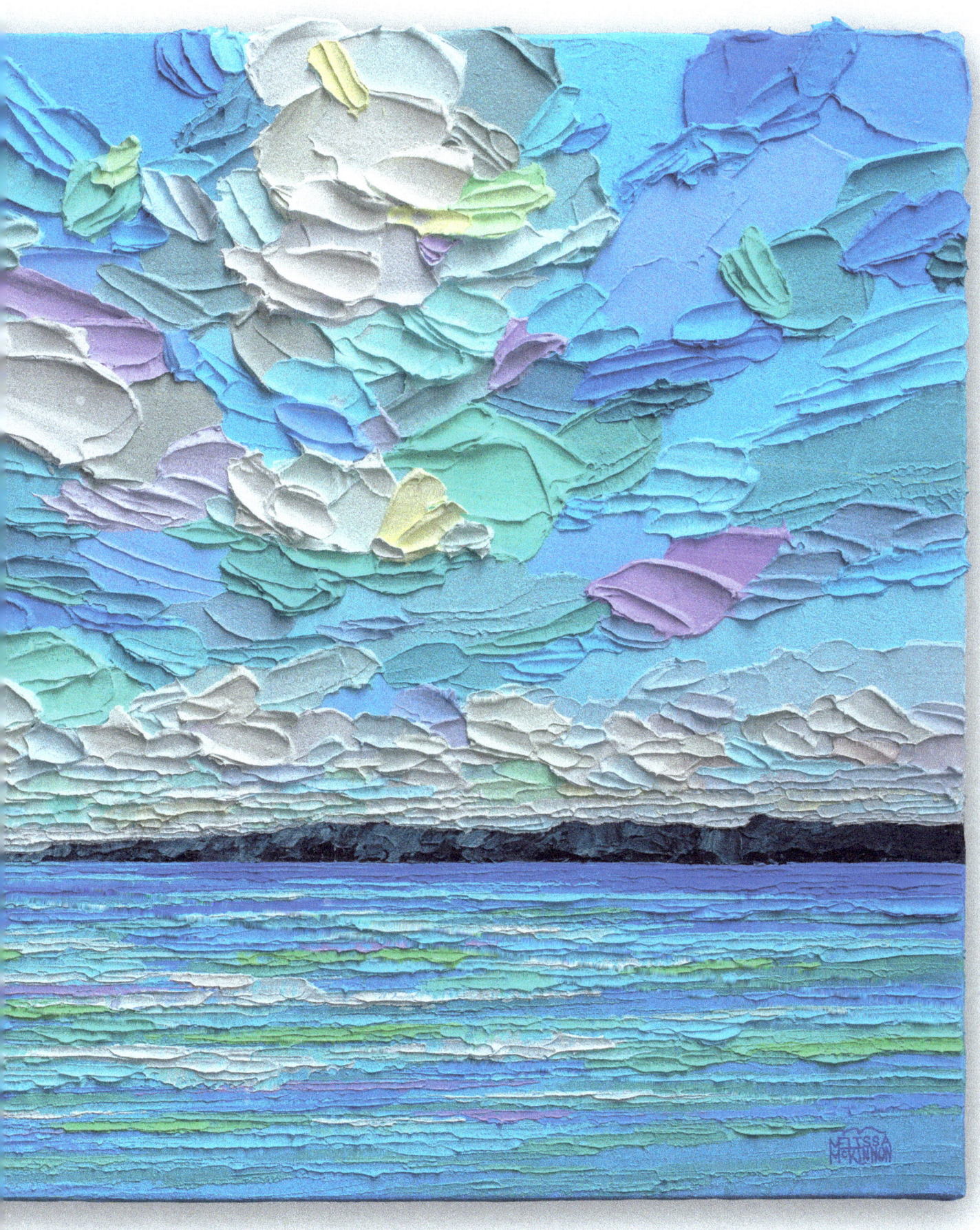

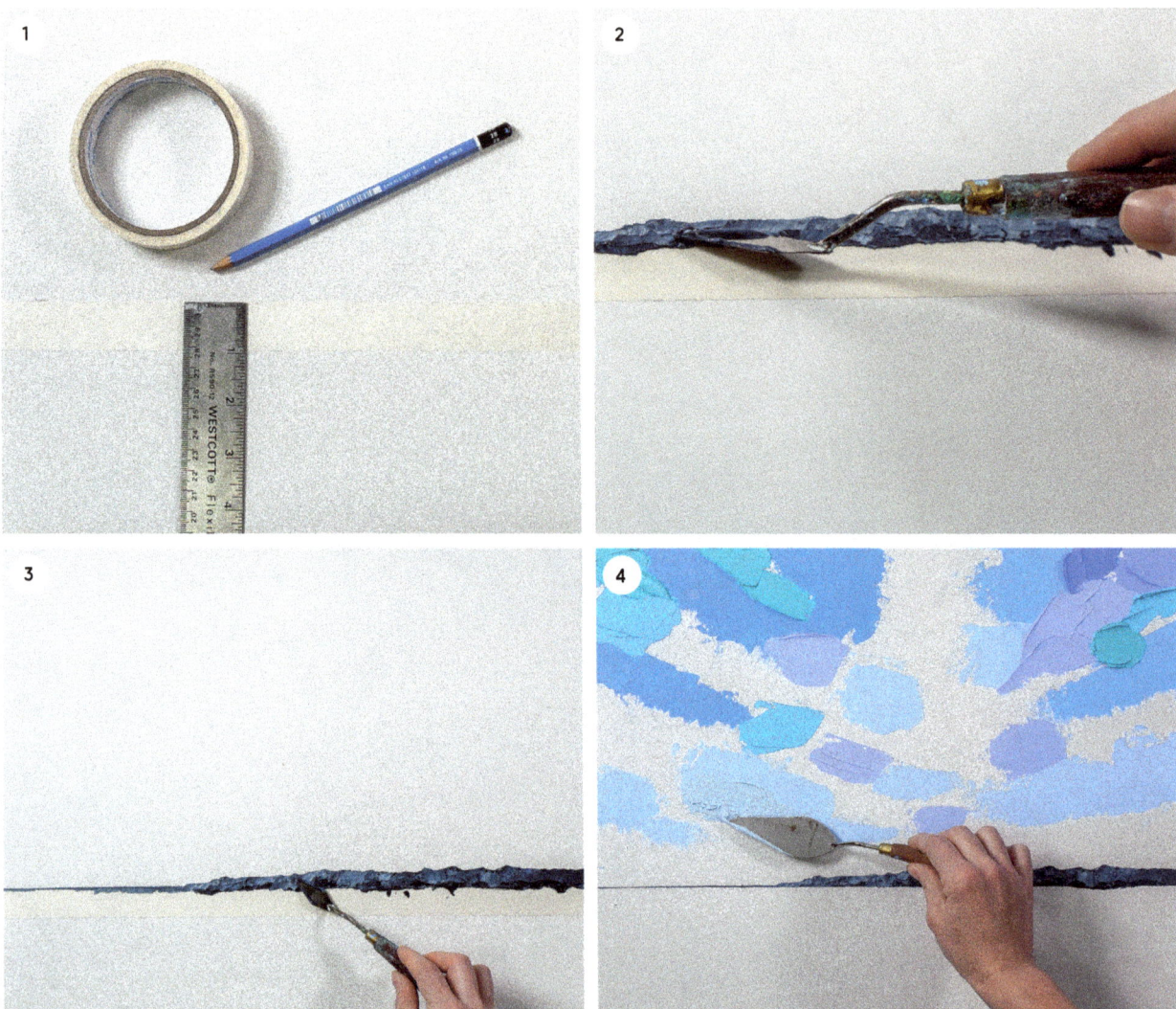

1. Measure 4½in (115mm) from the bottom of the canvas and apply a strip of masking tape below that line. This will indicate the horizon line.

2. Mix a blue-tone black by adding more phthalo blue (see Mixing Chromatic Black and Gray). Using a small diamond-shaped knife, apply a thin layer of paint above the masking tape line using the edge and tip of the knife to indicate land or rocks in the distance.

3. Add a small amount of white and with the underside of your knife, lightly graze the surface of the wet paint in a scumbling motion (see Mark Making) to add texture and highlights to the land formation. Allow the lighter color to mix with the darker color underneath for variation. The color

of the land will be darkest towards the edge of the canvas and slowly get lighter as it fades towards the middle. Make the land shape taller near one edge of the canvas and slowly taper it until it fades into a thin horizon line along the rest of the tape. Remove the masking tape.

4. Next, mix large amounts of three blues in three values (dark, mid-tone, and light; see Colour Mixing): phthalo blue, ultramarine blue, and phthalo turquoise. Starting with the dark blue colors, use a large spade-shaped knife to block in areas where you want blue sky to show. Keep your darkest values near the top corners and gradually add lighter values as you move down towards the center and horizon line.

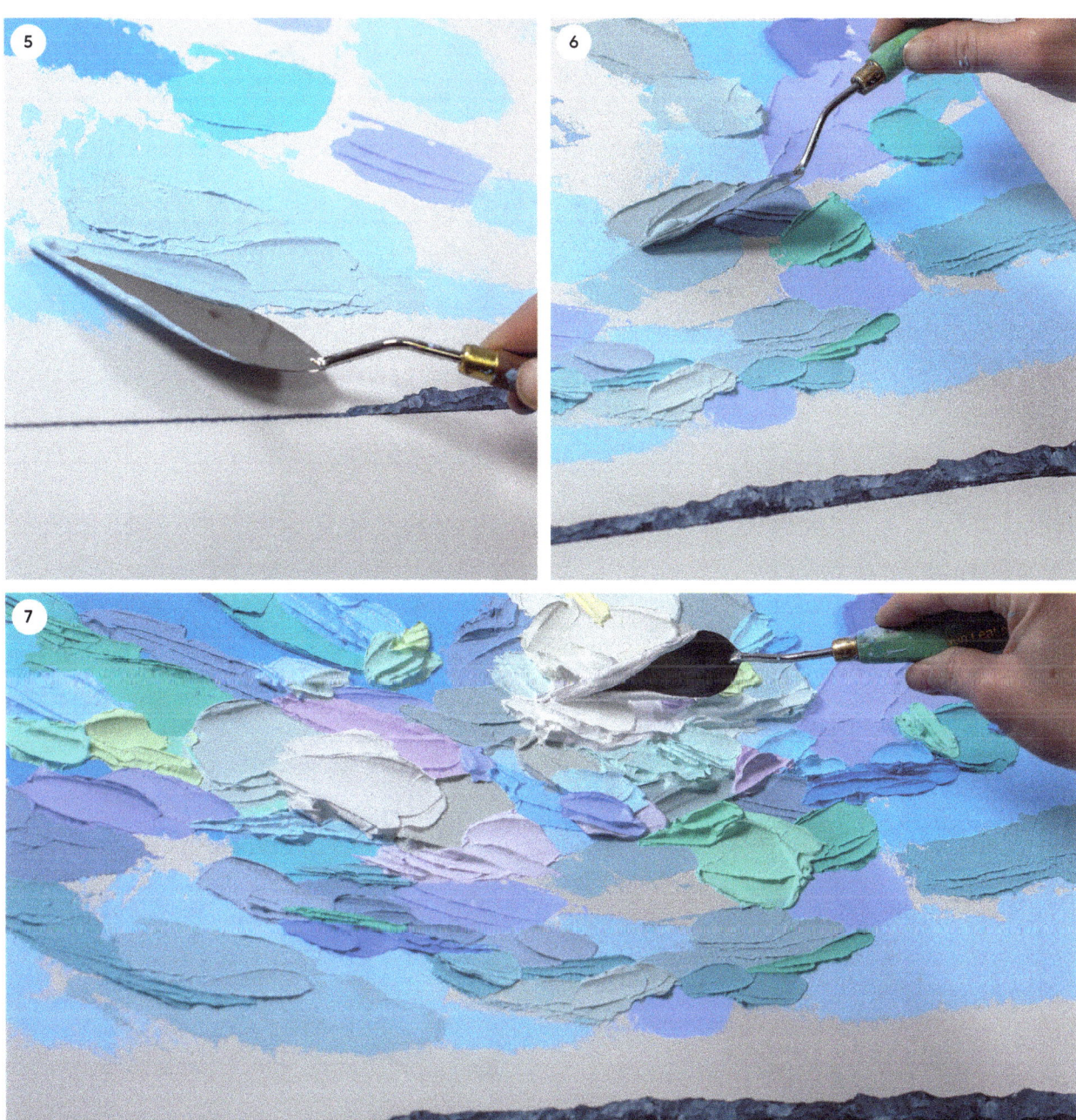

5. Keep these layers loose and thin because we will be adding multiple layers on top to build up texture. Be sure to use all three blues and vary the size and shape of your strokes.

6. Next, create shadow colors by adding some of your mid-tone blues to the chromatic black you've already mixed. Using a medium spade-shaped knife, block in various shapes and sizes to indicate shadow areas of the clouds in the background.

7. Use the remaining mid-tone blue colors to fill in the background with more cloud shapes. Alter the colors with small amounts of cad yellow light, magenta, and white to create a variety of new colors. Magenta and ultramarine blue will create a range of purple and pink hues. Phthalo turquoise and cad yellow light creates a beautiful aqua color that will bring warmth to your sky.

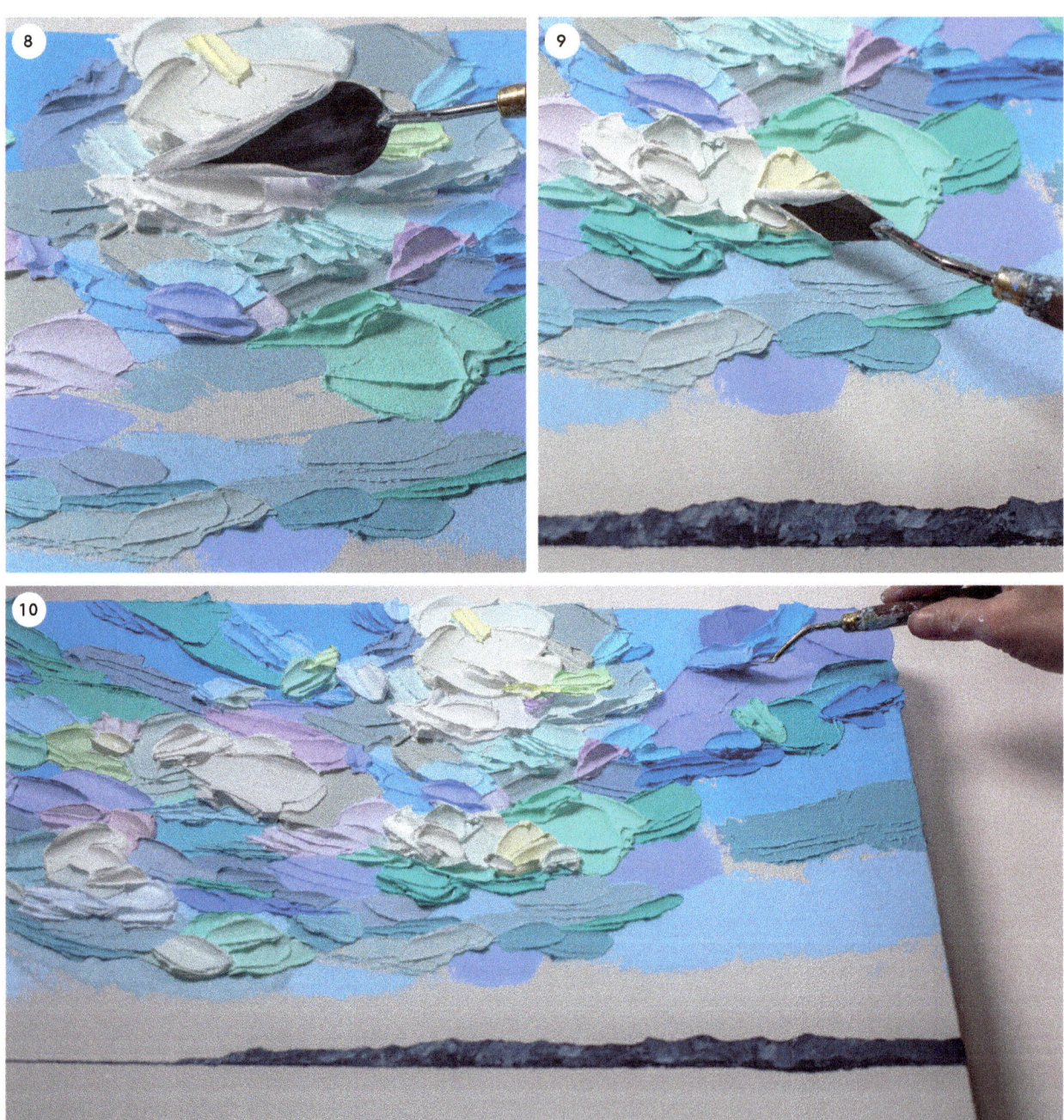

8. Mix a large amount of white with a hint of cad yellow light. Using the medium knife, start adding your lightest clouds using large, thick strokes of white (see Techniques).

9. Switch to a small diamond-shaped knife and continue adding layers of smaller clouds.

10. Once you have the main cloud shapes blocked in, assess the composition and add smaller details to the rest of the sky, filling in holes and covering rough edges with the diamond-shaped knife. You can add pops of color in contrasting values to make those areas stand out or look for areas that could be blended more. If you want to blend two areas together, like this junction of ultramarine blue and phthalo blue, try mixing the two colors together and add a touch of gray. This will harmonize the color and help the different marks visually blend into one larger shape.

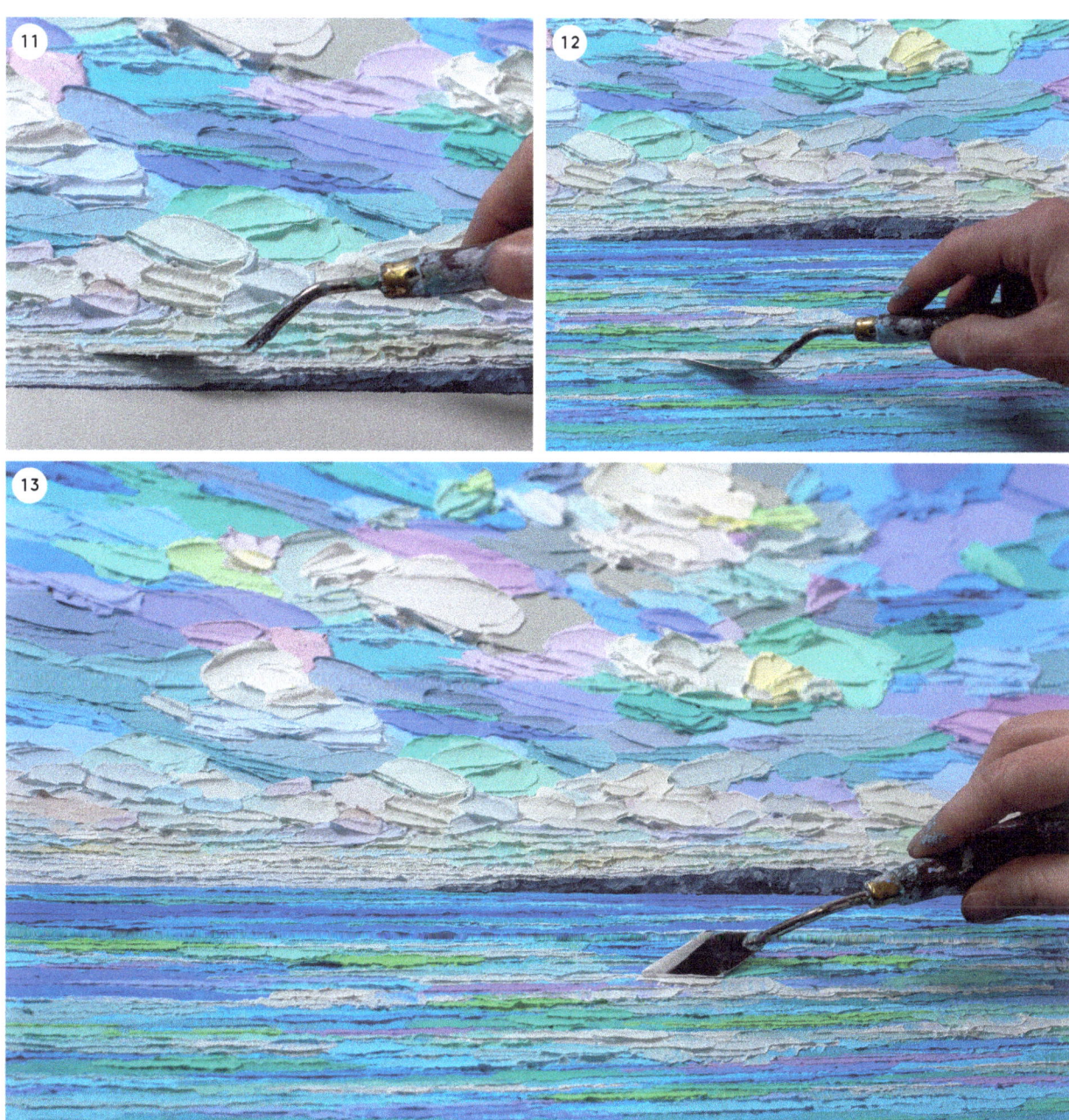

11. To finish the sky, fill in the area just above the horizon line with smaller and lighter cloud shapes to create a seamless transition. Near the horizon, use the straight edge of the knife at an angle to make your marks smaller and thinner as the clouds recede into the distance.

12. To create the suggestion of movement in the ocean, use the line technique (see Techniques). Starting with your darkest blues, begin applying the paint in horizontal lines across the bottom of the canvas below the rock line. Lighten the values as you move toward the bottom of the canvas. Continue to apply any colors you have left over from the sky.

13. Lastly, add small touches of white to the lightest areas in alternating lines to suggest waves or highlights on the ocean.

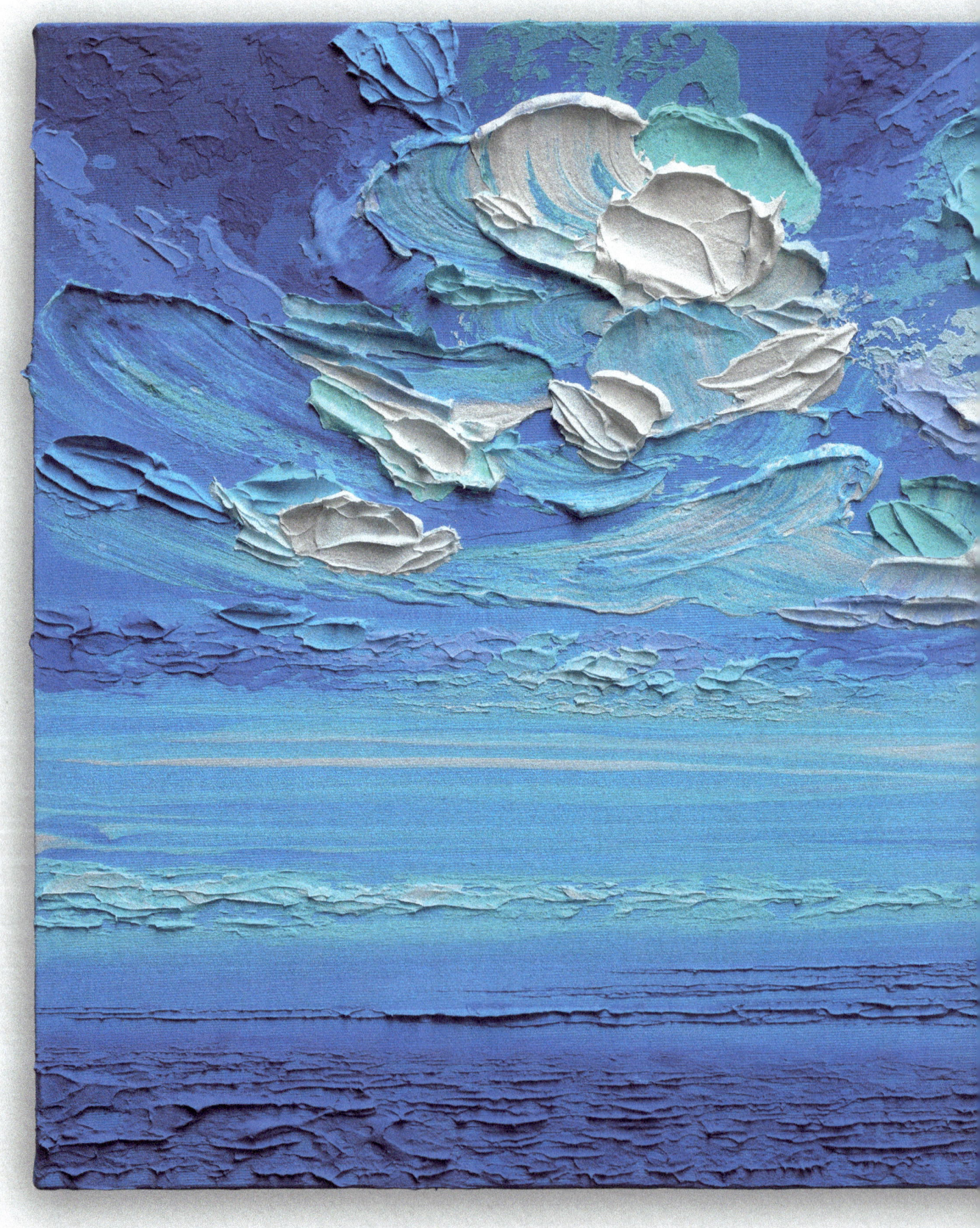

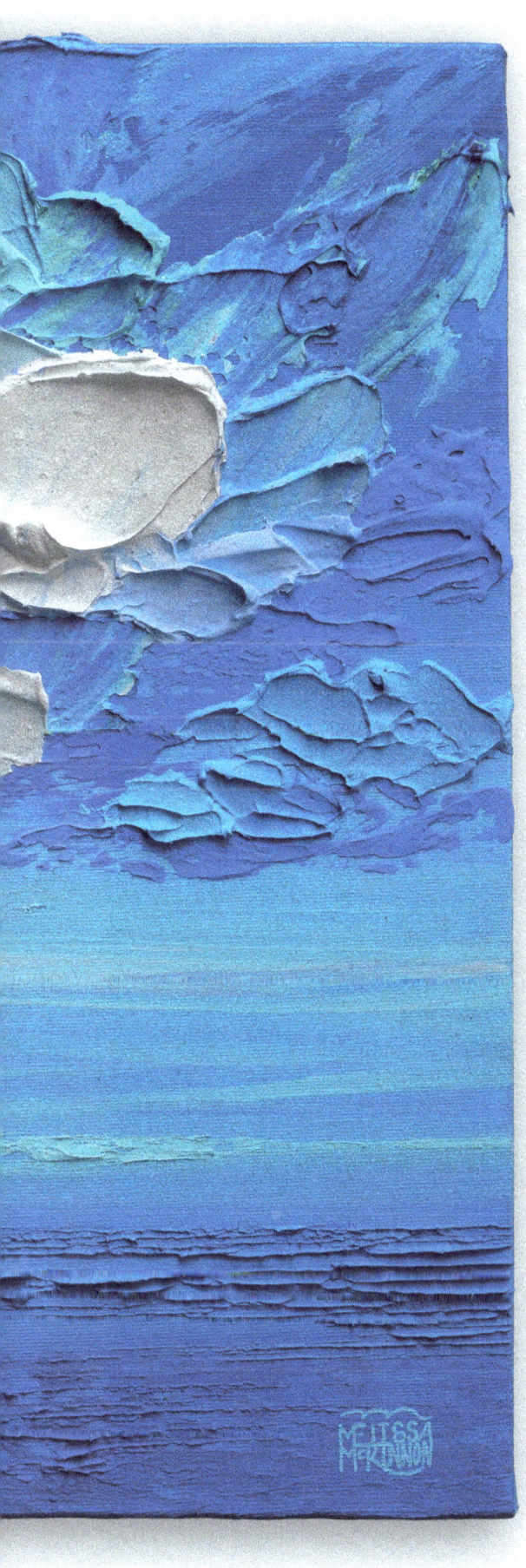

Dancing Clouds

What do you do with all that leftover paint? This fun painting will spark your creativity and, most importantly, use up leftover paint. In this project, I'm going to show you an alternative approach to the seascape we made in At the Water's Edge, but I encourage you to throw caution to the wind and experiment. Try a different subject matter, knives, colors, and methods of applying paint to the canvas. Learn to loosen up and to be expressive with your strokes, overcoming the fear of making mistakes and being too precious with your painting. We'll apply multiple colors of paint at once to create unique blended strokes.

Color palette

- Titanium white
- Phthalocyanine blue (green shade)
- Leftover colors from At the Water's Edge

Tools and materials

- Large flat synthetic brush
- Medium spade-shaped knife
- Small diamond-shaped knife
- 16in x 20in (40.5cm x 51cm) canvas
- Molding paste or gel medium to thicken paint where needed (see Mediums)

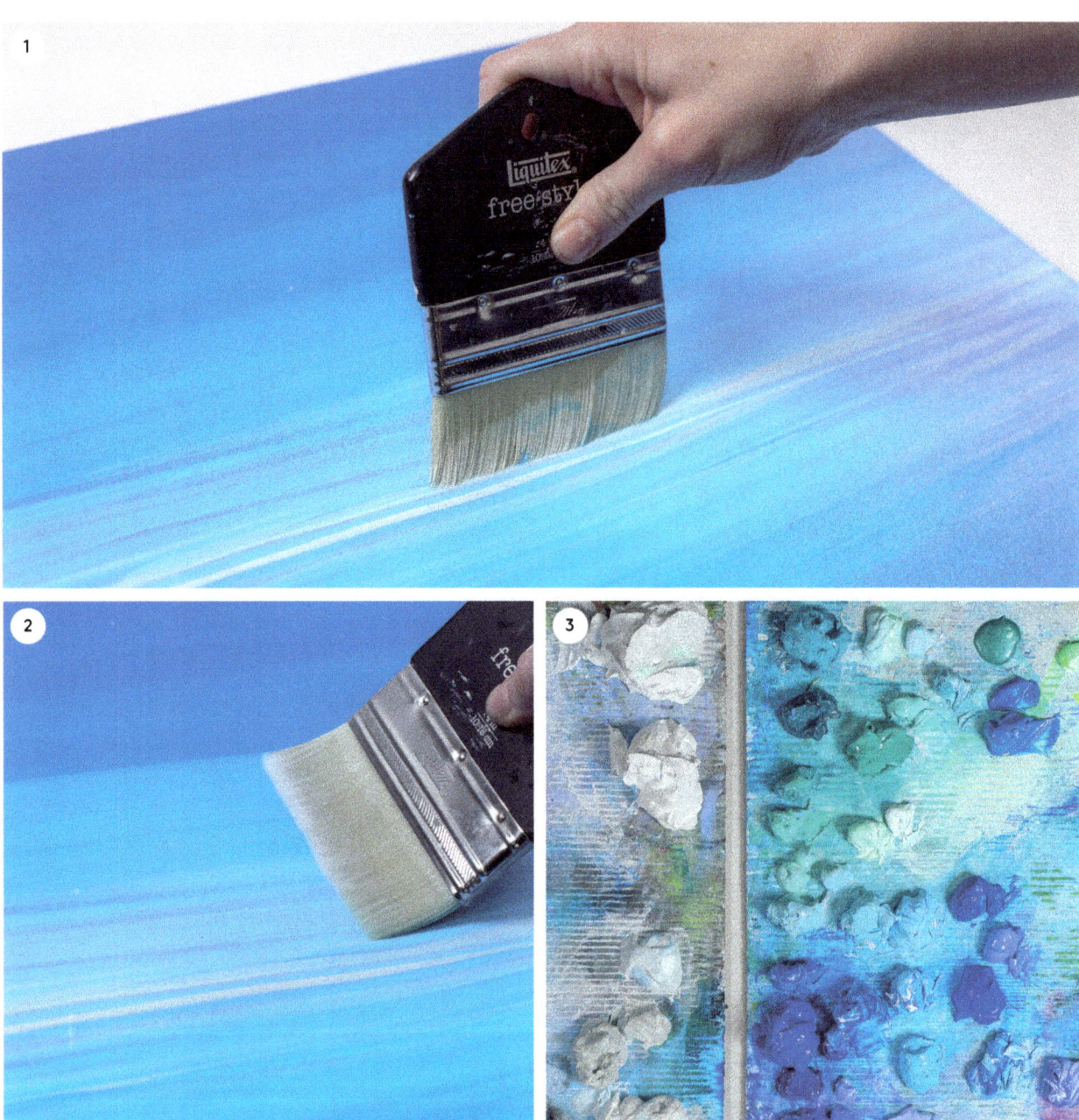

1. We are starting with the blending with a brush technique (see Techniques). Use a large flat brush to cover the canvas with a layer of phthalo blue. Add a generous amount of titanium white two-thirds of the way down the canvas. Glide the brush in a horizontal, side-to-side motion to blend the white into the wet layer of blue underneath. Blend the white outwards toward the top and bottom of the canvas to create a smooth transition of color.

2. Once you are happy with the gradient, load your brush with more white and add the indication of sweeping clouds or ocean waves along the horizon line. As you can see in my painting, I have left some strokes partially blended. Let the painting dry completely.

3. Now we can experiment with adding expressive, abstract cloud shapes. I'll be working with the colors leftover from the At the Water's Edge painting but you can use whatever palette inspires you.

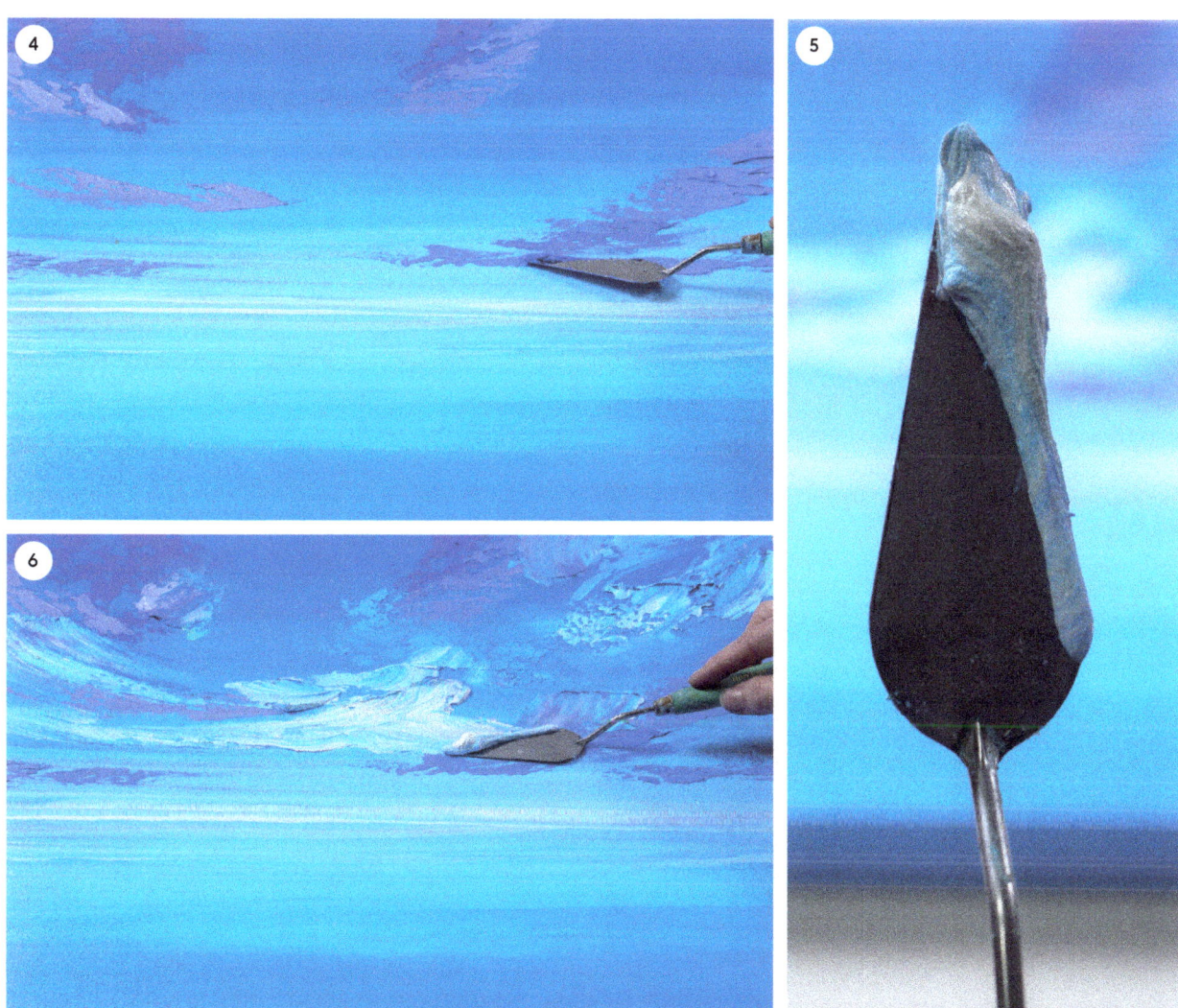

4. Using a medium spade-shaped knife, apply dark ultramarine blue in sweeping strokes, scumbling (see Techniques) across the surface and allowing the paint to skip and leave holes for the background to show through. To create a sense of energy and movement, I'm applying the paint in large strokes, working from the outside edges of the canvas toward the center.

5. Using a pile of mixed paint, load your palette knife with a generous scoop. If you prefer to have more control over the colors selected, you can load several individual colors onto your knife to achieve the same effect.

6. Apply the paint in a single stroke and then keep repeating. Notice how the colors blend in spontaneous patterns, no two strokes will ever be the same.

7. Switch to a small diamond-shaped knife to apply smaller cloud shapes. Even though my knife is smaller, I'm using more paint to create thicker strokes.

8. Switching back to a medium spade-shaped knife, add large yet short strokes of white to the cloud shapes. There happened to be some phthalo blue left on the palette knife from earlier and I chose not to clean it before loading the white paint. When I applied the first stroke it left an interesting blend of dark blue against the white, which I kept in. However, if I didn't like it, I could've scraped off the paint, cleaned my knife and applied the stroke again. Another option would be to let the original stroke dry a bit and apply another layer of pure white over the top, covering the blue streak and adding even more texture.

9. Continue adding white clouds in various shapes and sizes, some blended, some pure white, then assess the colors and composition of your sky. Add any additional details you'd like to see. I scumbled a few layers of ultramarine and phthalo blues of different values to transition from the large voluminous clouds to the softer white strokes of the underpainting.

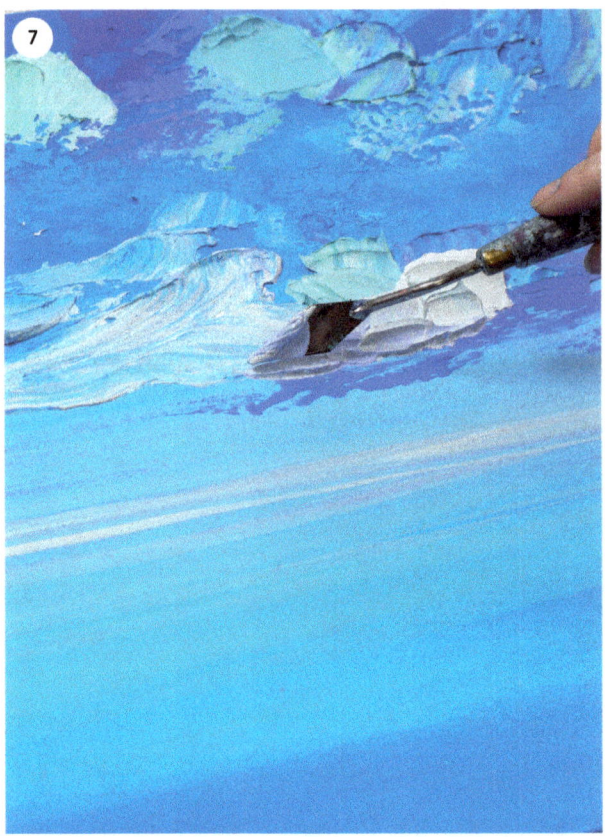

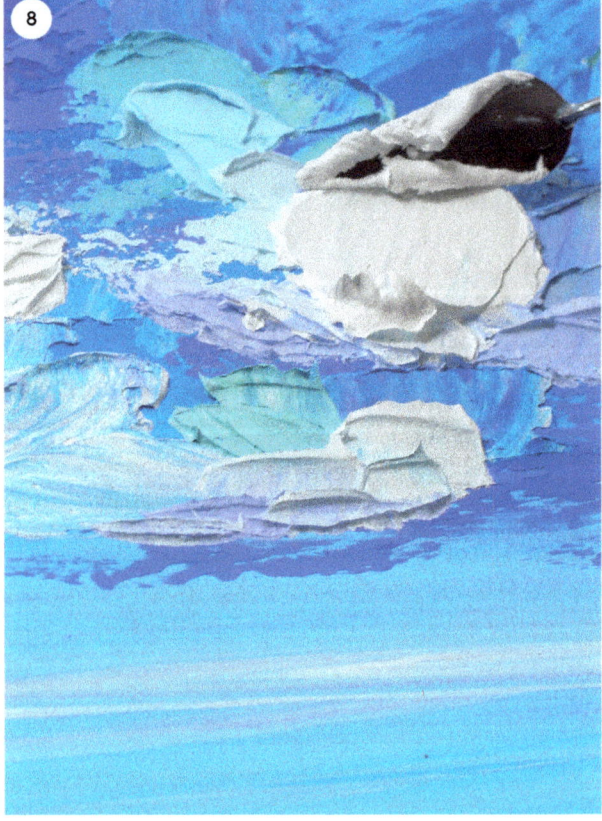

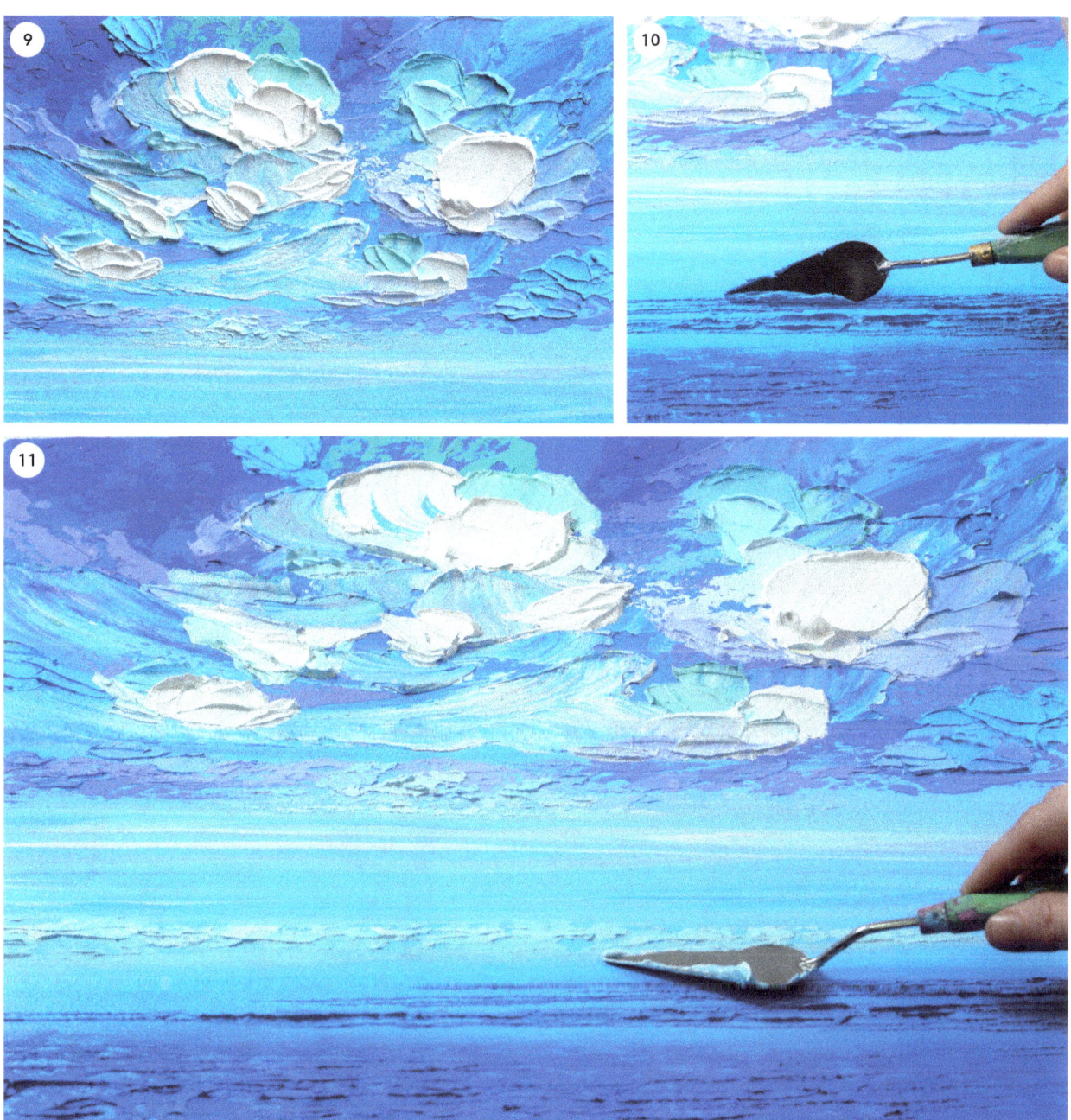

10. Using the edge of the knife, add lines (see Techniques) of pure dark ultramarine blue to the bottom of the canvas to suggest water or waves. I really like how the ultramarine is a similar value but a different hue from the phthalo blue underneath. This kind of subtle contrast adds interest and helps to balance some of the other bold choices I've made for this painting. Continue using the line technique to fill the bottom of the canvas with loose strokes and a generous amount of paint.

11. Assess the composition and make any changes to enhance the painting. I felt there wasn't enough interest in the lower half so, as a finishing touch, I added another layer of scumbled paint in light phthalo blue above the water lines, repeating the clouds shapes above and bringing more balance to the composition.

Majestic Mountains

Spending time in nature is a huge source of inspiration for me and it's a reprieve from the hustle and bustle of city life. I'm fortunate to live near the majestic Canadian Rocky Mountains and I love to explore them in every season. Here, I'm going to show you how add vibrant color and create textural mountains using simple layers with a palette knife. We are also going to revisit our aspen and birch trees, using a slightly different technique for the leaves, explore warm and cool colors, and enhance contrast with color and value.

Color palette

- Titanium white
- Cadmium yellow light
- Cadmium yellow medium
- Cadmium orange
- Quinacridone red
- Cadmium red medium
- Phthalocyanine blue (green shade)
- Ultramarine blue
- Permanent green light
- Phthalocyanine green
- Burnt sienna
- Chromatic black or Payne's gray

Tools and materials

- Large round natural bristle brush
- Medium spade-shaped knife
- Small diamond-shaped knife
- Pencil or chalk
- 16in x 20in (40.5cm x 51cm) canvas
- Molding paste or gel medium to thicken paint where needed (see Mediums)

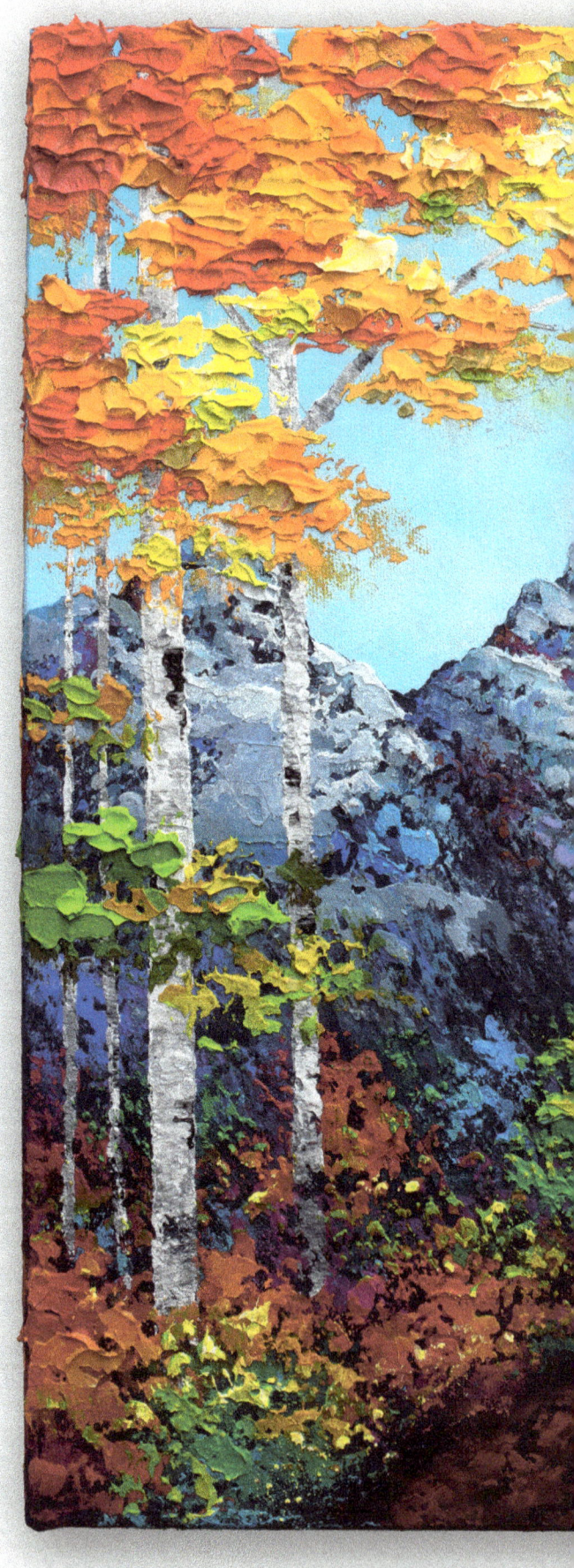

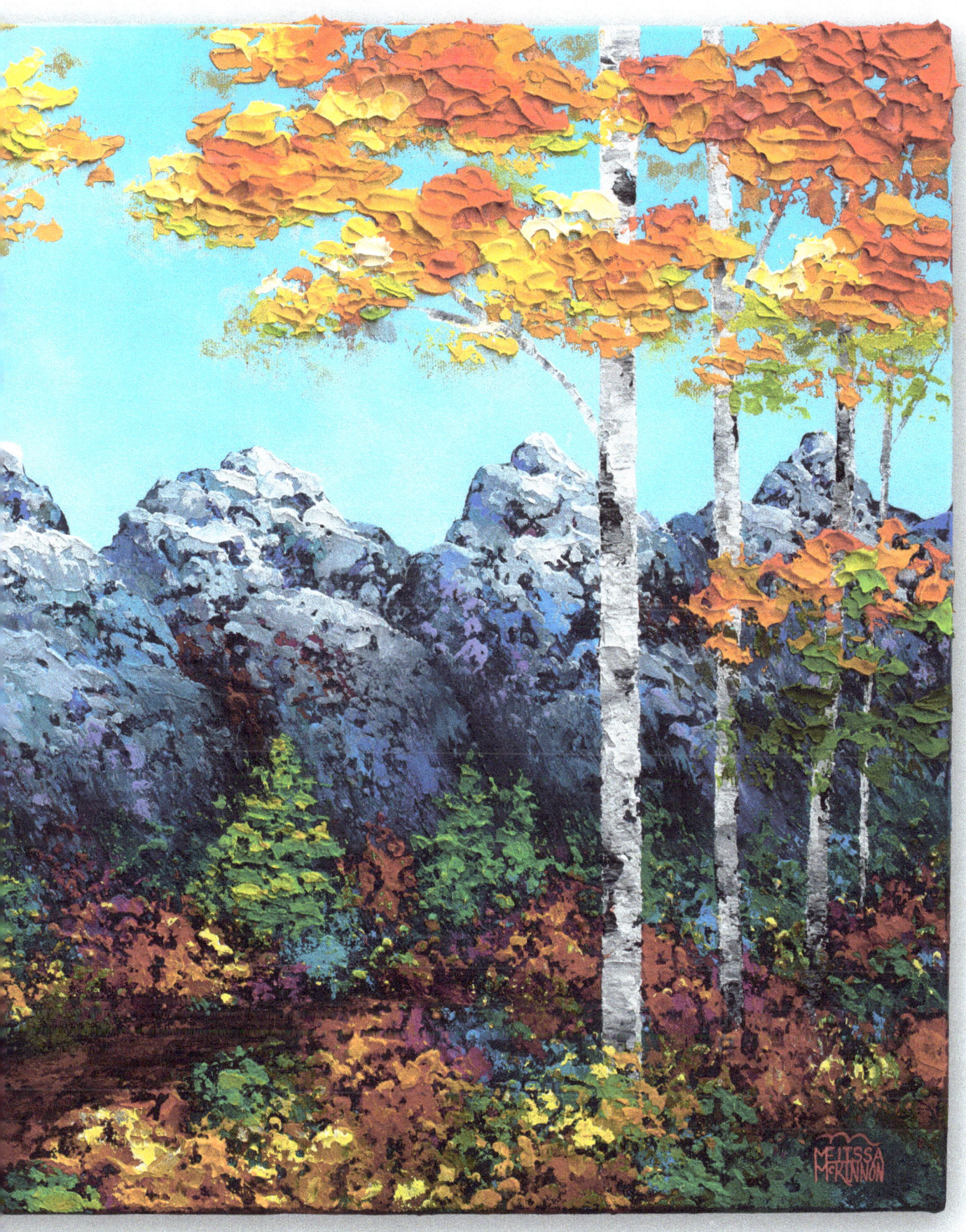

1. Using a large round brush, apply a mid-tone phthalo blue (no medium added; see Color Mixing) to the top half of the canvas using the blending with a brush technique (see Techniques) to block in the sky. Add soft fluffy clouds by applying more white to your brush and blend from the bottom up in a circular motion. I plan on adding a lot of texture in the mountains and surrounding foliage so I'm going to keep my sky fairly soft and blended, but you can create any type of sky you prefer. Allow to dry.

2. Use a pencil or chalk to draw in the size and shape of your mountain range. You can draw from your imagination, a photo, or from life.

3. Mix a cool-tone chromatic black (see Mixing Chromatic Black and Gray) and use it to cover the entire surface of the mountain range with the flat side of a small diamond-shaped knife. Use the tip and edge of the knife to refine the peaks and cover the pencil lines with accuracy. Apply the paint generously to create a textured surface.

4. Next, build more texture by adding several layers of paint in ultramarine blue, phthalo green, quin red, and burnt sienna. Use a medium spade-shaped knife to loosely apply the colors to the mountains in a scumbling motion (see Techniques) working from the top down. Allow the knife to skip over the bumpy texture below allowing some of the color underneath to show through. At this stage, begin to block in the ridges of the rock formations. I like to leave the texture loose and chunky near the top and apply more pressure as I move toward the bottom of the mountains creating a smoother sweeping effect.

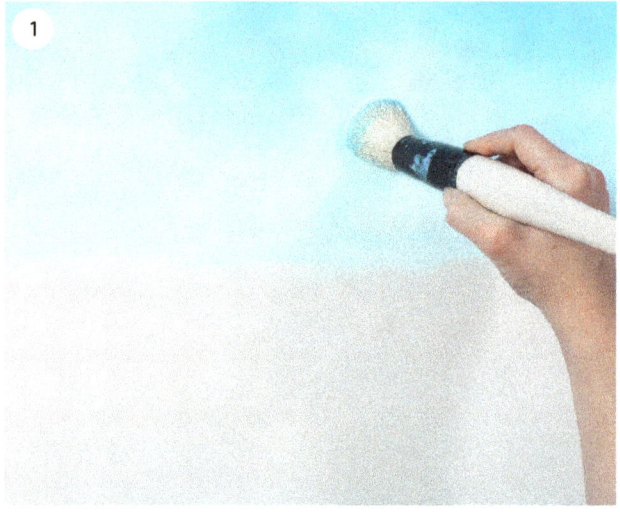

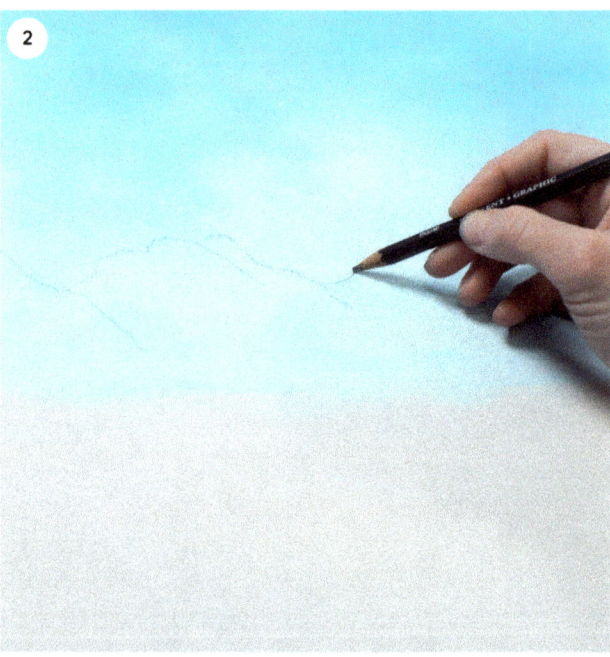

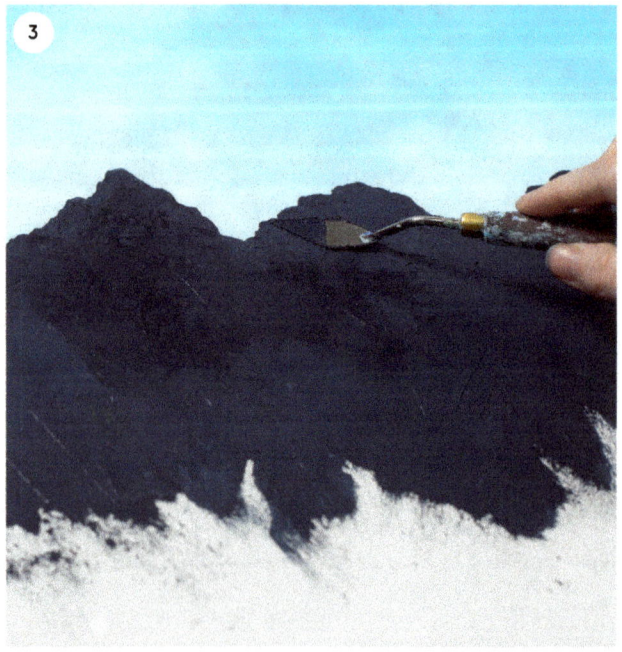

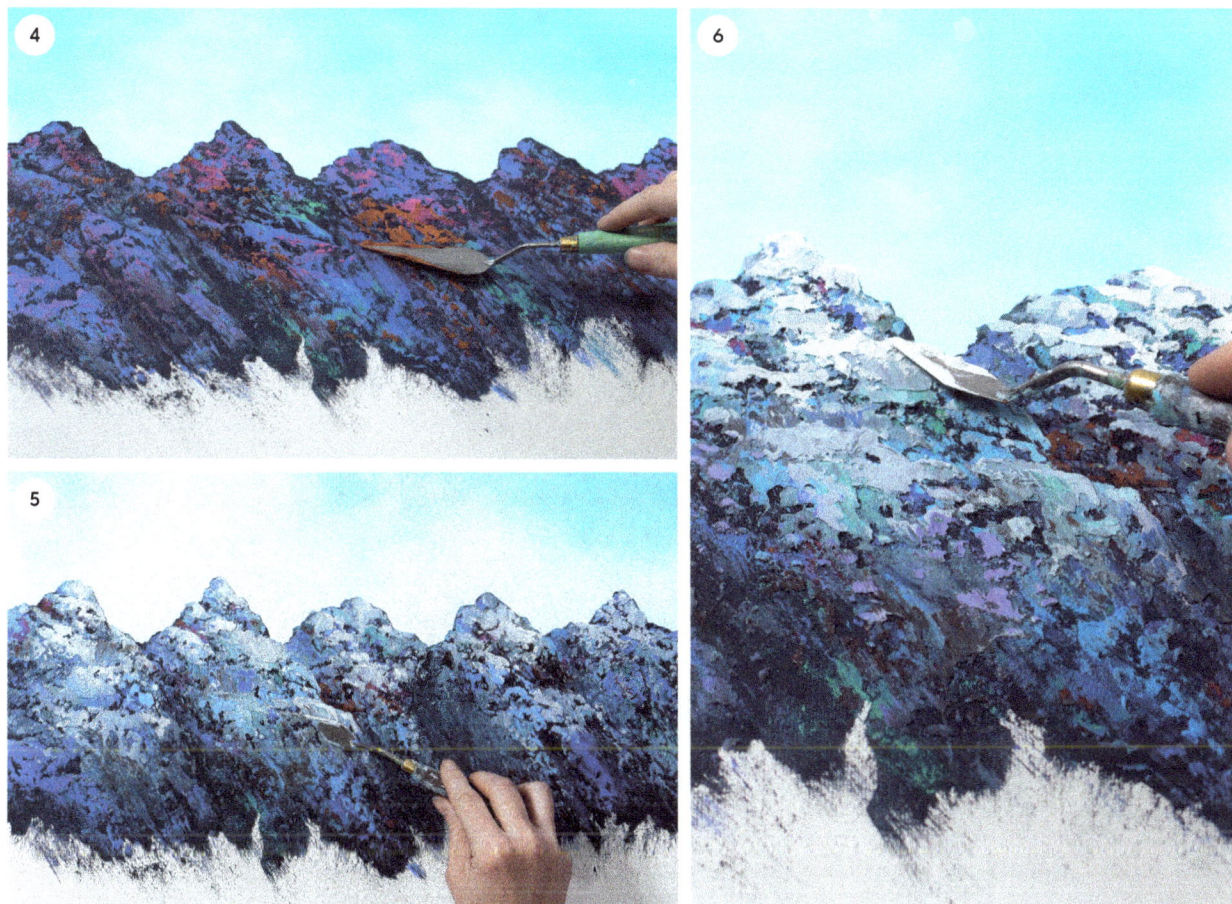

5. Mix a light bluish-gray using white, phthalo blue, and a touch of chromatic black. Using a small diamond-shaped knife, apply the color in a scumbling motion starting at the top of the mountains and fading toward the bottom, giving the indication of snow. Allow the knife to graze over the texture underneath leaving bits of black and color showing through. Allow the color to mix with the wet paint underneath creating new colors and gradients. Think about the shapes and angles of the mountain rock and glide your palette knife in the direction of the sloping mountain. Continue applying the light bluish-gray where you think the ridges would be, leaving the shadow areas dark.

6. My light source is coming from the right-hand side so I'm applying a cool white (white with a touch of phthalo blue) in a similar scumbling motion, focusing the majority of the paint on the right-hand side of the top ridges where the sunlight would hit the mountains.

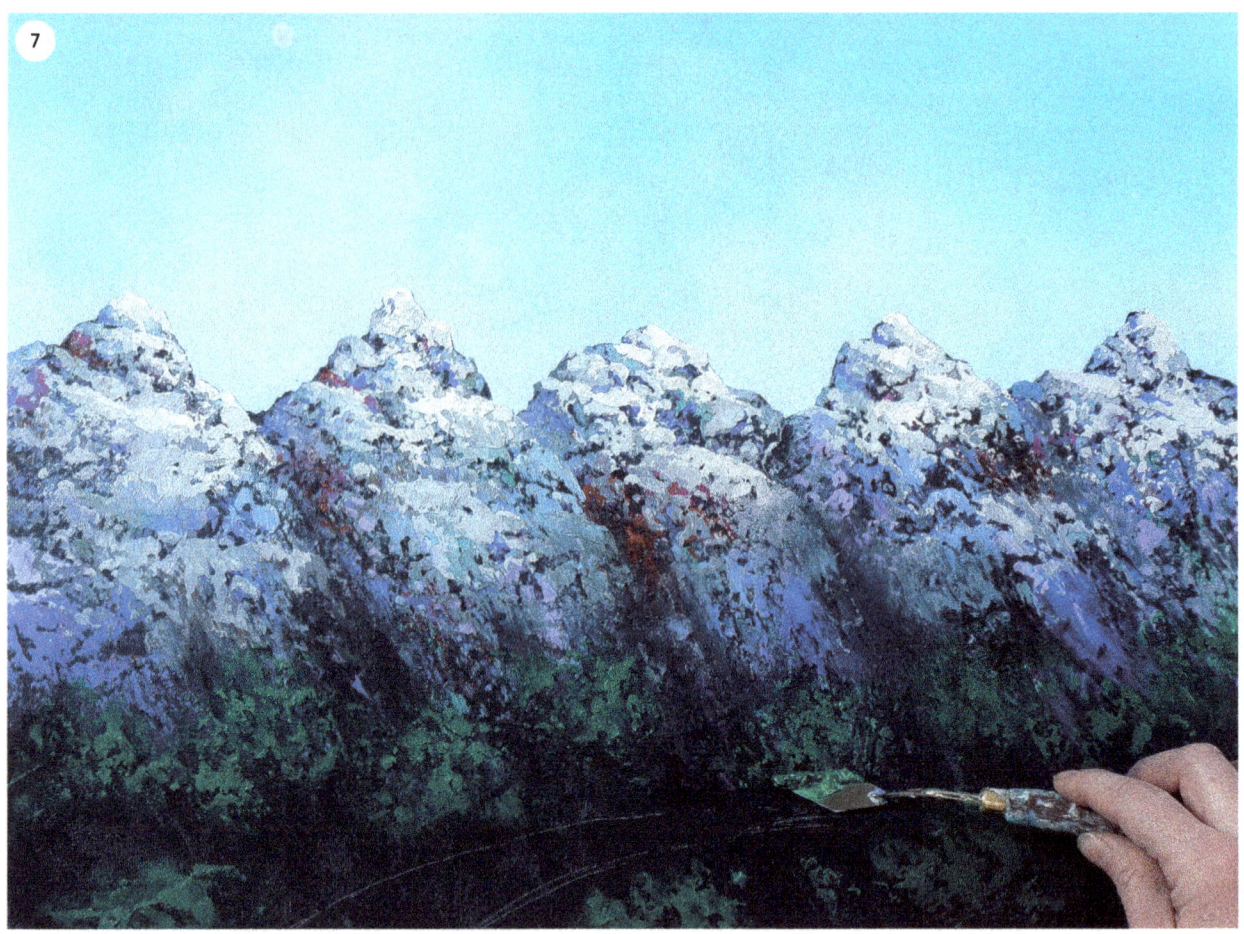

7. Next, we're going to create a forest in the distance with a few larger trees in the foreground to frame the composition. Decide where you want your tree line to be and how much of the mountains you want to keep. I want lots of trees in the foreground with a pathway leading into the landscape so I'm going to coat the bottom half of the painting with a layer of dark gray. I'm applying the color in the same direction as my sweeping mountains, slowly fading the color upwards to blend in with the mountains. This will visually push them back in the distance and give me a nice dark background to create the forest. While the paint was still wet, I used the tip of my knife to scratch the outline of a path, then added a scumbled layer of dark phthalo green in random patches to suggest the beginning of a tree line.

8. Next, scumble burnt sienna with the back of your knife to block in the pathway, allowing it to mix with the wet gray paint underneath. Let it dry slightly then apply another layer of burnt sienna, this time letting it scumble without mixing with the paint underneath to add highlights and dimension to the path. If you have leftover color on your knife, you can scumble it into the forest area with the phthalo green – the more color and texture the better! Continue to build up the foliage in the forest by adding layers of blue, green, and red, in abstract patches using a scumbling motion. Layer the colors from dark to light creating the suggestion of pine trees and foliage. I tend not to clean my palette knife in between colors and allow them to mix on the canvas creating new color blends as I go.

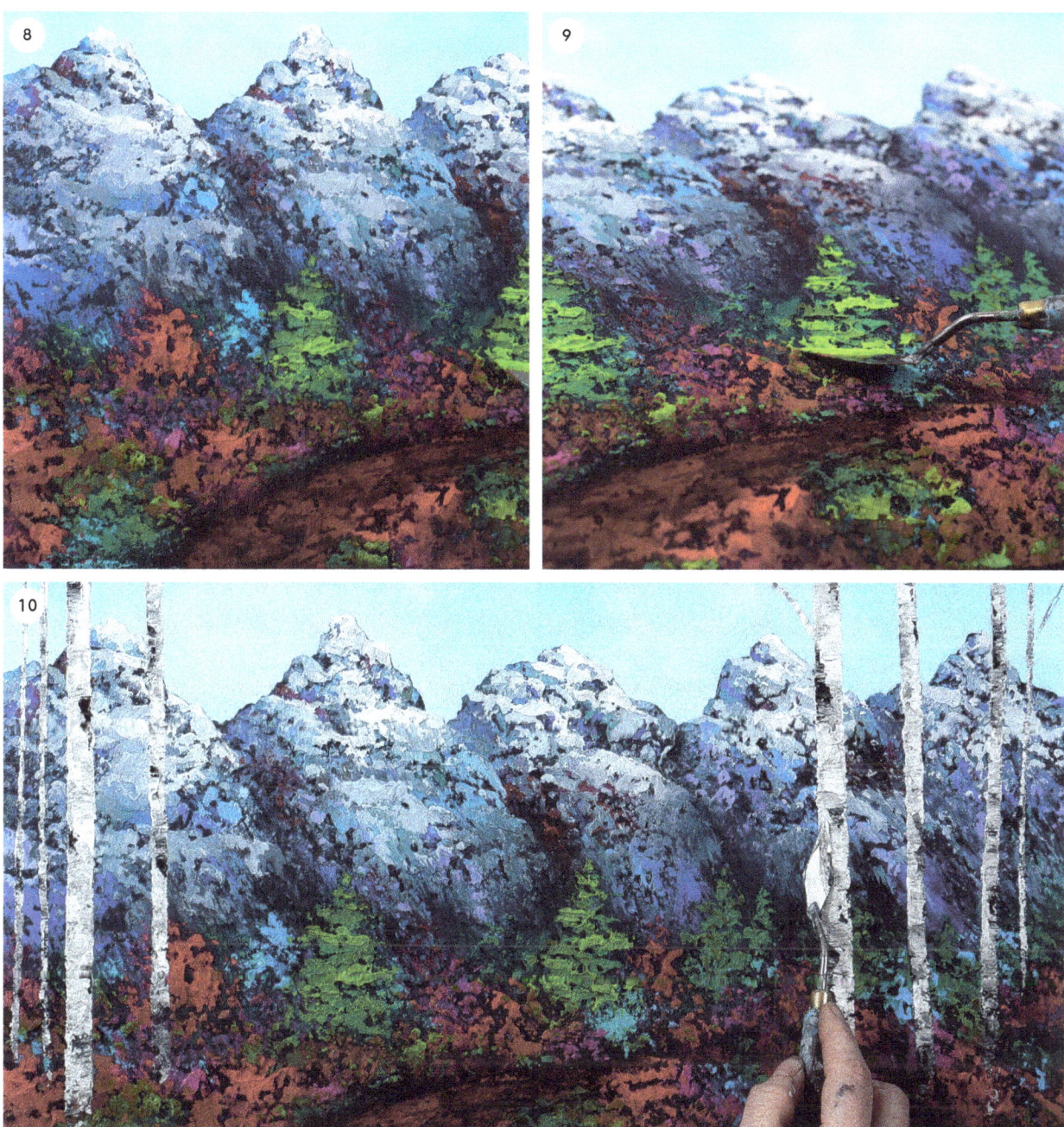

9. Next add a few individual pine trees. Load your knife with paint and use the edge to tap the color lightly on the canvas in a sideways zigzag motion, widening your strokes as you move down to create a triangular shape. Mix at least three shades of green for the pine trees. Start with dark phthalo green and add cad yellow medium to warm it and layer that over the top. Next, apply permanent green light with a touch of cad red medium to desaturate it, then add yellow and apply it in another layer.

10. Next, add a few large birch trees on either side of the canvas, using a small diamond-shaped knife to blend black and white paint to create tree trunks (see Journey into Autumn). Remember to vary the size of the tree trunks and add a few skinny branches extending toward the center of the canvas to create an arching canopy of trees which will frame the mountains.

11. Add highlights to trees and foliage in the foreground using lighter greens, oranges, and yellows. Add yellow and a touch of white to the colors you've already mixed to create lighter tints. By this time, the texture underneath should be dry, and you can lightly scumble your knife over the top and the bumpy texture will pick up random bits of paint to add highlights.

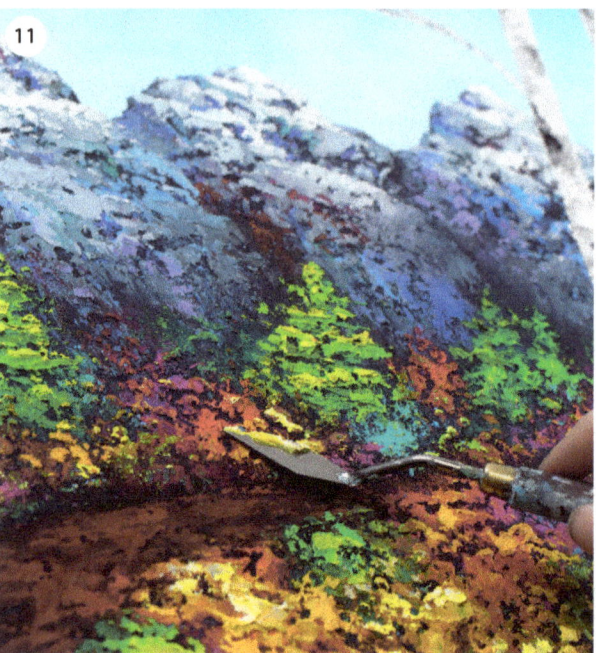

12. Next, add abstract leaf shapes to the trees. Load a small diamond-shaped knife with dark quin red and apply it to the canvas using the daub technique (see Techniques). Start at the outer corners and work towards the center, applying the leaves in small clusters. Next, layer cad red medium and cad orange in a similar pattern, allowing the colors to mix wet-on-wet to create new colors and shades. Continue the same process with the cad yellow medium, cad yellow light, and white, working your way towards the center of the canvas. Adding a small amount of the blue color from the sky background to your paint will desaturate it, making a nice shadow color and balance the vibrancy of the leaves.

13. Mix a light yellow and add small highlights toward the center of the tree canopy.

14. Add a few small clusters of leaves further down the tree trunks. I've added some of the green color used for the forest to tie the birch trees in with the foliage in the foreground. Review your composition and add any finishing touches.

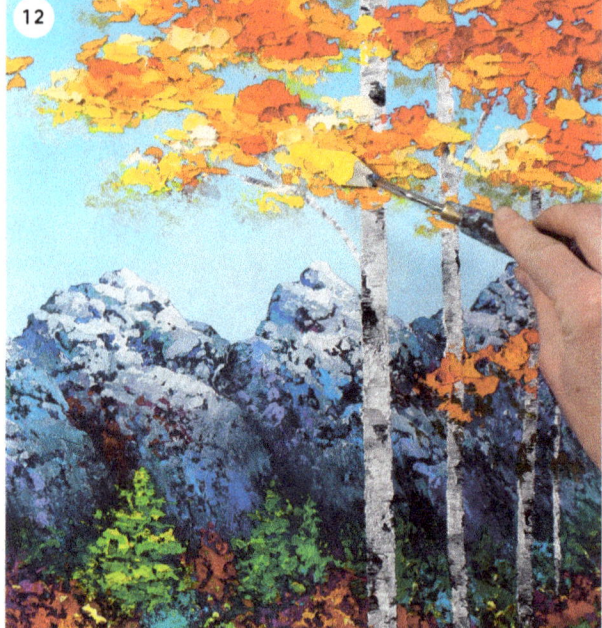

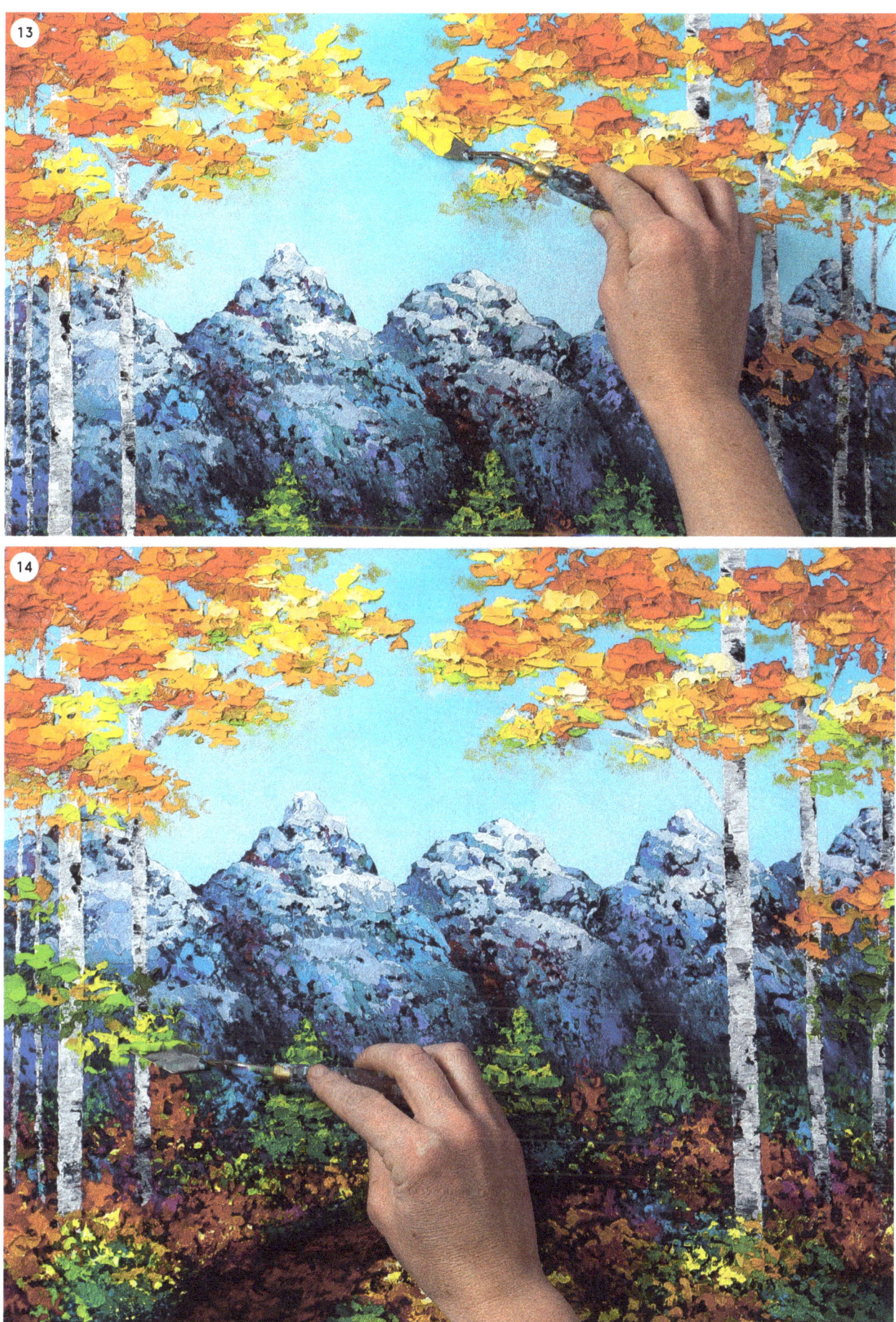

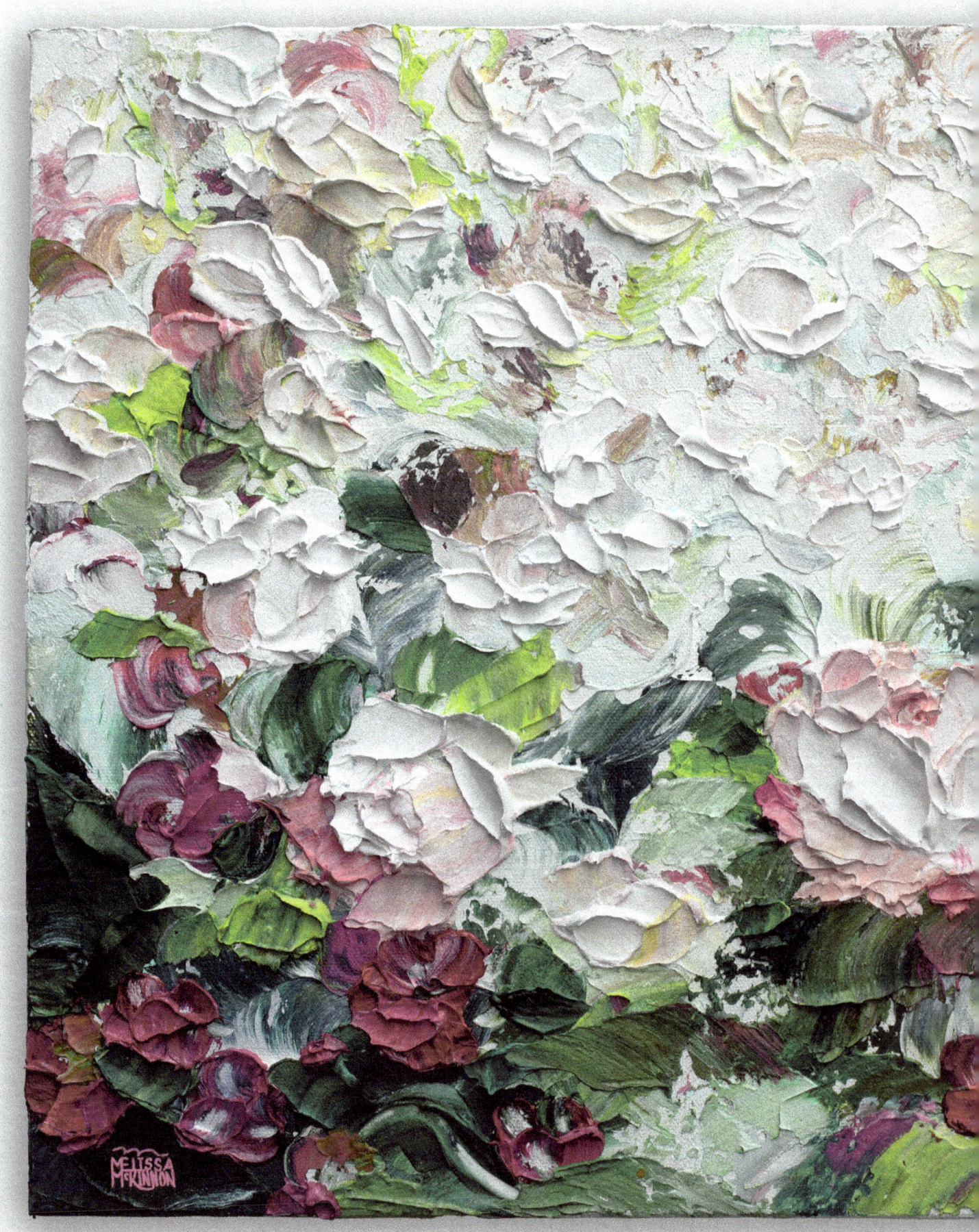

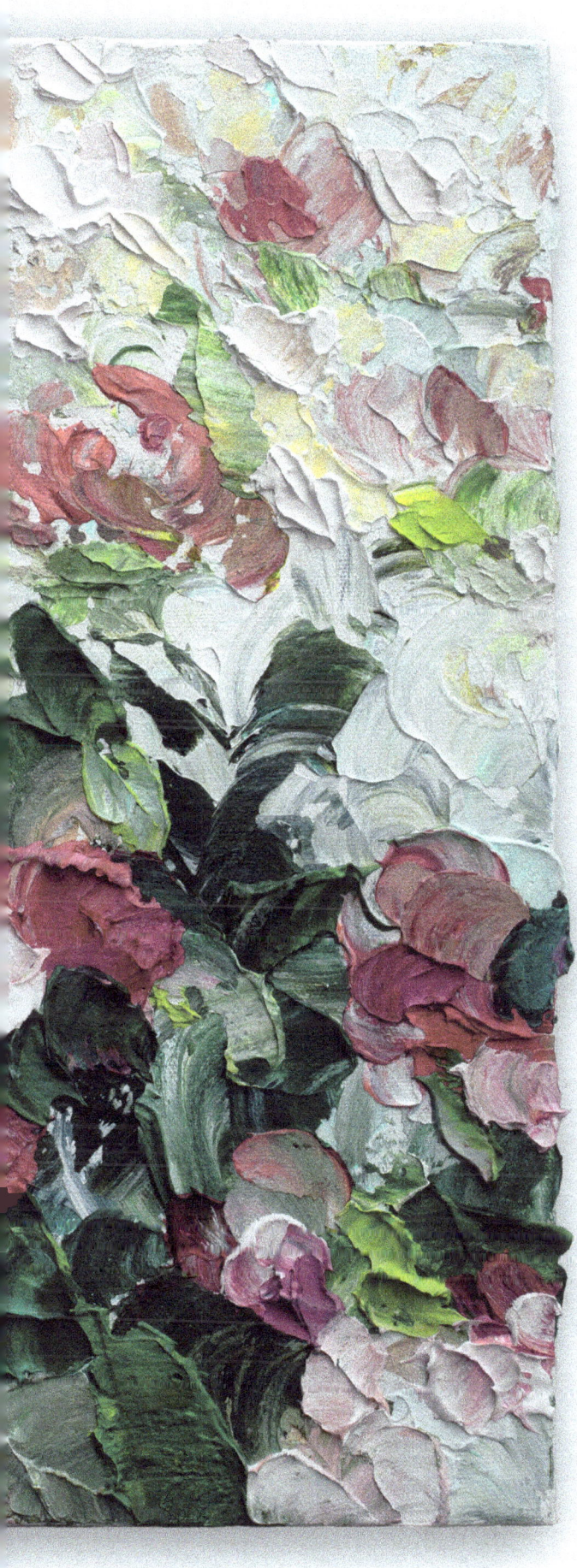

Where the Wild Things Grow

My floral paintings are an exploration of bold color, raw feminine energy, and passion that's found in nature. I want to capture that burst of energy and beauty before it disappears, telling a story of life and death, softness and strength, beauty and imperfection. The experience of enjoying fresh flowers is fleeting, but with a few strokes of paint we can appreciate their beauty forever. For this project, we'll use lots of paint to create an ultra-thick surface and work wet-on-wet, mixing colors directly on the canvas.

Color palette

- Titanium white
- Cadmium yellow light
- Cadmium yellow medium
- Quinacridone red
- Quinacridone magenta
- Alizarin crimson
- Permanent green light
- Phthalocyanine green
- Olive green
- Raw sienna
- Chromatic gray or Payne's gray

Tools and materials

- Medium spade-shaped knife
- Small oval-shaped knife
- 16in x 20in (40.5cm x 51cm) canvas
- Molding paste or gel medium to thicken paint where needed (see Mediums)

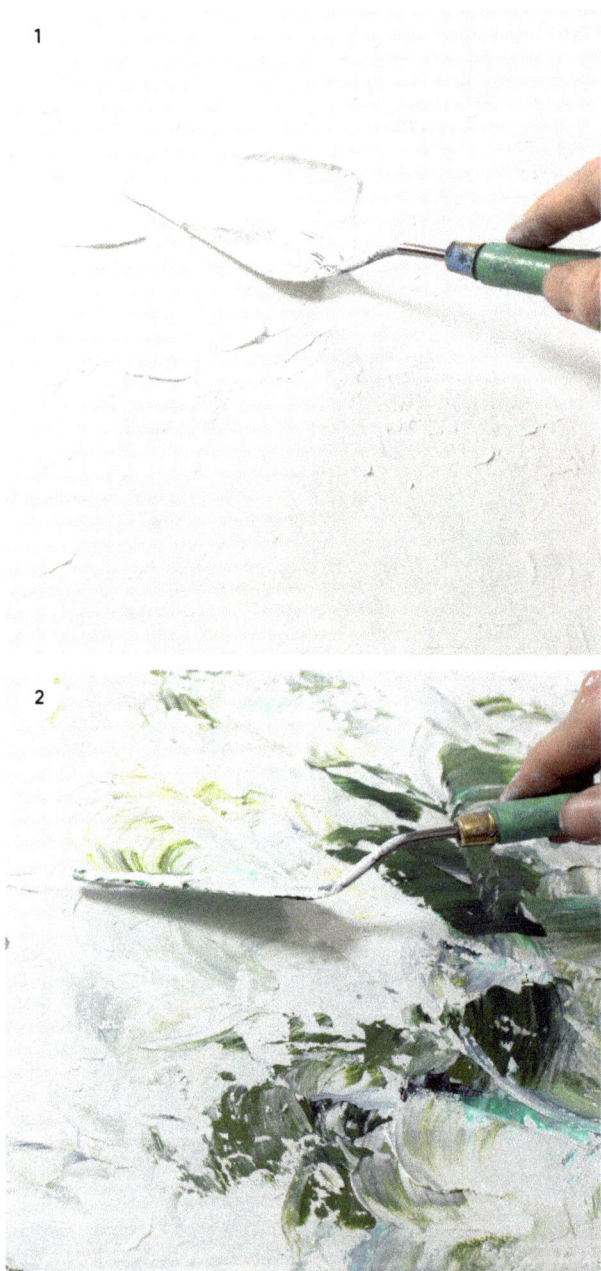

1. Use a medium spade-shaped knife to coat the entire surface of the canvas with a thick layer of titanium white and gel medium using random textured strokes.

2. To add shadow areas for the green foliage, apply a few strokes of dark gray (see Mixing Chromatic Black and Gray) in a sweeping motion to the bottom corners of the canvas, changing the direction of your strokes as you go. Continue the same process with phthalo green, olive green, and permanent green light. If you add too much green or the colors become muddy, you can always add white back in to lighten it up and start again with another layer.

3. Notice how the knife picks up some of the wet white background, making each continuous stroke lighter than the previous one. Use that to your advantage to create interesting marks and new color blends. Experiment with your strokes (see Techniques) – try pushing and pulling the paint. What happens when you change the pressure of your stroke or scumble the knife across the wet paint? Continue to add layers of green, working your way up the canvas. Try to create a variety of soft blended areas as well as thicker individual marks.

4. Using a small oval-shaped knife loaded with alizarin crimson, begin to apply small single petal strokes among the dark green leaves near the bottom of the canvas. Notice how each stroke blends with the green and white wet paint underneath. Without cleaning the knife, pick up new colors such as quin red, magenta, and raw sienna, allowing them to blend with each stroke.

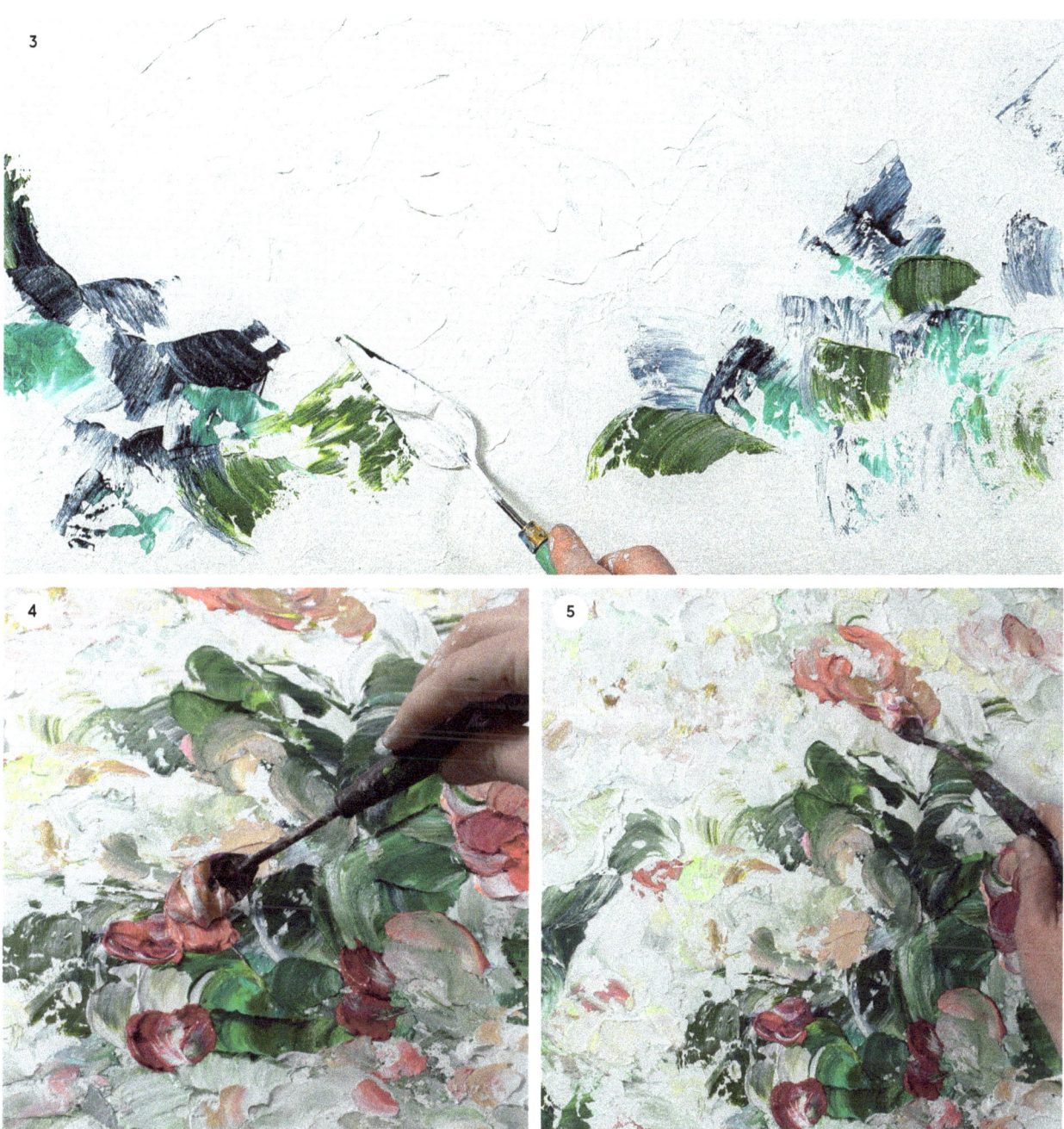

5. Next apply loose petal shapes in various sizes around the canvas. Adding small amounts of cad yellow medium and cad yellow light will lighten and warm the colors, giving even more variety and interest to your strokes. Keep the darkest shades near the bottom of the canvas and allow the knife to pick up bits of white paint as you move towards the top of the canvas, lightening colors as you go.

Notice the new shades of green and pink being created. You can wipe the back of your knife on areas of white paint to add little flecks of color to the pale background.

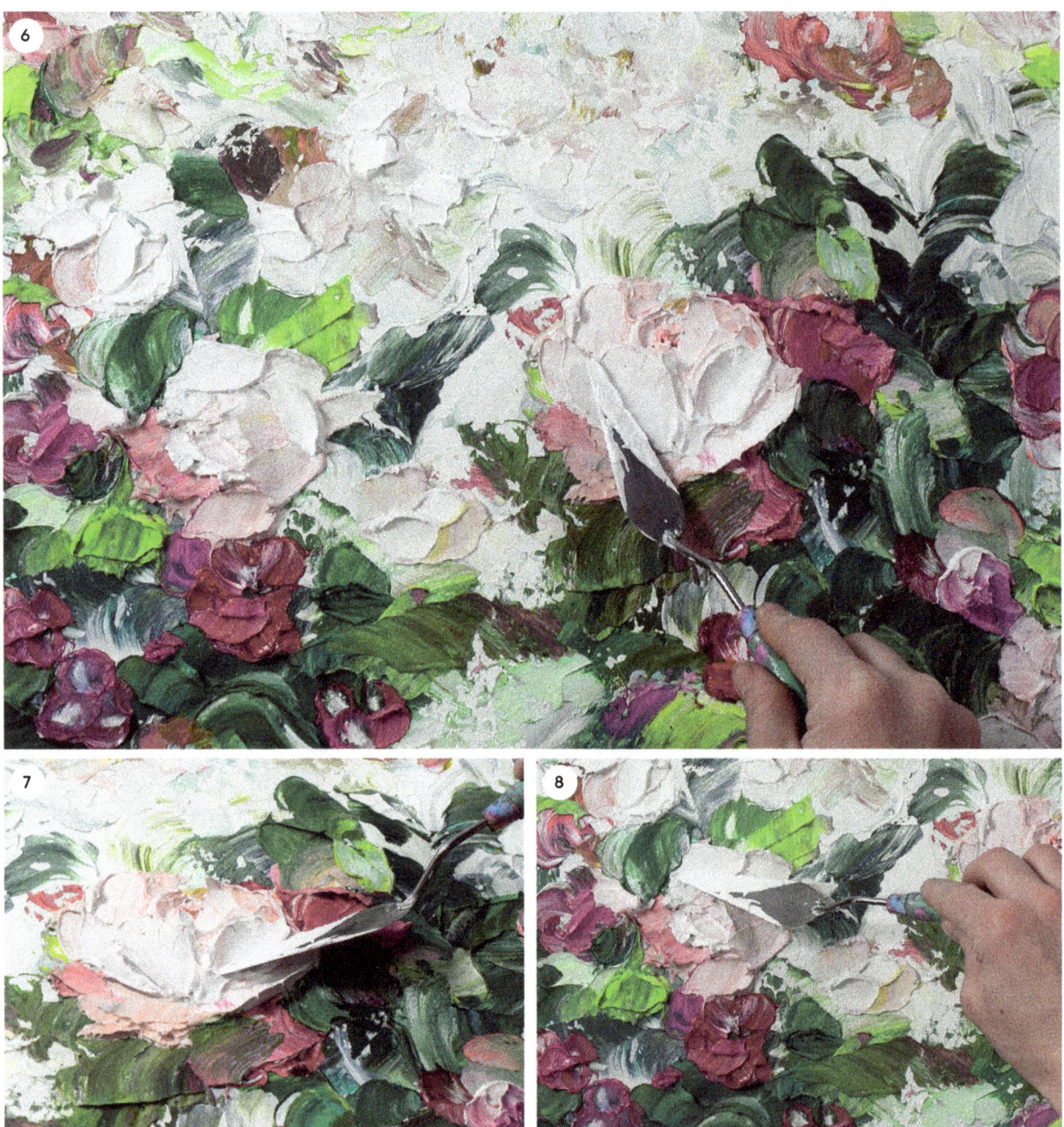

6. Before you add the main flowers, assess the composition and color balance of your painting. Add additional leaves to areas that may need to be filled out, especially under the area where you plan to place the main flowers. I mixed two bright greens using cad yellow light with a touch of phthalo green and permanent green light. I added small leaf shapes around the composition where I felt it needed more variety and brightness. These vibrant pops of color help draw the viewer's eye around the composition.

7. Next, add a few large flowers to the bottom half of the painting using the same process we used in steps 4 and 5 of Spring Blossom. Mix a couple of mid-tone and light pinks using quin red and magenta mixed with white and a touch of cad yellow light. Add molding paste for added volume and a different texture. Starting with a mid-tone pink, apply broad petal strokes with a medium spade-shaped knife to create the base of each flower. Allow the different shades of pink to mix with the white and green layers below. Continue

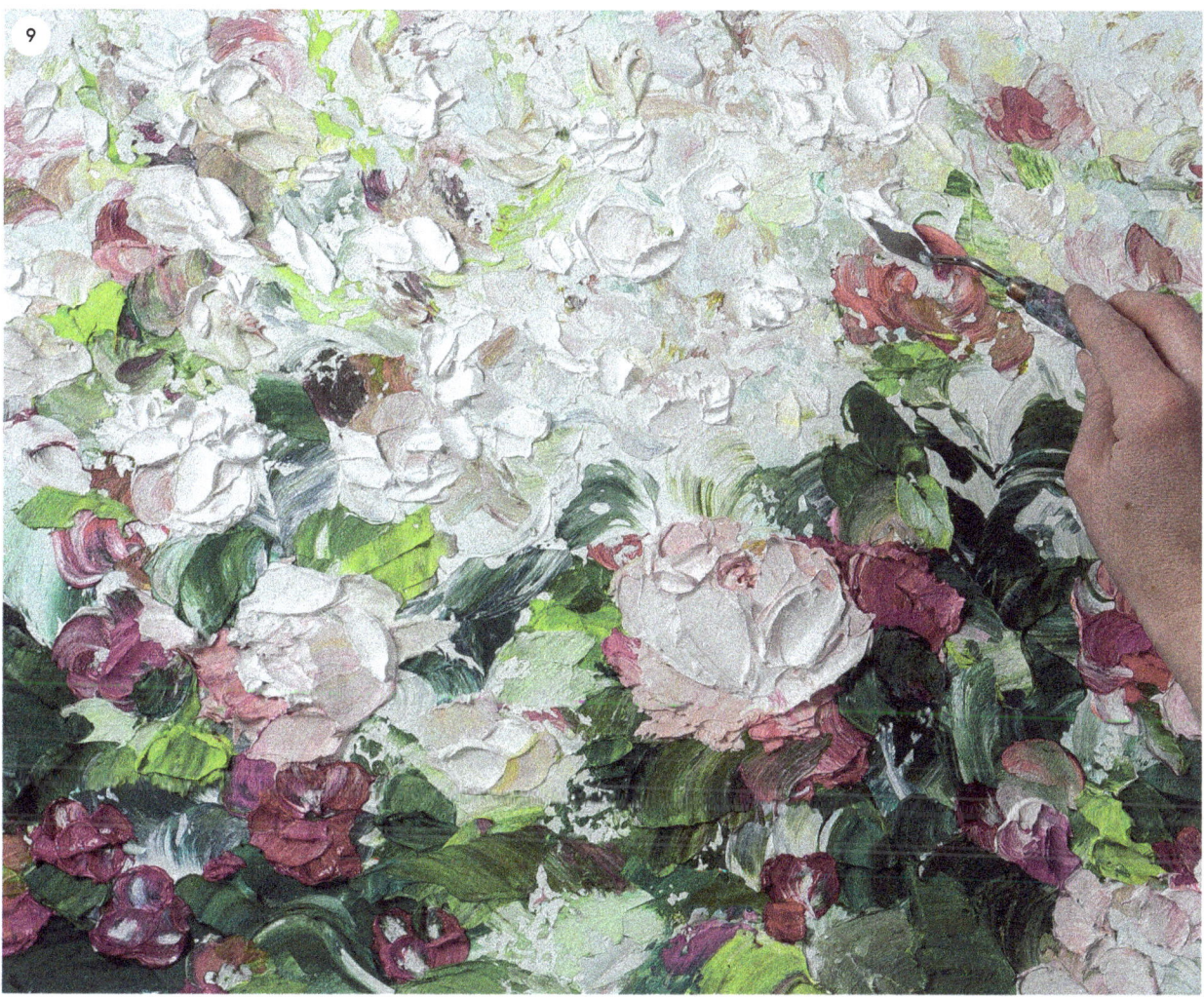

adding petals using the lighter shades of pink and white. Vary the size, shape, and direction of the petals.

8. Continue to add leaf details and smaller flowers to the background. Use the color and pattern of the background as a guide to where to place your flowers. Look for shapes and textures that could be turned into an abstract flower by adding a few individual petals on top.

9. Assess your composition and add finishing details. Fill in areas that could use more texture with daubs of white petals.

Kaleidoscope Sky

I've always loved the impressionist style of Monet's landscape paintings. Full of energy and movement, the abstract nature of this style of painting creates a conversation with the viewer, leaving them room to fill in the shapes and interpret the scene. Using small daubs of paint, we are going to infuse the sky in this project with color and movement. This will help loosen up our painting style, practice mixing color and value, and learn how to create texture with a brush as we did in Impressionist Brush Work (see Techniques). Heavy body acrylic paint is ideal for this project, but if you're using regular acrylic paint, mix a small amount of gel medium or molding paste in with the color.

Color palette

- Titanium white
- Cadmium yellow light
- Cadmium yellow medium
- Quinacridone red
- Quinacridone magenta
- Phthalocyanine blue (green shade)
- Ultramarine blue

Tools and materials

- Medium flat synthetic brush
- Small round natural bristle brush
- Chalk
- Heavy body acrylic paint (see Mediums)

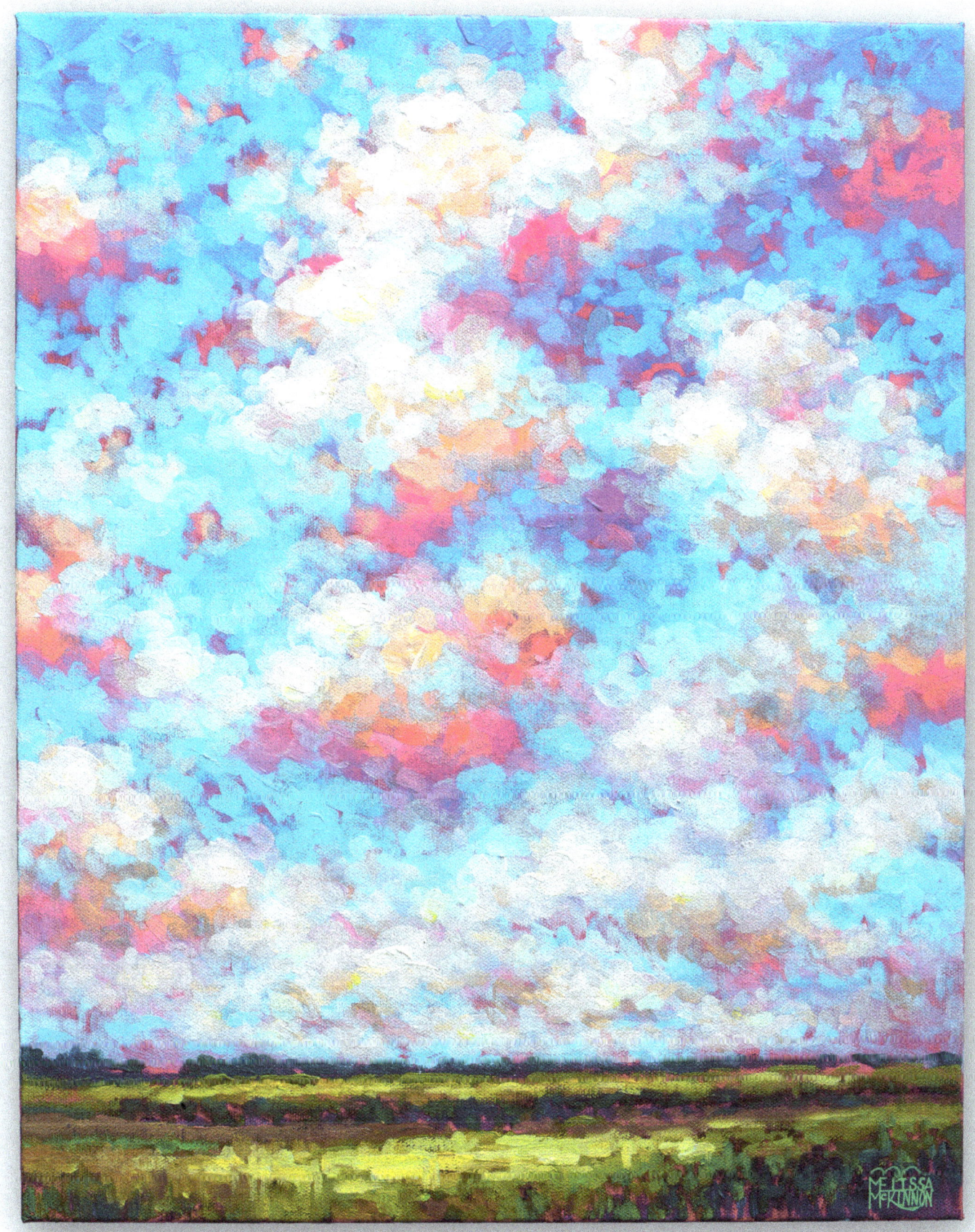

1. Using a medium flat brush, coat the entire canvas with a layer of bright color. I'm using magenta not only because it's my favorite color, but it has a beautiful vibrancy and transparency that allows the white of the canvas to show through, letting the color glow. It's fine if the color isn't blended perfectly because most of this layer will be covered with brushstrokes and only small areas of the background color will show through.

2. You can either loosely sketch your composition using a piece of chalk (see Composition) or dive right in and start painting. I usually paint from my imagination and create the composition as I go, however, you might feel more comfortable using chalk to loosely outline the horizon line and some of the cloud shapes to give you a general sense of the composition.

3. Mix a dark blue-gray using ultramarine blue, magenta, a small amount of cad yellow light, and white. Using a small round brush, apply the paint in short strokes to block in the shadow areas at the bottom of the clouds. The light source is coming from the top left corner so the shadows are on the bottom right of the cloud shapes. Remember to alternate the size and direction of your brushstrokes (see Impressionist Brush Work) and slightly alter the color by adding small amounts of magenta or yellow as you pick up more paint from your palette, transitioning from a blue-gray to a purple and pink gray. Lay down multiple strokes at a time, allowing the background to show through in some areas.

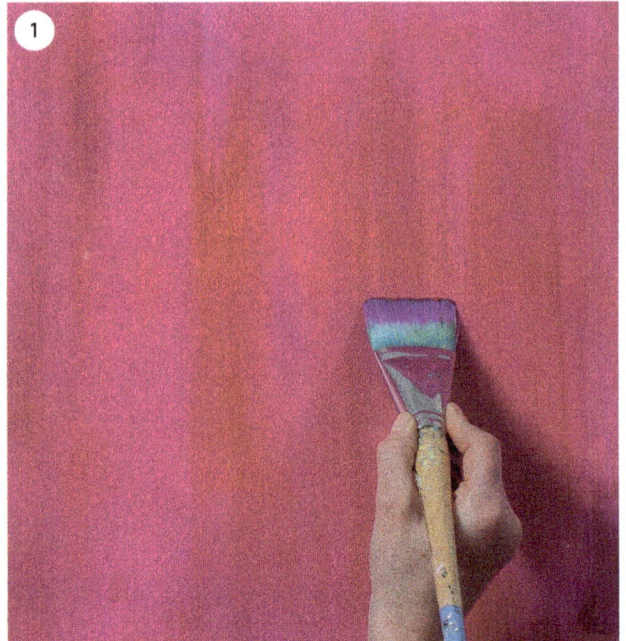

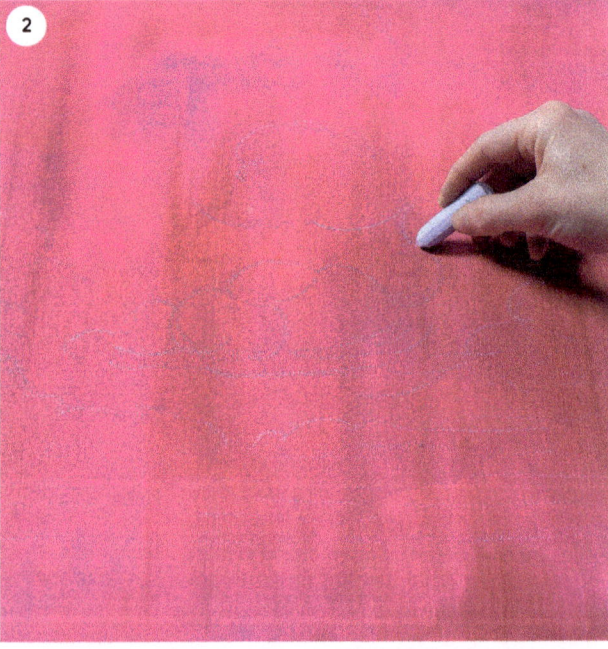

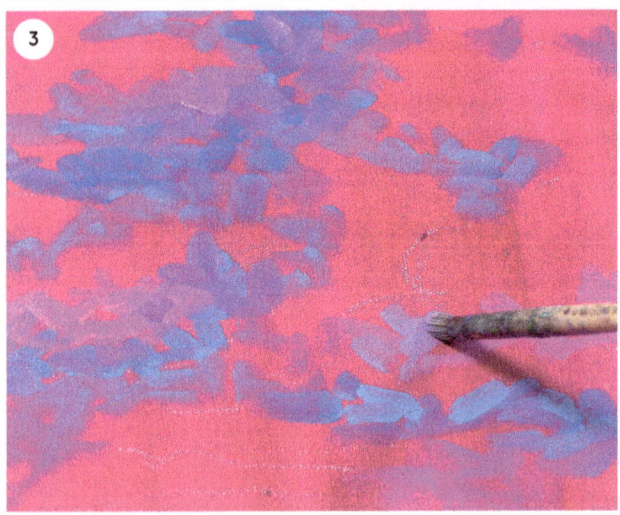

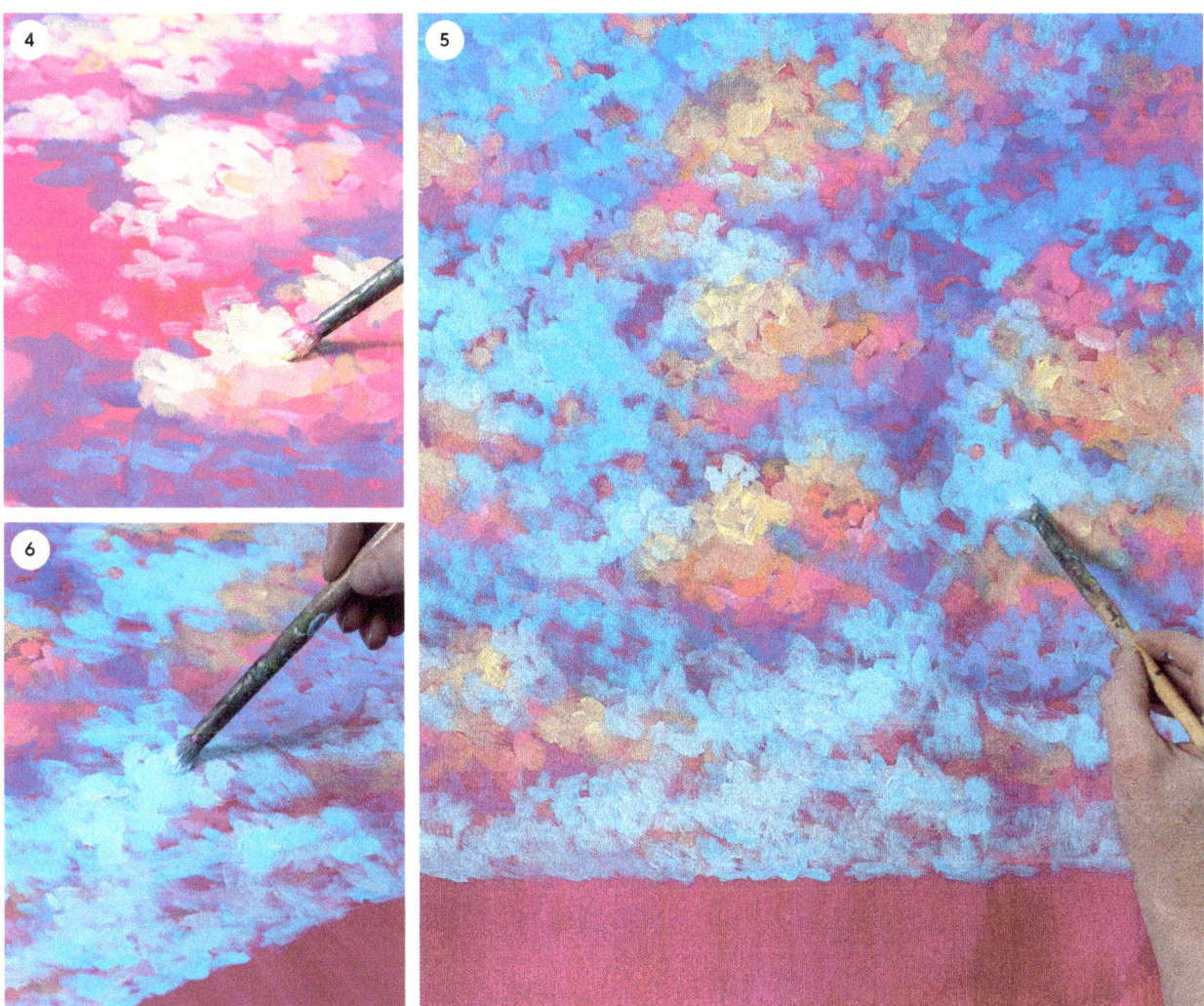

4. Mix a mid-tone pink using quin red (see Color Mixing) and use this color to fill in the body of the clouds. Add small amounts of cad yellow medium and white to add warmth and lighten your color as you move towards the light source at the top of the cloud clusters.

5. Next, mix a mid-tone phthalo blue. Starting at the top of the canvas, begin adding strokes for the sky, working around and cutting into the cloud shapes you have roughly blocked in. Notice how the pink color of the background changes the appearance of the blue paint especially with thinner strokes of paint.

6. Continue to add increasing amounts of white to your sky color as you work your way down the canvas toward the horizon.

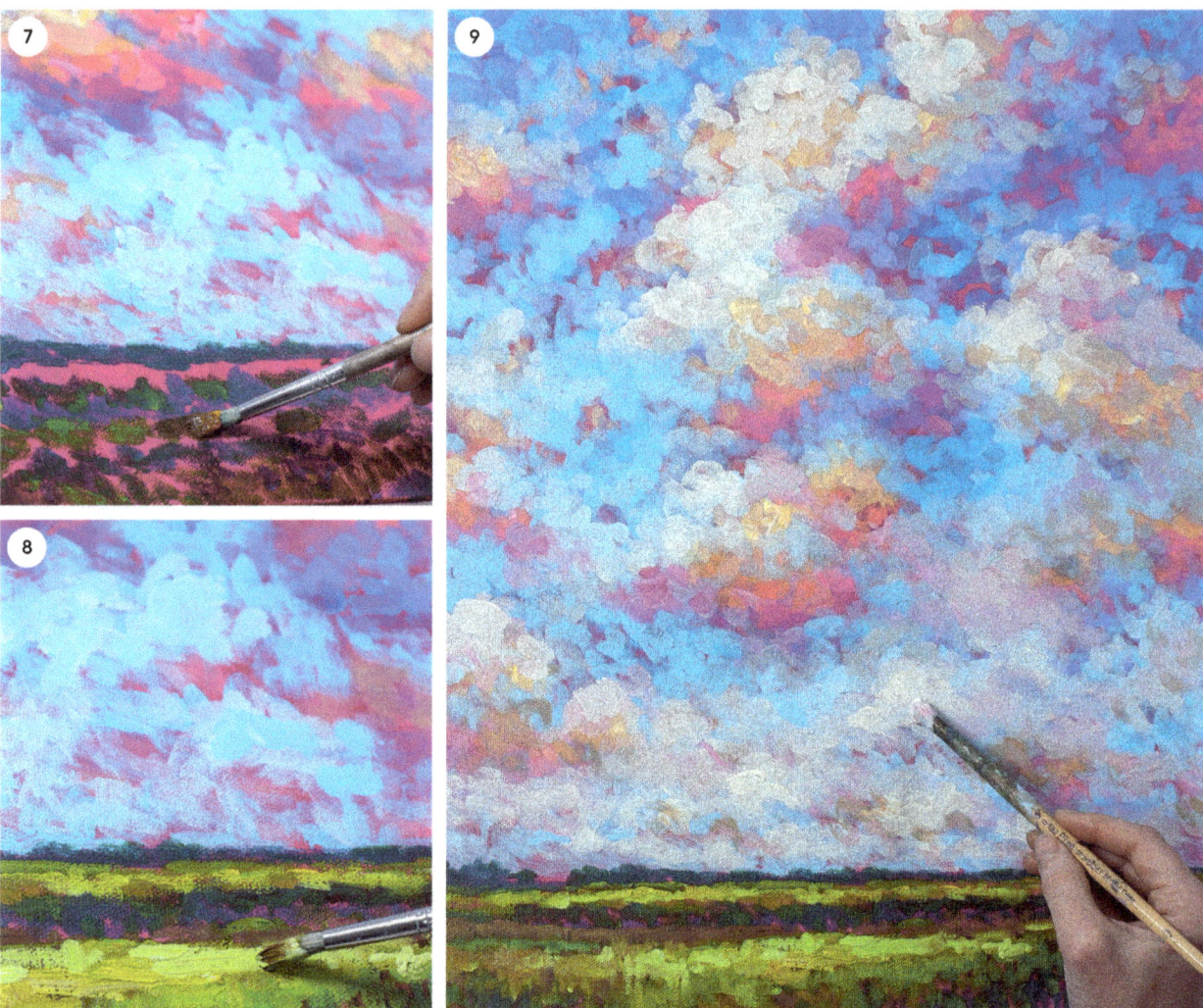

7. Mix a dark green using phthalo blue, a small amount of magenta, and cad yellow medium. Using the tip of your brush to create smaller marks, block in a dark tree line along the horizon just below the clouds. Add increasing amounts of magenta and yellow to warm and lighten the green shade. Continue to add rows of color to indicate grassy fields.

8. Next, add a small amount of your green mixture to cad yellow medium and cad yellow light to create lighter shades of green and continue to add rows to the fields. Add a small amount of white to lighten the colors as needed.

9. Mix a highlight color using white and a touch of cad yellow light. This will add dimension to the sky and refine the shape of the clouds. Apply small strokes starting at the top of the clouds where the sunlight would be the strongest. With each brushstroke, add in a color or two of the warm tones you used for the body of the clouds, creating additional variations of white, cream, and gray. These subtle variations in color will help blend your highlights in with the rest of the cloud. Adding a touch of the blue we used for the sky will help blend the edges of the clouds with the background. The more brushstrokes you add and the more variety of color you use, the more blended the sky will appear. Keep adding colors of different values until you're happy with the shapes of the clouds and the overall composition.

10. Use this last stage to enhance the contrast in your painting, add smaller details, and re-apply any colors you may have lost or covered too much of in the last stage. I added small brushstrokes of white to the lightest part of the clouds to make them stand out and little pops of vibrant color in a few areas to help draw the viewer's eye around the canvas

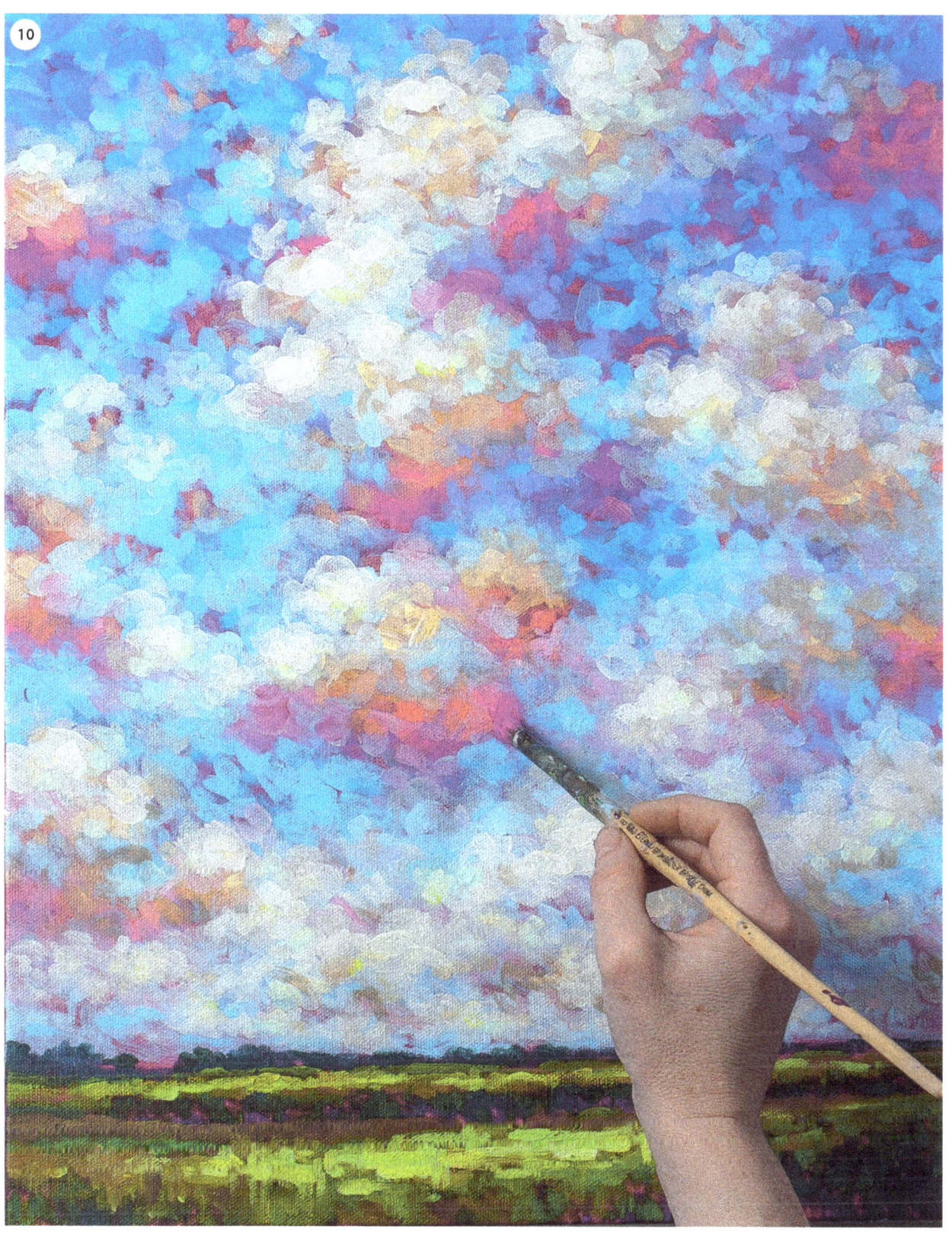

10

Under the Desert Sky

I've been referred to as a mad scientist when it comes to my painting practice, so I'm excited to show you lots of experimental techniques. In this project, we will create a desert landscape using the textured wood panel we've already prepared and paint on top of the absorbent surface using thin washes of color. We'll use the surface to create an abstract landscape, using a variety of mediums to make interesting textures. We'll learn different techniques to apply and remove thin washes of color to enhance the textured surface.

Color palette

- Titanium white paint
- Golden high flow transparent yellow iron oxide
- Golden high flow transparent red iron oxide
- Daler Rowney FW ink in red earth
- Liquitex ink iridescent rich bronze
- Golden high flow transparent brown iron oxide
- Liquitex ink in burnt umber
- Payne's gray ink

Tools and materials

- Small flat synthetic brush
- Large flat synthetic brush
- Medium spade-shaped knife
- Molding paste
- Water in a spray bottle
- Rubbing alcohol (70 to 99 percent)
- Paper towel or soft clean cloth
- Wood panel from Creating a Textured Background

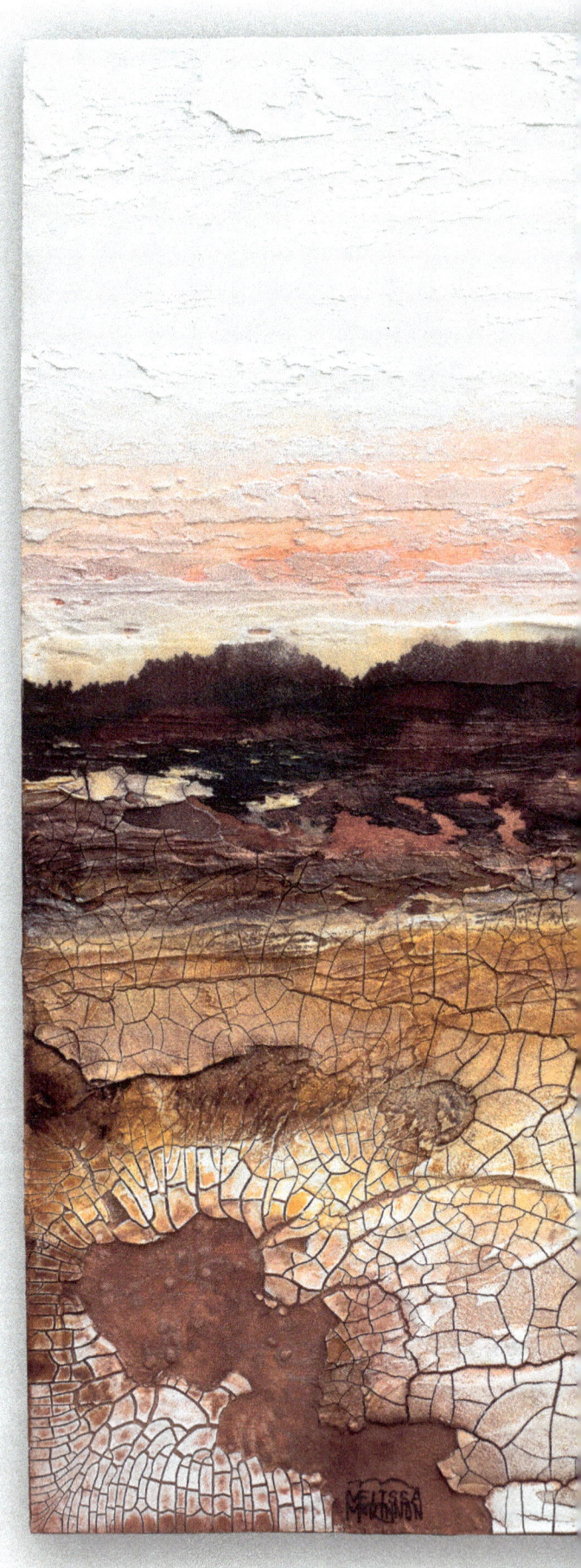

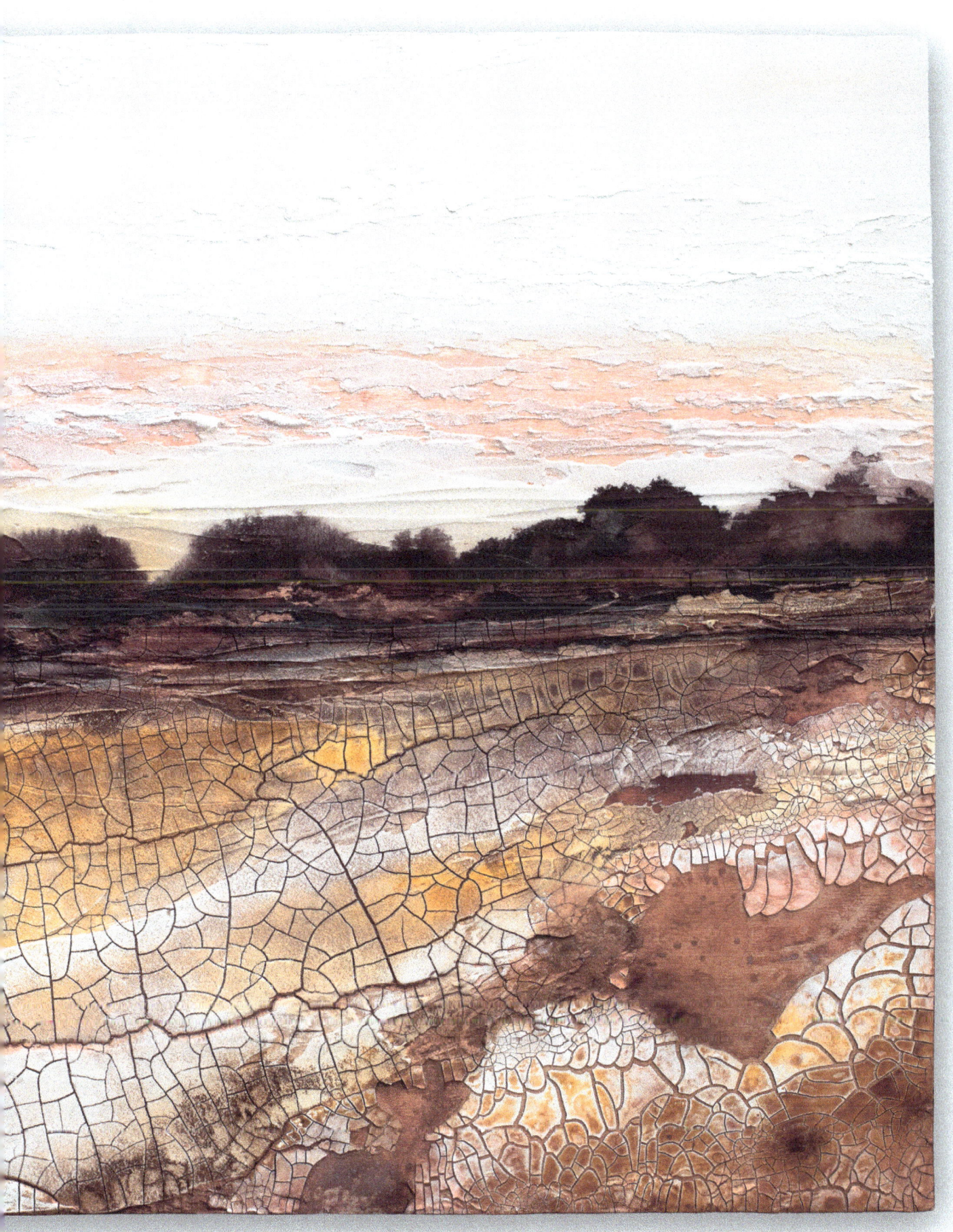

1. To allow the paint to flow on the textured background, mist the dried crackle paste with water from a spray bottle. Add a few drops of transparent red iron oxide and iridescent rich bronze to the lower corners, spreading the paint with a small flat brush. Notice how the color soaks into the cracks and surface of the paint. This is where the magic starts to happen. You don't have a lot of control over where the paint flows but as it dries, it will create unique and often unexpected effects. If you've applied too much color, you can use a paper towel or clean cloth to gently tap on the surface of the panel to remove the wet paint.

2. Apply burnt umber along the horizon line to indicate a darker rock formation in the distance.

3. Add transparent yellow iron oxide with a clean brush (so the browns don't muddy the yellows) in selected areas above and below the horizon line. This transparent color has a warm golden glow and will mix beautifully with the other colors.

4. Next, add a few drops of transparent brown iron oxide straight from the bottle onto the horizon, allowing it to mix with the wet burnt umber. In my painting, there was a ridge of raised texture that I wanted to emphasize, so I added the brown ink in drops along the ridge letting it flow and pool in abstract shapes, hoping it would create interesting patterns as the ink dried.

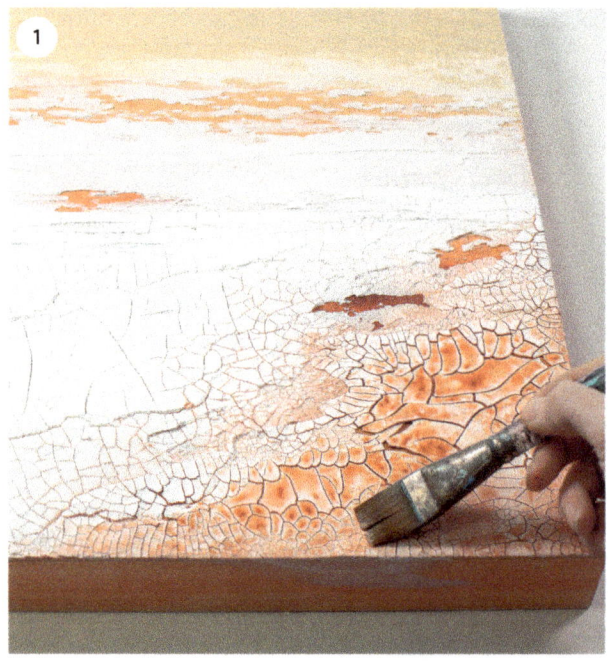

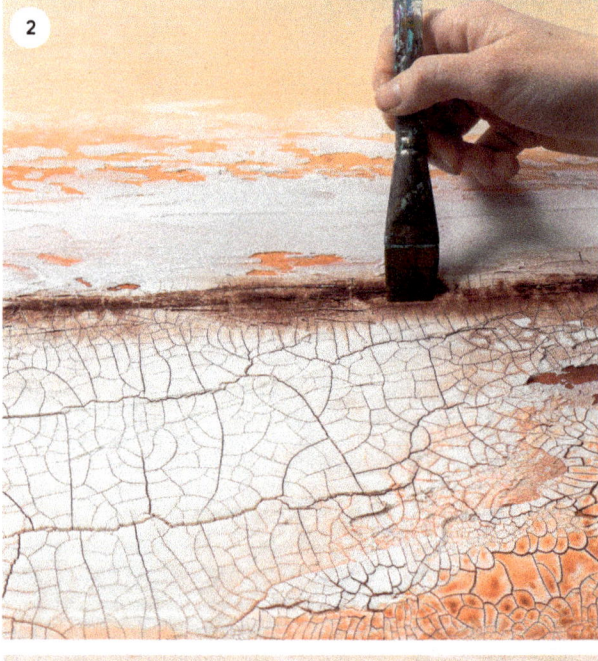

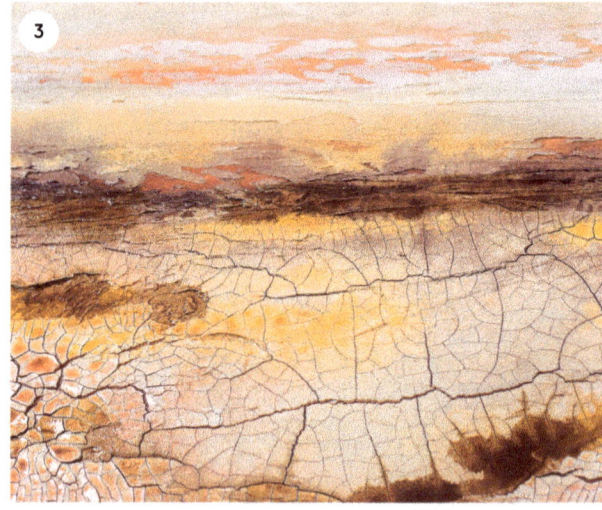

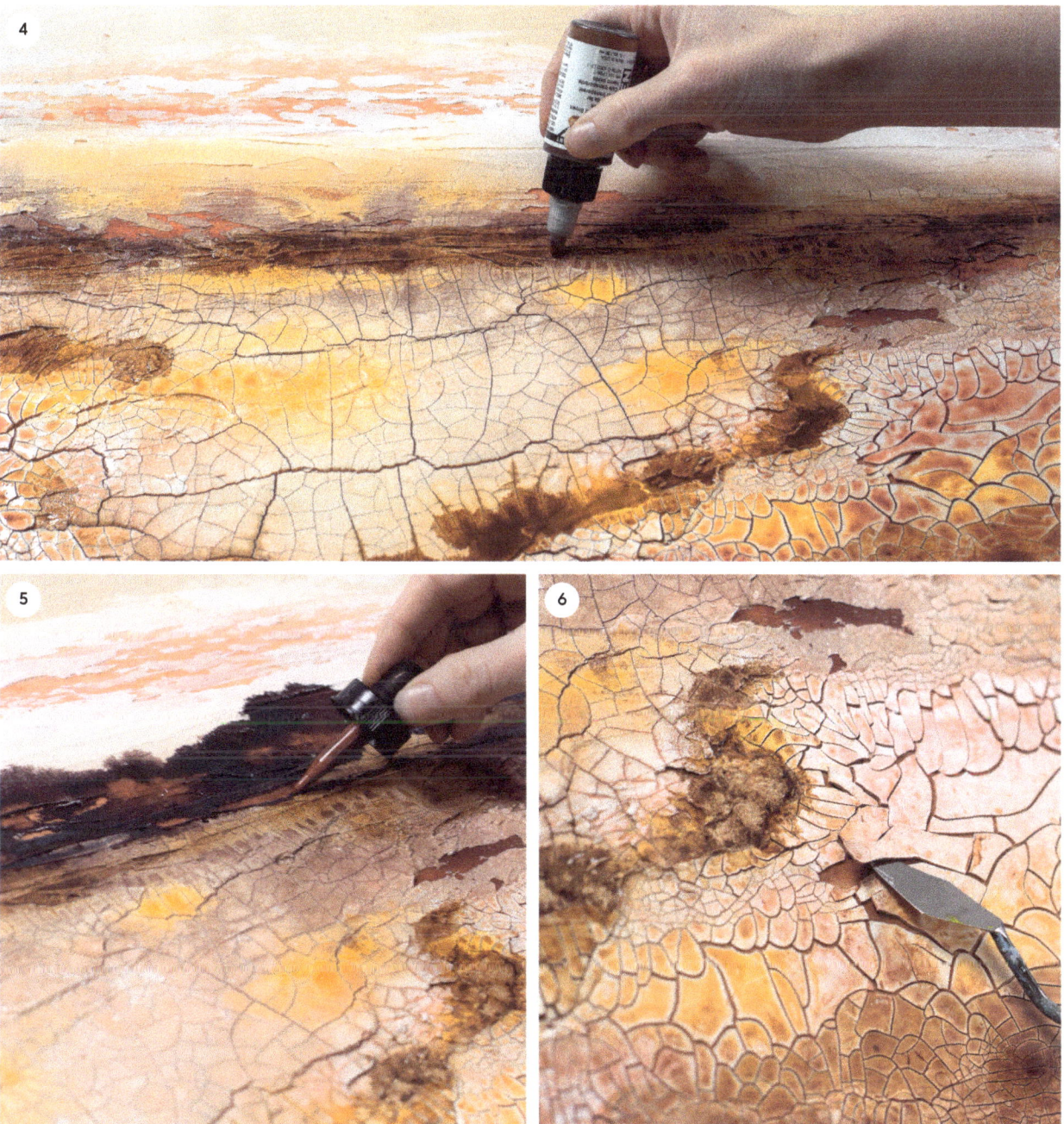

5. Add Payne's gray and red earth straight from the bottle in drops along the horizon to deepen the color. Allow the inks to mix and blend creating interesting effects as they dry.

6. You can use a knife or other hard tool to remove some of the crackle pieces to reveal interesting patterns underneath and create another layer of depth in the painting. I felt that the texture was too heavy and uniform at the bottom, so I removed some of the pieces to create a more interesting shape that reflected the contours of the land.

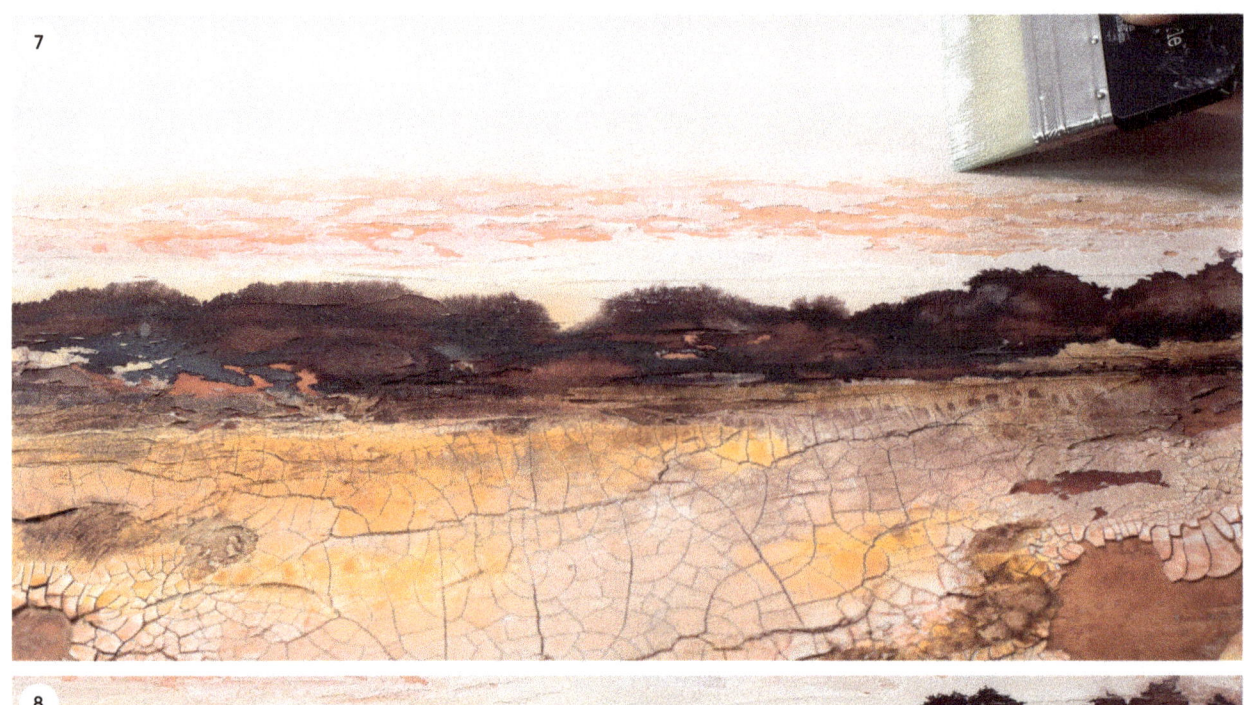

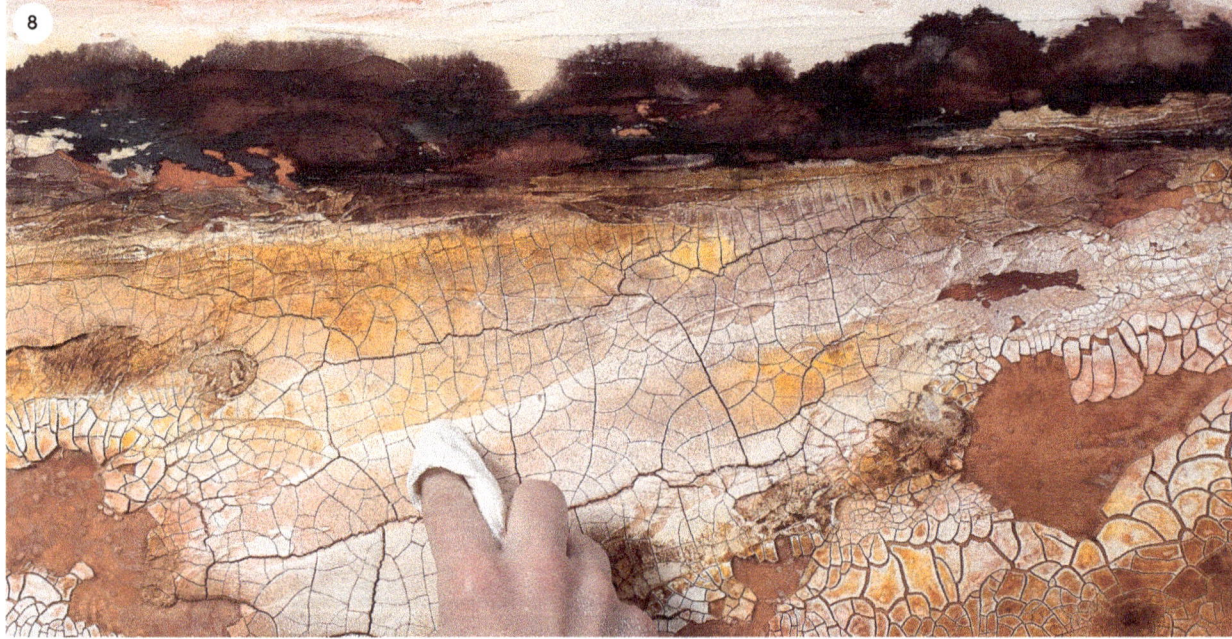

7. Next, use a large flat brush to apply a thin coat of white acrylic paint to the sky allowing it to softly fade into the copper-colored clouds. Keep this layer very thin by mixing the paint with 30 percent water to allow some of the wood grain underneath to show through. You could apply a thicker, more opaque coat of paint but I like that the wood grain pattern adds to the visual texture of the landscape. You can also see what the canvas looks like with some of the crackle pieces removed.

8. Next, we're going to use rubbing alcohol to remove some of the dried paint and further enhance the surface of the crackle paste. Wet a paper towel or clean, soft cloth with rubbing alcohol and tap, dab, or rub the surface of the crackle paste to remove some of the paint. How much paint is removed will depend on how firmly you rub. With a light touch, you can create some interesting textures by tapping or dabbing the surface. By adding more rubbing alcohol and rubbing firmly, you can remove quite a bit of the

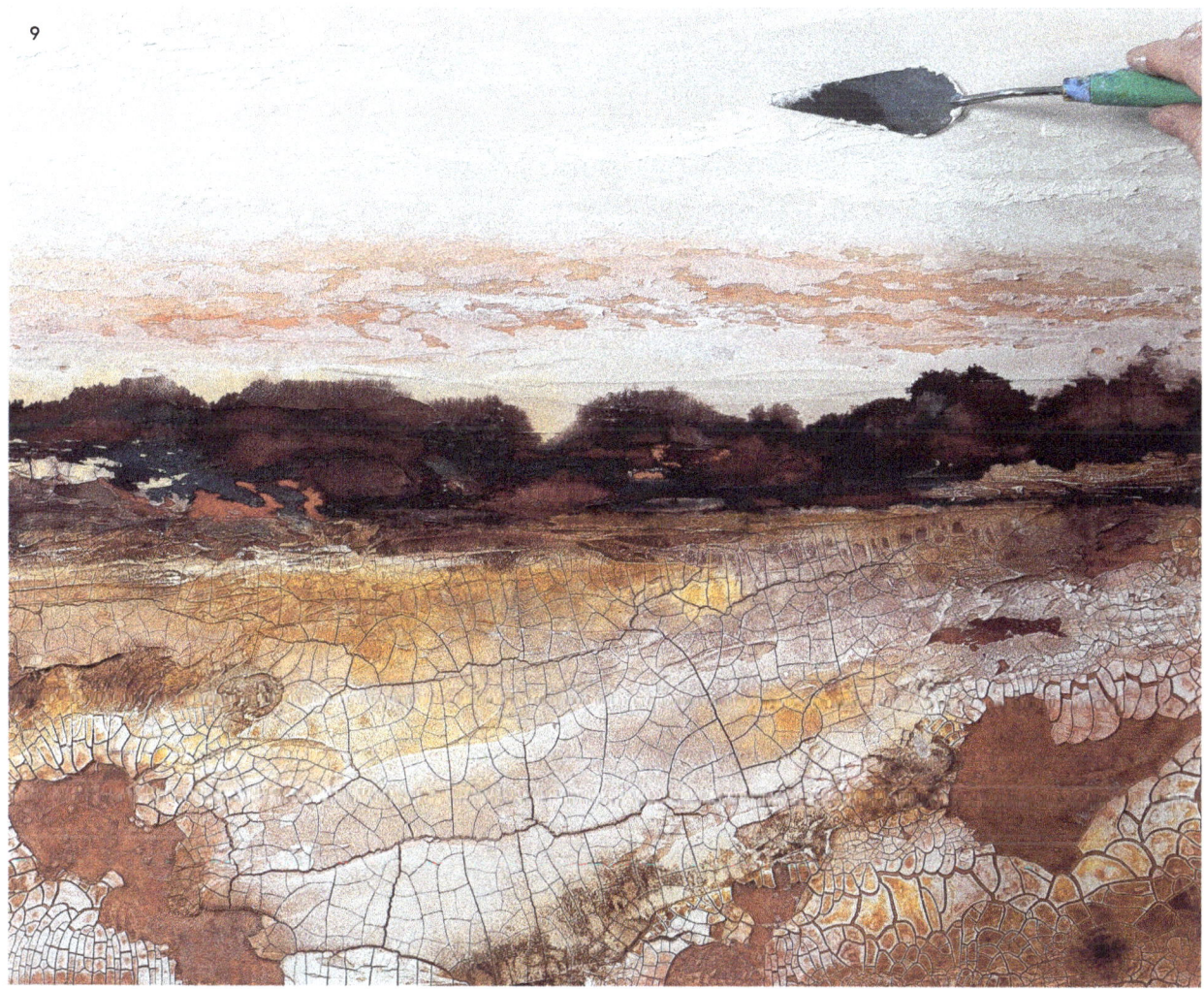

9

paint. This is a good option if you feel like you have added too much paint, it's too dark, or you just want to add some interesting textures. You can repeat the steps, adding and removing paint, over and over until you are satisfied with the surface of the painting. The more layers you add, the more interesting and complex the surface becomes.

9. To finish the painting, add some impasto clouds to create more dimension in the sky. To do this, mix molding paste with a few drops of the transparent yellow iron oxide and red earth, and apply it with a medium spade-shaped knife in a sweeping, scumbling motion (see Techniques) across the top portion of the sky.

Finishing

Once you've had fun and created your paintings, you need to think about how you are going to preserve and present them. Here are some useful suggestions.

Edges

Don't forget to finish the sides of the canvas. Options are to continue the painted image onto the side of the canvas or paint it a solid color.

Sign

To sign the front of your painting, use a paint marker or thin brush and acrylic paint diluted with water to make it flow more easily. Sign, title, and date the painting with pencil on the back.

Drying

The surface of the acrylic painting will be dry to the touch within a few hours, depending on the thickness of your paint. However, the paint underneath will take much longer to dry and finally cure. Wait one to two weeks before applying varnish.

Varnish

Apply liquid varnish with a flat synthetic brush or use several coats of an aerosol spray varnish to seal the surface of your painting and protect it from dust, minor scratches, and UV light.

Wire

Small paintings can be hung with a saw tooth hanger or d-rings and wire.

Care for paintings

- Seal with varnish to protect the painting.

- Frame to protect the edges.

- Keep out of direct sunlight to prevent colors from fading.

- Never use solvents or cleaning products, they could damage the surface of the painting.

- Dust paintings with a clean microfiber cloth or new soft paintbrush.

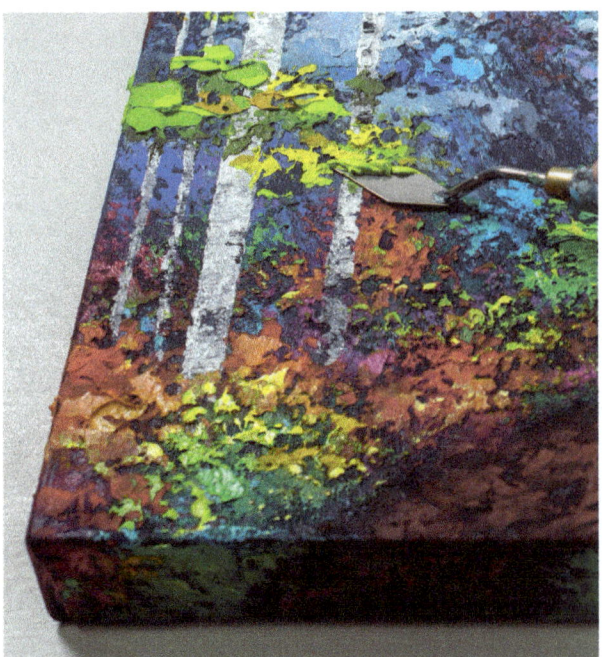

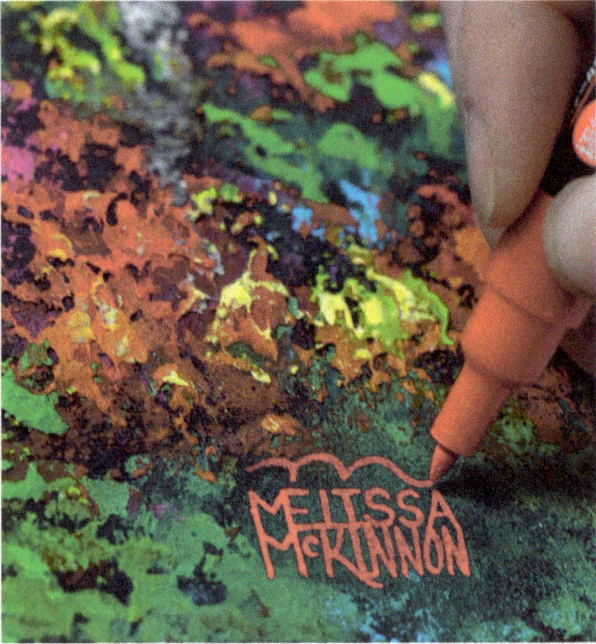

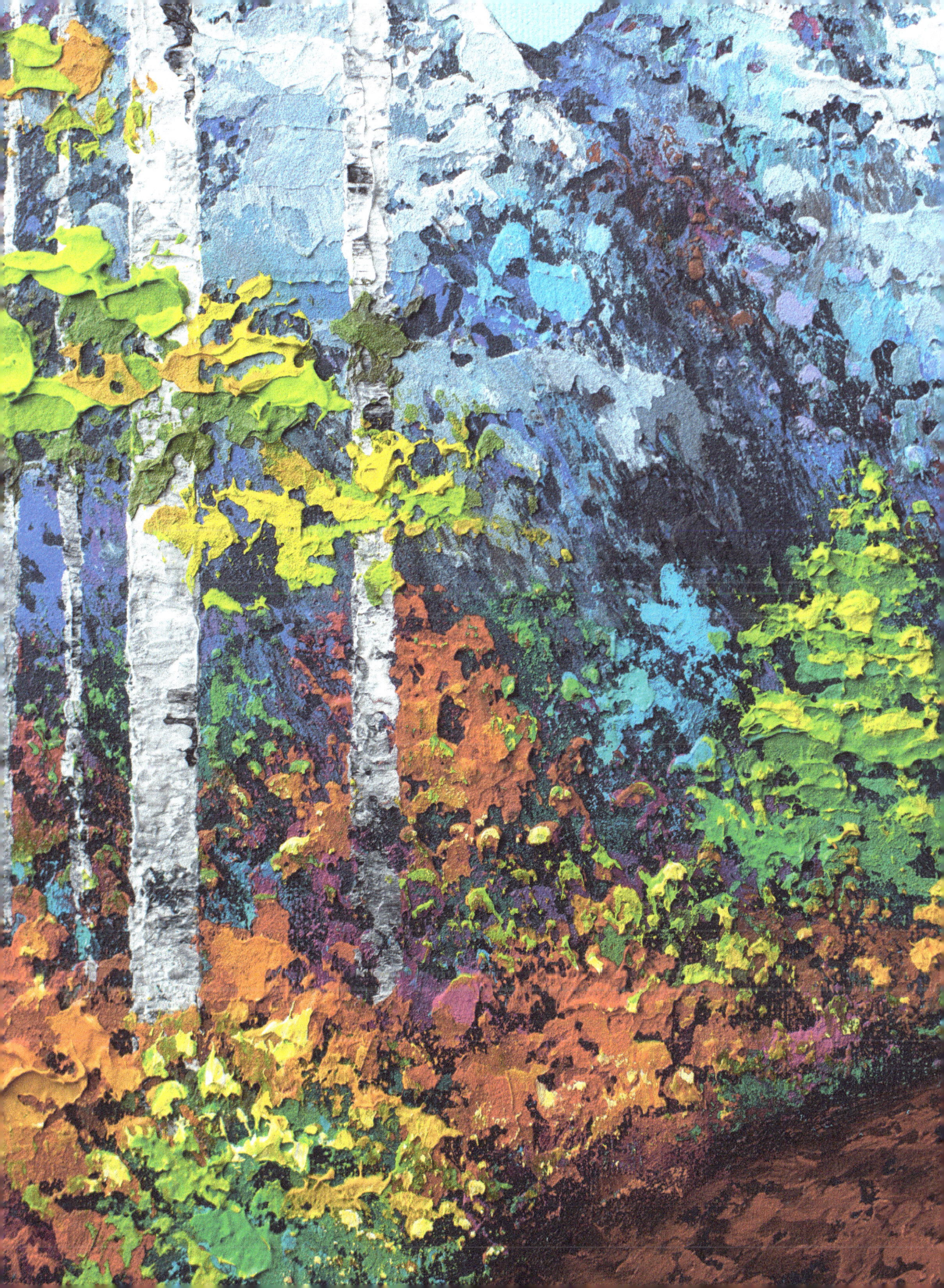

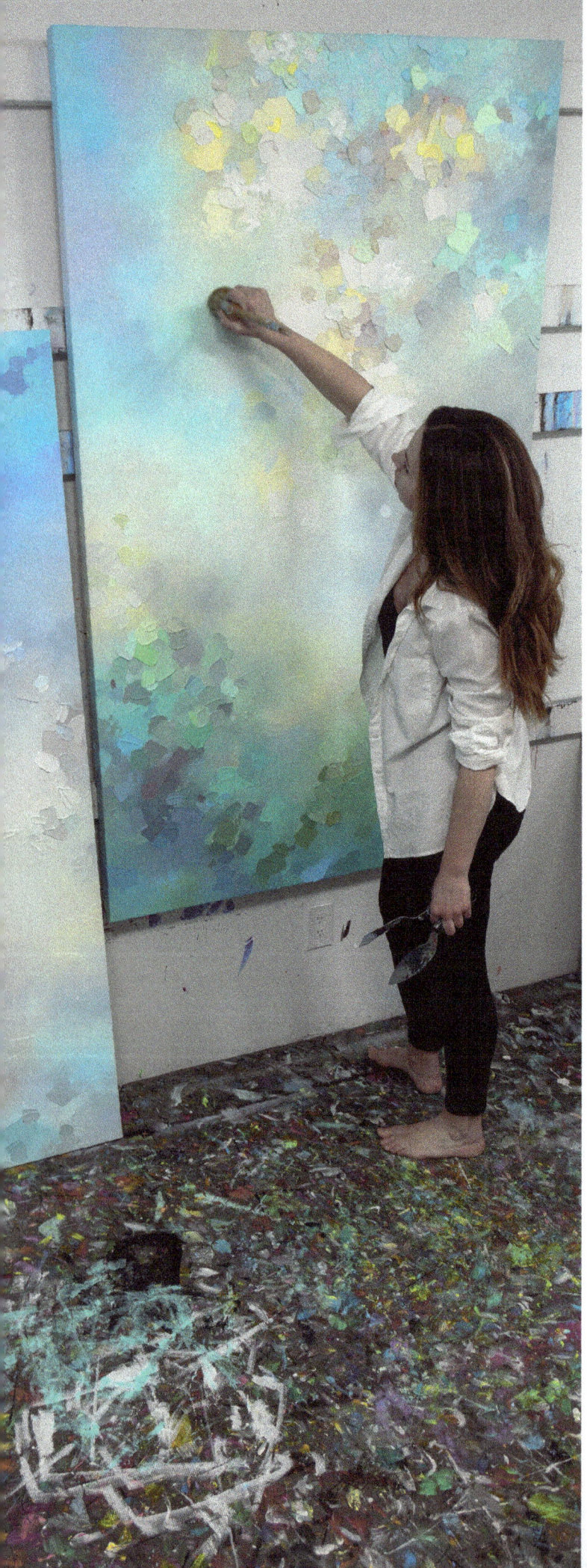

About the author

Melissa McKinnon is a contemporary landscape artist with a signature style that celebrates color, texture, and movement with layers of rich, vibrant paint. Inspired by her Canadian roots and grounded in her natural-born creativity, Melissa paints the trees, skies, mountains, oceans, and florals that bring joy to her, and beauty to the walls of collectors worldwide.

You can find her paintings, prints, videos, and online classes on her website

www.melissamckinnonart.com

Tag her on social media:

Instagram: @melissamckinnonart

Facebook: MelissaMcKinnonArt

Pinterest: mmckinnonartist

Acknowledgments

This book is dedicated to my daughters Isabella and Valentina, my biggest inspirations. Thank you to my husband, Miguel and Mom, Claudia. This book wouldn't have been possible without your assistance, support, and encouragement.

Using my work

The exercises and projects in this book are for educational and practice purposes only. I encourage you to use them as inspiration to develop your skills as a palette knife artist. At first, you might want to follow along step-by-step until you get the hang of it and that's okay. However, as soon as possible, I urge you to break free from the constraints of copying and start exploring your own inspirations and interpretations of the world around you. Every artist is unique – from the way you hold your palette knife, to the marks you make intuitively, to the colors you're drawn to, to the way you see the beauty in the world, and how you express it through your art.

Index

A DAVID AND CHARLES BOOK
© David and Charles, Ltd 2022

David and Charles is an imprint of David and Charles,
Ltd, Suite A, Tourism House, Pynes Hill, Exeter, EX2 5WS

EU GPSR Authorised Representative:
Logos Europe, 9 rue Nicolas Poussin, 17000,
La Rochelle, France
Email: contact@logoseurope.eu

Text and Designs © Melissa McKinnon 2022
Layout and Photography © David and Charles, Ltd 2022

First published in the UK and USA in 2022

Names of manufacturers and product ranges are
provided for the information of readers, with no
intention to infringe copyright or trademarks.

A catalogue record for this book is available from the
British Library.

ISBN-13: 9781446309377 paperback
ISBN-13: 9781446381847 EPUB
ISBN-13: 9781446381830 PDF

Publishing Director: Ame Verso
Senior Commissioning Editor: Sarah Callard
Managing Editor: Jeni Chown
Editor: Jessica Cropper
Project Editor: Clare Ashton
Head of Design: Anna Wade
Designer: Lucy Waldron and Nick Leggett
Pre-press Designer: Ali Stark
Art Direction: Lucy Waldron
Photography: Jason Jenkins and Melissa McKinnon
Production Manager: Beverley Richardson

David and Charles publishes high-quality books on
a wide range of subjects. For more information visit
www.davidandcharles.com.

Share your makes with us on social media using
#dandcbooks and follow us on Facebook and
Instagram by searching for @dandcbooks.

Layout of the digital edition of this book may vary
depending on reader hardware and display settings.

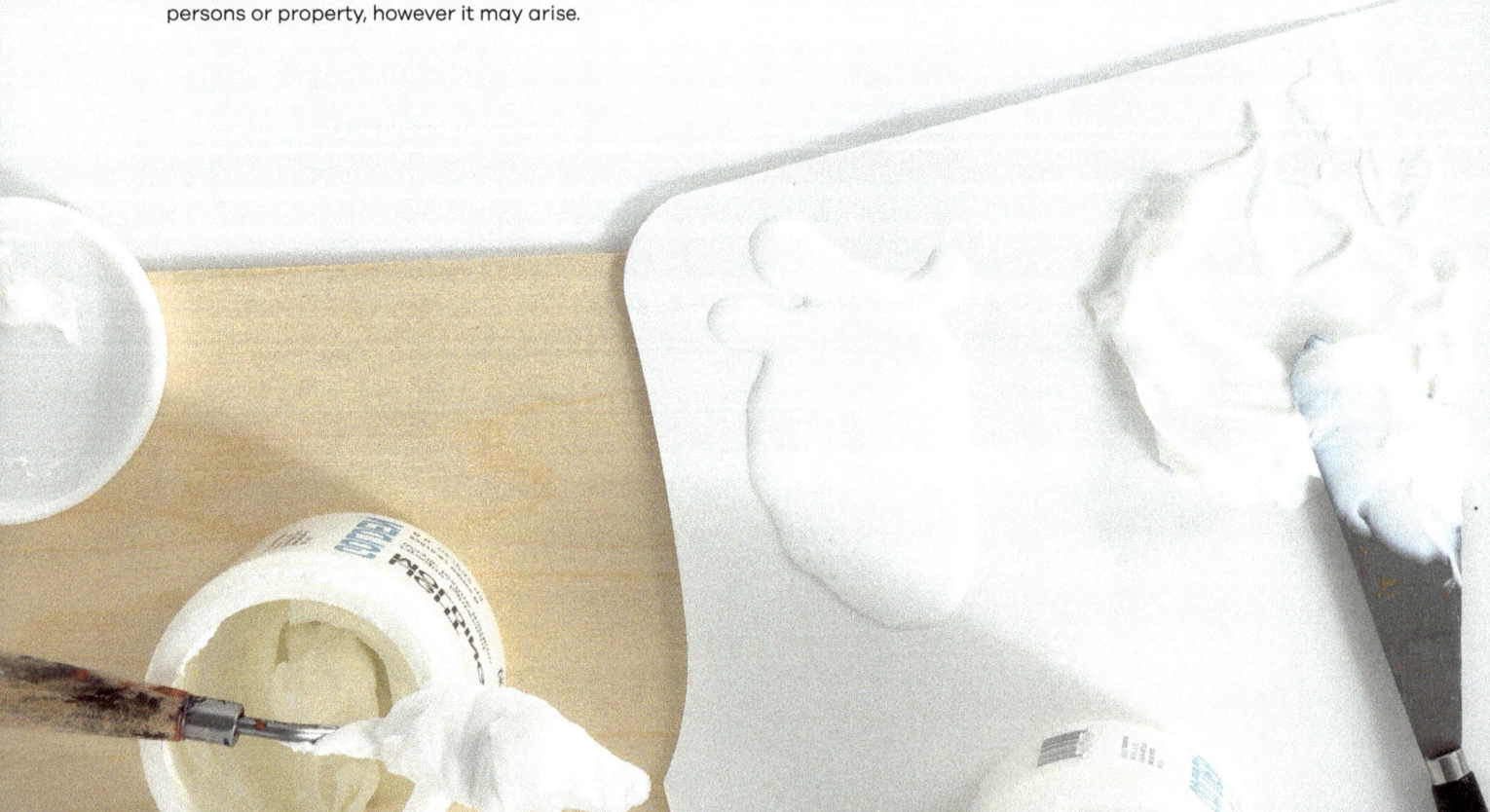

www.ingramcontent.com/pod-product-compliance
Lightning Source LLC
Chambersburg PA
CBHW050940200526
45172CB00024B/1375